MW01268880

The Complete
Guide to All Cats

The Complete Guide to All Cats

Ernest H. Hart

and

Allan H. Hart, B.V.Sc.

With Illustrations by Ernest H. Hart

CHARLES SCRIBNER'S SONS
NEW YORK

Copyright © 1980 Ernest H. Hart and Allan H. Hart

Library of Congress Cataloging in Publication Data

Hart, Ernest H
The complete guide to all cats.

Includes index.
1. Cats. 2. Cats—Diseases. I. Hart,
Allan H., joint author. II. Title.
SF442.H37   636.8   79–28427
ISBN 0–684–16493–0

1 3 5 7 9 11 13 15 17 19 VC 20 18 16 14 12 10 8 6 4 2

Printed in the United States of America

To Katie, April, Stephanie, and Matthew,

and all the lucky people
throughout the wide world
who are owned by cats

Ode to a Cat

His is that peerless
integrity
neither moonlight nor petal
repeats
his contexture

—PABLO NERUDA

Contents

Preface

This is a book for the cat owner and breeder, the novice and the experienced ailurophile. It is a book fashioned to be all things to all cat fanciers, for it contains information pertinent to the many facets of general cat care, including selection, diet, husbandry, and supervision in sickness and health. In the chapters on cat diseases you will find the latest scientific findings on feline ailments, prognosis, nursing, and medical approach.

Other sections, such as the chapters on feline evolution, cat varieties, genetics, exhibiting, breeding, and catteries, are for the seasoned breeder and show fancier. Here, too, will be found relevant information about feral cats, large and small, of forest and jungle. We have also delved into other areas of cat culture—the cat in folklore, in the occult, and in the arts; feline physiology; the geriatric cat; and cat lore—to avoid the dull tone often found in books of basic information and general care.

Through exhaustive research and the compilation of extensive data, we have attempted to provide you with a completely comprehensive and fully illustrated volume that will serve as the most important work of feline reference on your bookshelf.

Seldom could two collaborators have found so much pleasure in their literary partnership as have we, for this book represents an alliance between father and son, each prominent in his own field of endeavor, and both eager to combine their talents in this volume. We anticipate that you will enjoy reading it as much as we have enjoyed writing it.

ERNEST H. HART
ALLAN H. HART, B.V.Sc.

CHAPTER I

What Is a Cat?

Scientifically, the cat (domesticated) is of the class mammalia, order carnivora, family *Felidae*, genus and species *Felis catus*. In more conventional terms, Webster's dictionary defines *cat* as "(a) a carnivorous mammal *(Felis catus)* long domesticated and kept by man as a pet or for catching mice and rats; (b) any of family *(Felidae)* including the domestic cat, lion, tiger, leopard, jaguar, cougar, wildcat, lynx, and cheetah."

Felis catus.

Definitions! Just words that don't begin to tell us what a cat really is. We will have to delve much deeper to discover the true nature of a creature so complex as the cat.

The *Felidae* family to which the domestic cat has been definitely assigned includes species that vary greatly in size from the 600-pound Siberian tiger to domestic breeds that weigh only 5 to 15 pounds upon maturity. The *Felidae* are typical mammals: they are four-footed, warm-blooded, air-breathing, viviparous vertebrates that nourish their young after birth with a secretion called milk supplied by the mother's mammary glands.

All *Felidae* are flesh-eaters and therefore classified as carnivora. They possess the sharp, strong dentition that is typical of predatory animals. Their thirty teeth (sixteen in the upper and fourteen in the lower jaw) —lethal and necessary equipment for these fierce hunters of the night —are all pointed and arranged in the proper order to pierce, sever, and tear. All cats, feral and domestic, possess rounded heads, large round eyes, and pricked cupped ears. With one exception they have separate-toed feet *(fissipeda)* with sharp, retractile claws; the cheetah's claws are not fully retractile, however. *Felidae* feet are also digitigrade: cats walk on their tiptoes, a way of locomotion that lends itself perfectly to the silent stalk and stealth of their hunting style. Their abundant whiskers *(vibrissae* or vibrasse) are sensitive adjuncts to the cat's remarkable nocturnal vision, superior scenting ability, and uncanny auditory sense.

More words! Information—yes. But mere jargon that does not yet even begin to evoke the basic essence of puss as we know him, or bring into clearer focus the unique creature of so many facets that we call the cat. Perhaps if we journey through time, back to beginnings, and trace the tangled origin of the *Felidae,* we will find clues that will lead us to the answer of that most pertinent question, *What is a cat?*

GENESIS OF THE FELIDAE

A great philosopher once declared, in a fit of ridiculousness, "From the past we can find the answers to the present and the future"; or perhaps this apt quotation was spoken by a great fool (it is frequently difficult to discern one from the other). Fool or philosopher, the homily is eminently forgettable yet pertinent to the question *What is a cat?*

The progress of any living creature that has survived the prodigious vagaries of evolution and environmental change over the awesome gulf of time that saw the development of animal life on this globe deserves our interest.

We will pass quickly over the multi-million-year reign of the monstrous dinosaurs during the Triassic period of the Mesozoic era roughly 190 million years ago. With our lifespan of "three score and ten," most of us cannot grasp the meaning of such an awesome multitude of millennia. But as the thunderous tread of the giant reptiles lessened and finally ceased, a number of smaller dinosaurs slowly succeeded through mutational and selective change in escaping the rigid genetic formula that had led to the extermination of most of their species. These new creatures, the Synapsida, became an evolutionary bridge between reptiles and mammals.

Reptilian cold-bloodedness changed to a system of bodily temperature regulation, scales gradually evolved into feathers and hair, the cerebral cortex—the area of the brain dedicated to patterns of intelligent behavior—began to develop. The Age of Mammals had begun.

An explosion of varied life forms all struggling to find a survival niche in a brutal world of tooth and claw followed. The earliest carnivorous creatures were, in general, small, furtive, arboreal, nocturnal, and more intelligent than their contemporaries; among them skulked and snarled the ancestors of man and his future animal companions, the cat and the dog.

The Age of Mammals began approximately fifty-five million years ago in the Paleocene epoch of the Cenozoic era, an era that continues to the present. Small and furtive mammals erupted into evolutionary change and advanced indomitably in a savage test of existence through numerous biological levels by means of variation-produced mutation, natural selection, superior reaction to stimulus, and species radiation to fit vacant or newly emerging ecological niches. Mammals were destined to survive, grow, specialize, and finally conquer the earth in the slow but vicious struggle for species continuance.

Small, arboreal, carnivorous, the *Miacidae* were ferret-like forest dwellers and the ancestors of many predatory mammals, including the *Felidae*.

Cats evolved from archaic forms of viverrines such as civets and genets. This picture of a modern spotted genet shows the similarity.

At one period great flightless birds, *diatrymas* or terror cranes, were the nemesis of mammals. Eight feet tall, with huge beaks and claws, these rapacious carnivorous *aves* declined and disappeared when some of the carnivorous mammals representing the early *Felidae* became large enough to fill the *diatrymas'* ecological nook. The family *Miacidae*, one of the early, true carnivorous clans, were small forest-dwelling, arboreal creatures, rather ferret-like physically. They are important here because they were the archaic ancestors of the cat. From these vicious little predators flowed a veritable genetic tide of plastic animal forms that eventually fashioned the early weasels *(Mustelidae)*, dogs *(Canidae)*, bears *(Ursidae)*, raccoons *(Procyonidae)*, hyenas *(Hyaenidae)*, civets *(Viverrinae)*, and cats *(Felidae)*. It was from an archaic desert civet form that the *Felidae* actually evolved and, proliferating rapidly, established the family in both hemispheres.

Some thirty million years ago, in the Oligocene epoch of the Cenozoic era, the saber-toothed cats emerged. Some were slim and agile, others were ponderous and totally formidable, such as the *Eusmilus*. That the different forms of cats fought among themselves is evident in a skull of a normal cat species *Nimravus*, found by paleontologists in the White River diggings. The skull exhibits a dreadful wound that could only have been inflicted by the saber tooth of the powerful and savage *Eusmilus*. There is no evidence that Asiatic or Old World cats were more primitive or more advanced then the New World genera. Family *Felidae* species seem to have reached the same progressive evolutionary plateaus and patterns throughout their distribution.

Taxonomists concur that the *Felidae* evolved during the Oligocene epoch into two distinct lines: *Hoplophoneus* or *Smilodon,* the saber-tooths; and *Dinictis,* the primal ancestor of the modern domestic cat. Fossil remains of *Dinictis* indicate that our cats of today have basically changed very little from the ancient ancestral type.

By the time of the Pliocene epoch of the Cenozoic era, about seven to ten million years ago, we find that the cat family had reached rather modern forms and that the present-day genus *Felis* had arrived on the scene through the descendents of *Dinictis.* The saber-tooth felines had also prospered, producing, among other giant cats, the widespread *Machairodus.* One gigantic species whose fossil remains were found in the United States possessed canine teeth the size of walrus tusks with a huge jaw-flange large enough to accommodate its monstrous saber teeth. *Ramapithecus,* an early hominid, had made the scene by this time and undoubtedly fell prey upon occasion to the large, voracious felines, so we can count these cats also as man-eaters or, in the modern lexicon, almost-person-eaters.

The Smilodons eventually became the victims of their own specialization: some forms grew so individualistic that they fed only on the blood of their kills. Although they successfully evolved over a period of almost forty million years, they were destined for eventual evolutionary extinction, first in the Old World and later in the Americas. Their huge canine teeth became larger and more swordlike, their bodies bigger, broader, and covered with thick, powerful muscle so that they had the teeth and strength to stab and pull down the monstrous creatures they sought as prey: the giant sloth *(Megatherium),* an archaic rhinoceros *(Diceratherium),* early hippos *(Teleoceras),* and even elephant forms such as the long-jawed mastodon *(Gomphotherium).* It is thought that the Ice Age sounded the death knell for the Smilodons. The huge creatures upon which they preyed became extinct during this period. The monstrous cats were too ponderous to hunt smaller, fleeter game successfully, and so they followed their former prey into oblivion, much to the relief, we imagine, of early man.

The Smilodons were not unique in the manner in which their species became extinct. They were but one of a host of ancient creatures that reached an evolutionary impasse that made further survival impossible. Evolution produces a process of new behavioral elaboration. Changes in the teeth and skeletal structures of archaic animals are indicative of alterations in their behavior patterns and must be equaled by significant modifications in the tightly integrated total of all their parts. When animals reach the end of their evolutionary process, frozen in a pattern of inefficient specialization, they become extinct.

The felids of the Pleistocene epoch, about one million years ago, are divided into three basic groups, the numerically largest of which developed into modern cat types. The *Felidae* of large size (lion, tiger, leopard, and so on) are labeled *Panthera;* the smaller cats, *Felis;* and the cheetah, *Acinonyx.* The last were distributed only in Europe, though it is almost certain that they had their genesis in Asia. The habitat of the other two genera was worldwide. The plains of North America in that long-ago time were stalked by the giant *Panthera artrox,* leopards and jaguars, while giant tigers and the huge cave lion *(Felis spelaea)* of Europe ranged throughout the northern areas. The *Homotherium,* displaying long forelegs and shorter, plantigrade hind limbs, gnashed its razor-sharp saber teeth, ranged widely, and preyed upon young elephants, a feat only equaled by a very few earlier Smilodons, and one no predacious species of today can boast of with the sole exception of rapacious man, who preys on all creatures, including his own species.

Among the many forms of *Felidae* that genetically diverged from archaic *Dinictis* and its issue were the small caffer or bush cat of arid Africa, *Felis lybica,* and the European wild cat *Felis silvestris,* the two feline species considered to be the direct ancestors of our modern domesticated cats.

It is interesting to speculate that of the many mammalian families fighting for an evolutionary niche those multitudinous millennia ago, the *Felidae* might very well have inherited the earth were it not for one other mammal—man. Beginning three to five million years ago, when the earliest open-country hunters and gatherers, the Australopithicines and *Homo habilis,* began to walk upright on the earth brandishing

Huge, powerful, and saber-toothed, the feline plantigrade *Homotherium* walked like a man on the soles of its hind feet and preyed on young elephants.

Small, but strong, the caffer or bush cat of Africa is one of the feral feline species thought to be a direct ancestor of modern domesticated cats, though the familiar tabby stripes are less distinctive, the head larger, and the tail shorter than those of its tame descendents.

the femur of an antelope as a weapon, man possessed a creative brain. And man's ability to walk erect freed his arms and his increasingly dexterous hands to hold weapons and use them as extensions of his body and servants of his will. As a few million years of swift evolution continued, man progressed strongly as a predatory animal. By thirty to forty thousand years ago, when the later *Homo neanderthalensis* had developed fully, man was the most feared and practiced predator on the face of the earth. He still is.

THE DOMESTICATED CAT

It is entirely possible, though there is no definite proof, that man adopted the cat as a pet during the latter part of the Neolithic revolution, which marked the beginning of the agricultural era. In the hills of Mesopotamia where this phase of man's cultural progress came to fruition, zoologists suggest that with the domestication of meat animals and the planting of grains, man may have begun to acquire small pets. It was an age of beginnings; barbarism was on the wane, and so was the hunter-gatherer existence. History's birth was not far beyond the horizon.

There is also some evidence that the ancient Sumerians domesticated small cats for the household and as rodent guards for their grain storehouses. Inlaid panels from that early civilization contain scenes of animals indulging in human activities that seem to have mythological significance. The Sumerians also invented a system of business accounting and plain counting, the latter probably developed in self-defense so they could keep track of the kittens born to their promiscuous cats! Evidence has been advanced that the Norsemen worshipped cats, and we know that Siamese cats were the royal and sacred temple cats of Thailand. Cats in India became religious symbols, and in Japan they guarded Buddhist temples against rodent invasion—witness the splendid Go-To-Ku-Ji or Temple of the Cat, in Tokyo. In Burma, cats were the adored of the priests and nobility and had their own human attendants. So we see that in his early contacts with man, the cat enjoyed privilege. Even in our day of monumental absurdity one must be a truly "fat cat" to be worshipped, adored, and tended by a staff of servants.

But the cat as a domesticated animal reached true recognition in Egypt, the vast, Nile-nurtured cradle of civilization. It is quite possible that individuals of the African bush cat *(Felis lybica)* took up residence in Egyptian grain storehouses to prey upon the mice and rats that fed on the stored grains and spoiled much more of the gathered crops with their droppings. It would be surprising if the Egyptians did not consider this feline activity eminently advantageous and, in the course of time, make overt gestures of friendship to the guardians of their grain. When a queen (a female breeding cat) gave birth, one can easily imagine the keeper of a storehouse appropriating one of the tiny balls of fur and bringing it into the home for the children to pet and play with. Soon no doubt the strange inner mysticism of the cat, the obscure wisdom and unfathomable wells of secrecy that seem to dwell in its eyes, attracted the attention of the priests and nobles: the aristocracy adopted the cat as an honored guest, and the priests as an object for deification. The cat's role swiftly diversified, and we see in early Egyptian tomb murals that domestic cats, trained to hunt birds, were popular partners of the ancient aristocrats indulging in this sport.

The span of Egyptian history helped broaden the cat's course. Barbarians seeking to conquer and grasp the great wealth that was Egypt's probably returned to their own lands with Egyptian cats as part of the spoils of war. The Middle Kingdom ended in the eighteenth century B.C. with the invasion of the Hyksos, a race of Asiatic barbarians who brought the domesticated cat of Egypt to Asia. The first known long-haired felines came from that vast continent. It is also entirely possible that some domesticated cat breeds originated in Asia as descendents of Pallas's Tibetan cat *(Otocolobus manul)*, and that they were later cross-bred with new arrivals from Egypt. The early long-hairs could fall into this category.

The Egyptians, constantly preoccupied with a shifting philosophy of life after death, never reached complete country-wide homogeneity in their religious concepts. Their major gods were members of the *Ennead* or Nine, but many local deities impinged upon each other's religious territories. In Heliopolis, the sun god Atum (Re) was deified; while Osiris, a legendary pharaoh, was named a god in a Delta township. The pharaohs were all given god status, sons of both Osiris and Re. Amon-Re eventually emerged as the most powerful of all deities. The gods had many reincarnations in Egyptian religious lore, returning often in the guise of animals or birds. The sun-god Re was reincarnated with a falcon's head, symbol of Horus whom the people of Behded worshipped as their most eminent deity. The cat was also deified, reaching that exalted estate as the cat-headed goddess Bast, with the center of this cat-cult worship in the town of Bubastis. The word "puss" may be a corruption of Bast, or it may be onomatopoeic, an imitation of the feline hiss. We think it is more likely that "puss" was derived from the cat's identification with Pasht, goddess of the

A bronze cat from Egypt (about 600 B.C.). In the background is a giant sculptured head of Ramses II from Abu Simbel.

moon and the sun, of good and evil. So amorphous was Egyptian religious thought that the cat was symbolically associated with both fecundity and virginity. This latter identification is undoubtedly what made Alice's Cheshire cat grin, for there is no creature more promiscuous than the cat.

The cat enjoyed its finest hour in Egypt. Worshipped and protected from all harm it became a haughty aristocrat, a creature unique. Anyone who dared to do injury to a cat was drastically punished, and when a cat died, the family mourned deeply, shaving off eyebrows and indulging in solemn rites. Mummified and buried in cat cemeteries, many cats were also laid to rest in special sarcophagi in the tombs of their noble masters and mistresses, often with mummified mice to dine on in the hereafter. (The Metropolitan Museum of Art in New York City displays such sarcophagi.) But it was the Roman writer Palladius who, in the fourth century, officially christened the domestic feline with the name *catus*. Statues depicted the Roman goddess of liberty with a cat at her feet.

Phoenician trading vessels, along with the conquering Romans, brought cats from Egypt and introduced them to Europe about 900 B.C. The Crusaders carried cats from the Orient and Asia, and the domestic cat spread to the far corners of the earth. The first records known of the planned breeding of domestic cats come from the Imperial Palace, Kyoto, Japan, dated A.D. 999. In that ancient country, cats controlled the rodent population in the granaries as well as the *rodentia* that feasted upon the cocoons of silk worms, the end product of which was an important Japanese industry.

Indeed, in Europe the cat was protected by law when first introduced to the continent. Throughout the world in the eleventh century, but particularly in Europe, a sudden social and intellectual advance included the cat in its development, and puss found a niche in the new needs of the people. When the dread Black Plague swept through Europe bringing death in its wake, cats were in great demand as killers of the flea- and lice-ridden rodent carriers of the disease. Once again the cat enjoyed great popularity.

Then during the Middle Ages mankind took a long step backward from the light of sanity and culture into the morbid gloom of madness. A new and in some aspects even more deadly disease was born in the brains of half-mad, flaming-eyed fanatics, and the cat fell from favor. Accused of association with the elements of evil, cats were cruelly purged by murderous religious zealots. But the time of travail passed and they again became household pets and eradicators of the filthy rodents that have pestered man from the time he first learned to store food. Yet the vicious brand that stamped the cat during the dark days of the Middle Ages, and during the celebrated Salem witch trials in our own country—when cats were named as consorts of witches and war-locks, linked with Satan worship, and considered guardians of the living dead—has not been completely eradicated. Cats, particularly black cats, have for centuries been considered by some superstitious minds as familiars of Lucifer and dabblers in demonology.

We can assume that the domestic cat was not introduced to the Americas until European ships touched these shores, for there is no anthropological proof that the early American Indians kept cats or attempted to domesticate any of the New World feral varieties of cats. The journals and records of early, intrepid travelers to the New World show that cats were brought here in their accustomed roles as pets and valuable defenders of a ship's edibles. Michele de Cuneo, a Spanish seaman who sailed with Columbus on his second voyage in 1493, when the first Spanish colony was established in Haiti, writes of the cats that sailed on that voyage to the West Indies. In South America the Indians were delighted with the small, tame felines that came from Europe and protected their stored maize and tubers from rodents. The Aztecs named the cat *"Mizton,"* or Little Lion, because of its general physical resemblance to their native mountain lions.

This condensed statement of the origin, evolution, and history of the feline family suggests that the cat has had a checkered career as a domestic creature, its fortunes swinging like a pendulum from one extreme to the other. Through it all the cat has never lost its aplomb, characteristically increasing in numbers until today there are more than forty million domestic cats in the United States alone. Over thirteen million kittens will be born this year.

Yet even with this knowledge of the past, of the origin, evolution, and history of the family *Felidae,* we are basically no closer to answering our original question, *What is a cat?* than we were before. Perhaps words and knowledge are not the answer because they tell us *about* the cat, but not what a cat *is.*

Let's try an experiment.

Put this book down for a moment and look at your cat.

What do you see? What do you feel when your cat's eyes meet yours, that sudden inner warmth spreads through you, and a thin web of rapport binds you momentarily together?

Well, now you know—words are not the answer. There are no words in any known human tongue that can truly describe what your cat is to you; that feeling of deep emotion at once solid and amorphous, the inner response beyond the limits of man-made speech to interpret.

Now you have found the answer to the question *What is a cat?*

CHAPTER 2

Characteristics of the Cat

Over the millions of years it took to fashion the family *Felidae*, the needed characteristics were refined, attuned, and molded to definition. Thus the evolution of the species as predatory creatures with highly integrated structures resulted in a mosaic of special attributes that fitted them—large, medium, or small—into their distinctive rapacious niche.

The domestic cat is a remarkable animal possessing singular characteristics. Highly intelligent, unrestricted, captivating, quiet, sensitive, poised, and self-sufficient, cats combine all these sterling qualities with affection for their human families. Basically the cat is very clean, intolerant of abuse and neglect, has a hidden well of nervousness, does not require planned exercise to keep fit, and is dignified or playful and fun-loving according to its desire of the moment. Perhaps the most telltale characteristic the cat exhibits, one with which it is born and which it displays throughout life, is a supercilious smile of counterfeit respectability.

No two cats are alike: each has its own individual personality, different from any other cat, even its siblings. An uncle of ours used to say, "When there is a cat in residence, boredom leaves the premises."

Physically lithe and superbly balanced, the cat is a night hunter and climber, and utilizes its sharp, retractile claws for both these purposes. The gathered stealth and patience as it stalks its prey, and the speed and power of its pounce and strike, are incredible, and to its quarry inevitably disastrous. Strangely, however, though predators by instinct, the young of the family *Felidae* must nevertheless be taught to hunt.

A typical short-haired, domestic *Felis catus* is approximately 30 inches long including a 9-inch tail, and can weigh up to about 20 pounds, though all weights and measures vary considerably with the breed and the individual cat's condition. Coloring varies, too, and a whole delightful artist's palette of hues and combinations can be found. The tabby, perhaps the most common, inherits a direct color pattern from the domestic cat's wild progenitors *Felis lubica* (sometimes referred to as the Libyan cat) and *Felis sylvestris.* Tabby stripes are basically of two varieties: narrow vertical bands that accent the colored areas of the body, and broad longitudinal stripes and/or blotches on a fairly light base color. Albino cats with blue eyes are frequently deaf, a fact initially reported by the eminent naturalist Charles Darwin.

Cats are ancient advocates of self-determination. Even though they have shared intimate household relationships with man, as has the dog, unlike the dog they have retained their spirit of independence. Canines are instinctively pack animals and give fealty to their human masters as they would to the leader of the pack. Cats are genetically solitary creatures, who condescend to offer you their presence and, upon occasion, their esteem or love (if you have earned it), but owe absolute allegiance to no one and so are completely autonomous. Because of this basic proclivity, cats can become feral quite easily and, after adapting to a wild existence, often attain added bulk and growth. Reports suggest that feral domestic cats sometimes reach the dimensions of the wildcat *(Lynx rufus)* of over 40 inches in length and 30 pounds in weight. In Thailand, wild specimens of the Siamese cat have been seen to be much larger than their domestic siblings. While in the feral state, they revert to basic behavioral patterns, becoming truly nocturnal, and are not easily observed. They have, however, been reported to frequent jungle growth surrounding ancient, deserted temples, where they probably purr to pagan gods.

Each feral species fills a bionomical territory on its own terrain, preying upon beasts proportionate to its size. Feral felines, particularly the "big cats," are the epitome of the specialized carnivorous killer. Their prodigious power enables them to prey upon animals of much greater size than their own. Their appropriate dentition, retractile claws, great strength, lithe balance, night vision, protective coloration, stealth, and speed all combine to fashion a perfect predacious creature. The lion in Africa, adapted to life in open plains, wears a coat that blends into the tawny landscape. It feeds upon herbivorous animals as large as the eland (an antelope weighing about 2,000 pounds and standing almost 6 feet tall). The leopard, an arboreal forest dweller, has a spotted coat that simulates the light shadow-dappling of tropical sun through the leaves and branches of jungle trees. The New World jaguar's pelage mimics the same kind of environment as the leopard's. The latter cat, smaller than the lion, preys upon medium-sized ungulates, antelopes, gazelles, and baboons. The huge tiger, a giant Asian cat, inhabits dense high grass country, where its striped pelage mimics the shade cast by high ground foliage. Its food is the large herbivorous ungulates and whatever other living creatures are available. The jaguar, like the tiger, has a wide range of tastes but prefers a diet of horses and other ruminants. Pumas (or mountain lions) also evince an appetite for horse entrée, but never pass up a gourmet dinner of sheep or venison. In North America, they fill the carnivorous ecological niche the jaguar occupies in South America and the leopard in Africa. The puma's coat blends well with the rock and sand terrain that is generally its habitat.

Lynx and bobcat dine on rabbits, birds, and rodents, and the smaller wild and domestic cats are addicted to a diet of rodents and birds. Incidentally, the domestic cat cannot roar but it can purr, and the larger feral cats are purrless though they roar with gusto. It is obvious that the family *Felidae* aids in the equitable numerical division of all other animal species until man, in his inimitable fashion, arrogantly upsets the balance of nature with bionomic fumbling.

DEFENSE

Cats of all sizes have a very effective means of defense when attacked by a large and dangerous adversary. Unlike any other animal, which would be in a very vulnerable position if knocked down onto its back with its soft belly and vital parts exposed, cats are more dangerous to their foes supine than when upright and facing their attacker. On their backs they can use as weapons the full scope of their armament: teeth, jaws, powerful front legs and claws, and their mighty, clawed hind-quarters. By drawing their hindquarters in toward their chests as their antagonist pounces, they rake the razor-sharp claws of their powerful rear paws through his underbelly while holding the attacker with their front feet and gripping his neck with their teeth. This maneuver results, with great frequency, in the disembowelment of their enemy, and is undoubtedly an effective method of immediately draining all hostility from the opposition. The truly giant cats would not have to engage in such activity since there are no other predators large enough to challenge their sovereignty.

THE CAT IN THE HOME

Cats in general, and domestic kittens particularly, are playful and exceedingly inquisitive. They will generally accept no territorial boundary lines and, unless trained not to, will leap onto tables, beds, bureaus, and kitchen counters to seek amusement. Although we speak frequently of the cat's self-sufficiency, and writers often stress the cat's aloofness and imbue it with an aura of absolute independence and disdain for its owner and the human race in general, such statements are apocryphal. Most domestic cats do not make a fetish of independence. If introduced to the household as kittens, they become quite fond of their human family and display their feelings openly. Yes, they are basically liberated creatures, but most cats become dependent upon their owners for sustenance, comfort, and love, and they offer their own affection in return. Not to understand the reciprocal balance of such an arrangement would be stupid—and the cat is far from being a stupid animal. Certainly if this were not true, the cat would never have attained such exalted status as a pet over the centuries.

An act that epitomizes the young feline's attitude of affection toward its human family is the offering of its first-caught mouse, dead, half-dead, or very much alive, laid at your feet (often to your complete disgust) as an expression of gratitude. The act is partially a boast of new-found prowess, but it is also a way of saying, "I bring you this fine, fat mouse because you are good to me and love me, and I am, in return, very fond of you."

Cats such as Silky, an Australian tom who walked fifteen hundred miles to his home in Melbourne after becoming lost in the Outback while on vacation, have been known to travel for weeks and months over hundreds of miles, braving vehicle-clogged highways, woods, and water to find the human families that had deserted them by moving from one state to another. What more can one say to illustrate the cat's intense devotion?

CAT COMMUNICATION

Cats cannot, of course, speak as we humans do, and if they could they would undoubtedly scorn to utter the insipid noises that people call conversation. But cats do have a dialect of their own, a form of body language augmented by vocal sounds that conveys definite meaning. Olfactory communication serves to announce a cat's presence or the boundaries of its territory, and to initiate sexual awareness in the opposite sex. Cats have the ability to produce a great variety of vocal sounds, all of which have meaning. Some are used to converse with other cats, but a number of these sounds are vernacular intonations directed at human friends and owners. Many cat fanciers vow that besides the generalized words cats use, each also has an extended vocabulary of its own.

By using their sinuous bodies, limbs, tails, voices, and eyes, cats can convey many meanings. Such simple signs as flattening the ears back against the skull with back arched, tail out straight, and lips curled while spitting or snarling indicate very clearly that puss is angry.

Purring usually accompanied by a gently waving tail means a cat is content, that all is right with the world. Dilated pupils, a fluffed-up coat and tail, together with an arched, rigid back, signify fear. Watch your cat during different environmental circumstances and through its reactions you will begin to understand its language. Actually, the cat's method of using auditory and visual signs as a means of communication is a legitimate and primitive process of imparting information; it parallels the method employed by early man before he learned to give vocal meaning to specific actions and articles and invented speech.

Cats instinctively know the value of soft physical contact, a benefit psychologists and psychiatrists have only recently discovered and now use in contact groups for disturbed people. The contact soothes and helps people to express a sense of sharing. Cats often softly pat the faces of their loved ones in a precious gesture of one-to-one rapport.

Domesticated felines are basically flower children and seem to adore all kinds of flowers. They are also natural retrievers and enjoy playing this game with their owners. Montaigne, in his *Essays,* remarks: "When I play with my cat, who knows whether I do not make her more sport than she does me?" The long-haired breeds enjoy pampering and take regal delight in viewing their world from a silken pillow. All cats are effete and vain, and indulge in constant self-grooming and cleaning. There are exceptions to this statement, as witness the roving, free-lance tom cat who offers fealty to no one and takes his pleasure wherever he finds it. Homeless, mean, scarred, disreputable, and filthy, feeding out of garbage cans and prowling the night alleys, he is a feline bum who can never be rehabilitated. How strange that cats should mirror man in so many characteristics!

To exercise and sharpen their claws, cats will indulge in what they consider an ecstatic pastime—digging their claws into any material and ripping. Unfortunately, too often the material cats use for this fun time covers your best couch or living room chair, so do not expect to keep your furniture unscarred if you keep cats. Scratching posts will take a good deal of this wear and tear, but they usually will not discourage cats from occasionally trying their claws on the furniture.

The cat's eating habits are fairly broad, though an occasional epicurean feline must be tempted with special foods. Unlike the dog, cats favor fresh meat in preference to aged, but they do not confine themselves to a very narrow menu. At one time we lived with a short-hair who, as a cantaloupe freak, would relish melon meat in preference to any other kind of food. We named her Cantaloupe Cat—what else?

Cats do not have nine lives as you have probably been led to expect. Like you and me and Patrick Henry they have but one life, and they seem to enjoy it to the fullest extent possible. The average length of life for a domestic cat is approximately twelve to fourteen years; but with good care, a reliable veterinarian, and a bit of luck, a cat's lifespan can be lengthened considerably.

You have undoubtedly noticed how often cats purr: from the time they are tiny kittens to the end of their days, they indulge frequently in this form of expression. Some purr quite loudly, others softly, and some vary the intensity of their purring. A record of cats purring could lull people to sleep better than any of the soporific remedies offered commercially. Cats purr when content, when playing, and even sometimes when hurt, but they make no sound at all when they hunt, earnestly or in play. Then they are as silent as mist rising from marshland, and they move with virtuoso grace. Cats indulge in tiny naps (catnaps, of course) during the day, which are completely efficacious because cats are able to relax completely. Deep though their sleep may be, at any time the slightest sound will bring them fully awake and immediately aware.

Occasionally one finds a feline (whether whole or neutered) whose temperament is truly intolerable; one who is actually mean and vicious and will scratch and bite whenever it is given the opportunity; who hisses, bares its teeth, and glares at the least provocation, real or imagined. If this nasty cat is a really magnificent specimen of the breed, do not despair. Instead, consult your veterinarian, who may recommend one of the new psychotropic agents that are administered orally. This therapeutic treatment could help improve the cat's disposition dramatically.

Cats are not stoic when it comes to pain, and when hurt they are for this reason not one of your veterinarian's favorite patients. But the cat when healthy and content can relax as can no other creature domesticated by man. This proclivity brings to the families with which cats live a feeling of quiet peace and calm that can actually reach and affect the humans in the household if they allow it and bring them a measure of composure. We can profit from our cat's deportment, and find an approach to living that can aid us in contending with the chaotic complexities of this frenetic century. No, the cat is not an answer to all our woes; but a knowledge of its ways and an ability to absorb and practice some of its philosophical somnolence may help us, to some small extent, in coping with the bewildering chaos of our time.

From earliest times our favorite felines have been labeled domesticated cats, and so they are, for they have accepted domestication in the dictionary sense. But from the scientific standpoint, a cat is not exactly a domesticated animal. Anthropologists define domestication in several different ways, but basically they agree that domestication is a process of artificial selection, which creates progressive change in the central nervous system and in anatomical structure. Hereditary behavior patterns are progressively modified and anatomical features not conducive to survival under natural conditions are developed. After a specific degree of domestication has been reached, the animal may be unable to survive under feral conditions.

This definition of domesticity does not fit the cat, which has not been basically changed or physically modified to any great degree. The majority of cats can still survive and prosper in the wild state.

The essential difference between the two most numerous of the domesticated animals that man has accepted into his household is obvious. The dog lives *for* its master, serving as a companion and vassal of man. The cat lives *with* us as a guest in our house, graciously accepting our hospitality as its just due and rewarding us with affection and the pleasure of its company.

Felines in Folklore and the Occult

THE CAT IN FOLKLORE

Folklore is the earliest oral tradition of man. Contemporary thinking to the contrary, it is neither simple nor aesthetically sterile. It was basically the approach of early peoples to superstition and events that were beyond their understanding. Folklore is also an effort to perpetuate tales of wisdom, humor, or earthy philosophy as a cultural dialect.

Stories of miraculous cats supplying poor and put-upon families with freshly killed rabbits are very common in all countries; and from many peoples have come legends concerning cats—some terrifying, some strange and bordering on the mystical, others amusing or pertaining to ethnic values or religious beliefs. Folklore is of the common people to a great extent, the uneducated, the farmers, laborers, those close to the soil; simple folk with uncomplicated lifestyles. It is composed of the legends of these people, their traditional beliefs, and is filled with inner symbolism, their fears of the unknown, the mysticism and terror of night sounds, and all the inexplicable incidents that are their ancient inheritance. These, and the common man's hopes and dreams, are the body and blood of folklore.

As an associate of man, the cat has had so varied and difficult a career that its continued domestication is remarkable. No other animal has become a part of so many strange and eerie tales and legends, no other creature has been elevated to the Olympian heights of godhood and, accused of satanic association, been plunged to the depths of torture and death. Why this has happened cannot be conveniently explained, for we know cats as innocuous creatures, sweet, mostly gentle, fine pets, and possessed of fewer vices than other animals.

Perhaps it is because man's fertile imagination envisions unfathomable mysteries lurking behind the cat's strange eyes. Perhaps man thinks he sees in their depths the reflection of forbidden knowledge or an eerie contact with strange worlds and supernatural occurrences. History teaches us that people in the clutch of fanaticism or fear lose hold of reality and conjure weird and twisted images that become, to them, surrogates for truth. It is also possible that within man's subconscious there lurks a residual ancestral memory of great killer-cats that preyed upon his progenitors when the human animal was more animal than human.

God or devil's own, the colorful heritage of the family *Felidae* lends itself splendidly to association with folklore and the occult.

Associated with folklore are the many ways in which the word "cat" has been woven into the myriad facets of our vocabulary. The language of mariners is rich in such usage: the cat's-head of a ship, cat's paw, cat-fall, cat boat. Many more terms and nautical articles borrow the feline name. Cats have long been thought by mariners to bring good luck to a ship, for they surely have performed a valuable service in controlling the numbers of rats aboard. There are many tales of ship's cats who somehow missed boarding before their ships left the docks, and who were waiting patiently on the same dock when the ship returned from a long voyage.

Horticulturists have adopted the word "cat" in naming many kinds of plants: the herb cat's-foot, cat-thyme, cattails, cat-briar, and a host of other agricultural growths.

There are so many ways in which the term "cat," or derivatives of it, are used that to name them all would stupefy the reader: kitty (as in poker), pussyfoot, catty (substitute for "bitch"), catty-cornered, cat's-eye, catfish, catnap, copycat, Cat Street (in Hong Kong), Catskill Mountains and numerous islands, capes, and coves, to name but a few of the words and landmarks that have been inspired by *Felis catus*. And in a multitude of dialects from all corners of the globe one hears a number of aphorisms—such as, "When the cat's away the mice will play."

Certain feline creatures known to folklore are called "magician cats." These are usually very-good-luck cats that can bring great wealth and good fortune to the lucky humans who treat them well. Dick Whittington's famous feline was a "magician cat," and there is no denying that puss did very well by our Mr. Whittington, if the tale is to be believed at all. Black cats have been considered lucky by some folk and unlucky by others. And you may be aware of the overwhelming number of inns, taverns, grog shops, and bars all over the world that have incorporated "cat" in their names: The Black Cat (or Le Chat Noir) is quite common, as are The White Cat, The Purple Cat, The Cosy Kitten, and so on.

Mummified cats, with rats or mice in their mouths, have been discovered in the walls of eighteenth-century houses in Europe, put there by the builders, probably at the request of the tenant, to protect the home from evil spirits—and possibly second mortgages.

Siamese cats were reportedly used as watch-cats in temples to warn the priests of intruders. The kinked tails and crossed eyes possessed by many Siamese cats (particularly in earlier centuries)

have been the subject of a bountiful array of stories and legends. One such tale concerns a Buddhist temple that housed a goblet from which the great Buddha himself had quenched his thirst. A pair of Siamese cats guarded both cup and temple, but the Buddhist monk who resided in the sacred premises was wont to quaff too readily and too long of the juice of the grape, and when he had done so, would wander away smiling inanely. One day, after his usual session with liquid forgetfulness, the monk wandered away and failed to return. Eventually, aware that it was necessary for all religious temples to house a guardian monk on the premises, the tom cat went in search of one, admonishing his mate before he left not to remove her gaze, for even an instant, from the hallowed goblet. The tom's search was a long one, and the female Siamese stared fixedly at the holy cup for such a long time that eventually her eyes crossed. When she slept she encircled the goblet with her tail so that it would not be stolen, and as a result could never again completely straighten that necessary appendage. When the male Siamese finally returned with a new guardian monk for the temple, he found a cross-eyed, kink-tailed female guarding the sacred cup. The story ends at this point, but it is our guess that the tom may have rued the day he left.

Of the many fables we have heard, two others concern the kinked tail of the Siamese cat. One tells of a Buddhist monk who was so forgetful that he tied a knot in puss's tail to remind him to remember. The author of that little pearl of folklore evidently forgot what it was the monk was supposed to remember. Another rather kinky story concerns a lovely princess who feared losing her priceless rings when bathing, so she removed them from her aristocratic fingers and strung them on the tail of her Siamese cat. She then knotted the end of the poor cat's tail so the rings would not fall off—perhaps because she did not want a ring in her bathtub.

Puss in Boots is a familiar classic fable, and *The Boy Who Drew Cats*, a Japanese fairy tale, tells us about a poor boy sent to the local temple to be trained for the priesthood. But the strange boy had no interest at all in theology, for he was consumed with a burning desire to draw pictures of cats. He drew cats everywhere and in every conceivable position, and the priests called him incorrigible and beat him severely, chanting that this was a temple and not a cat house. Finally, castigated to the point of becoming punch-drunk, the boy ran away from the temple to make his way in the world as a cat artist or catologist. One evening he came to a deserted temple in the jungle. Since cat portraiture was not very remunerative at the time, he decided to take advantage of a free lodging and stay the night. But, by candlelight, before he went to sleep, he painted cats all over the walls of the temple. Then, exhausted, he lay down and immediately fell into a deep sleep. He dreamed that night that there was a great and frightening struggle going on around him, and some fearsome Thing from an awesome beyond-world was reaching with slobbering, ravening appetite for his throat. When early morning light striped the temple floor, he awakened. There on the ground, close to his ragged blanket, he found the body of a giant, malevolent spirit-rat —and the mouths of the cats he had drawn upon the temple walls were dripping with fresh blood.

There is no dearth of tales told of Mohamet's cat, Muezza, a beautiful white puss that was the favorite pet of the great Prophet. And there is a Hindu fable the senior author heard in India with many complications, of which the pithy substance is a competition between two men of great virtue, and a bit of philosophy spoken gravely by the king of the gods to his favorite goddess, to wit: ". . . to steal a mortal's cat is indeed the most insufferable of insults." This story, we promise you, was much more interesting when told in Hindustani—particularly if one has no understanding of the language.

THE CAT AND THE OCCULT

The killing of a cat was considered a sin in many countries, particularly in ancient Egypt where the cat was deified. But in the folklore of China and Japan, cats have often been cast in demoniac roles. Oriental legends postulate the ability of cats to transform themselves into myriad shapes as they grow older, with the power to cast a curse upon an entire family unto the third generation. European legend holds that a cat who reaches the age of ten years can speak in human tongues if it so wishes, and at twenty years of age it becomes a witch. In other countries the killing of a cat is thought to release demons who had assumed feline forms. The released djinns would then wreak dire vengeance on the mortal who had destroyed their living body. And on Hallowe'en, the eve of All Saints' Day, even we enlightened twentieth-century sophisticates celebrate the specters that lurk in the night through the mediums of the broomstick-mounted witch and her black cat familiar.

The passage of the soul from a human being to an animal, and vice versa (metempsychosis), is the basis of occult folklore in India and other Oriental countries, and it is augmented by the belief that a mortal can become a cat after death. There are also many strange folkloric tales of reincarnated humans who used to be rats and who naturally exhibit an unholy fear of cats. The authors have known such

individuals, and they don't seem to change very much from one rein-
carnation to another.

Tales of talking cats are legion: Orientals ascribe to felines a host of
strange aptitudes, such as possessing supernatural powers and being
amorphous, as well as the ability to speak. Ailurophobes, of course, are
willing to accept any legends or philosophies that put puss in a poor
light, and because of their dislike of cats they have advocated the
persecution of felines as creatures commanding malevolent powers,
even though they may not truly believe such accusations to be genuine.

During the seventeenth and eighteenth centuries cats fell upon evil
times in Europe, and in the time of the Salem witchcraft trials here
it was not uncommon for cats, as consorts of witches, sorceresses, and
Satan, to be burned to death in the fiery climax of various kinds of
cabalistic celebrations. But cat historians, while lamenting the bar-
baric treatment accorded the cat, seem to forget the merciless fate that
befell their owners: poor eccentrics, senile old women, martyr-com-
plex visionaries, and bewildered, simple-minded, or retarded people.
Many such accused witches, under questioning, admitted that they
had frequently assumed the shape of cats. Needless to say, the "questioning" took the form of torture so brutal that the victim would have
confessed to anything.

There is a record of a trial in the Church Book of Bottesford, England, during which an accused witch, Joan Flower, and her familiar,
the black cat Rutterkin, were executed for causing the death of the wife
and children of a certain important gentleman through the agencies
of demonic spells and black magic. It was whispered at the time that
Joan Flower had been deflowered by the important gentleman—an act
that brought her wrath down upon him.

Cotton Mather, a thorough ailurophobe and the Joseph McCarthy
of his day, wrote wrathfully of transformations of "accursed witches"
into "demon cats." The grisly era spawned many gruesome tales of
witch-cats, as well as ritual recipes for witch's brews in which cats
figured as the main ingredient.

Tales of the cat's identification with the occult have come from
every corner of the globe, many with the same theme but slightly
different particulars. Stories of specter cats, haunted cats, cats that are
humans, and humans who become cats for nefarious enterprises and
lewd pursuits, are universal. The belief in the supernatural and occult
was fostered by mystics, and adopted and expanded by ignorance, fear
of the unknown, and a basic, primordial panic that still lives in man's
subconscious.

Of course, sometimes, one does wonder if the ancients saw something in the cat that we do not see; something that puss has learned
to hide over the centuries of his association with man; something that

caused the Old Ones to elevate the cat to deity status and later accuse it of a corrupt connection with the Prince of Darkness. One cannot deny the esoteric aura that envelops the cat, the sense of other-worldliness, of archaic mystery and unknown wisdom. And it does make one wonder—doesn't it?

CHAPTER 4

The Cat and the Arts

There have always been cultural barriers to an understanding and appreciation of the arts. But in the visual arts—painting, sculpture, architecture, design—that barrier is almost though not quite eliminated, for visual art is, by its very nature, a comprehensive language. In comparison, the cultural barriers raised in literature are much more apparent, simply because the written words of another ethnic system can lose much in translation and be shadowed by an alien philosophy. Music, too, arriving from a diverse cultural source, can seem to lack eurythmic value to an individual from a completely dissimilar society, while the dance, by contrast, is a visual experience and can be evaluated by all peoples even though the music that accompanies it may sound foreign.

Musicologists suggest that the musical experience probably originated in rhythmical body movements and oral chant sounds, and that instrumental music as melodic cadence did not evolve until the agricultural and pastoral societies came into being during the Neolithic period. The genesis of music and the dance therefore occurred simultaneously. Paleolithic musical instruments were very likely forms of flutes or flageolets, carved and hollowed creations of bone, bamboo, or wood; and possibly also some kind of percussion instruments such as drums and rattles. The initial percussion sounds were probably made by slapping the thigh or clapping the hands together. With the technological advances of the later Neolithic or Metal age, more complicated and diverse string instruments appeared.

As oral language developed, the chant sounds became phonetic, assumed word meanings, and were converted into songs. Oral music of diverse world areas is even more difficult to assess than instrumental music, for singers may ad-lib creatively, and local melodic sounds can be chosen to fit specific sectional music that might be audibly unmusical and strange to the untutored. An example is Spanish flamenco vocalizing, a form of specialized singing usually accompanied by guitar that is not often truly appreciated except by aficionados of this musical form.

Regardless of the section of the world a cat may come from and the types of oral music specific to the area, despite the ridiculous claims of ardent ailurophiles, cats cannot sing—and we challenge anyone to dispute this statement! Believe us, we have listened to a very wide variety of cats who have attempted to vocalize, some of whose owners even claimed them to have trained voices, and they were all insufferably awful. You never heard such discordant cater-wauling.

"Music and rhythm find their way into the secret places of the soul," Plato said, and perhaps the secret places of the cat's soul are filled with music, but it never seeps through to their vocal cords. It is a fact, though, that some felines seem charmed by certain kinds of music. But there is no doubt whatsoever that as vocalists they leave everything to be desired. Cats just cannot sing!

THE CAT AND MUSIC

Despite this lack in their vocal abilities, cats have been associated with music since early times. The Egyptians used a musical instrument called a seshesh that was fashioned in the shape of a cat. Musically, of course, there is the popular "Kitten on the Keys," and the old rhyme "The Cat and the Fiddle," though we doubt that puss would play an instrument with strings of catgut. But if one did, being aware of the habits of cats, he could very well be the ubiquitous fiddler on the roof.

In the final act of the ballet *The Sleeping Beauty,* by Tchaikovsky, there is a musical mélange of dancers and orchestra fabricating an amusing and animated meeting between two cats. John Wilson (1595–1674) wrote the orchestral *Funeral of the Calico Cat,* and Domenico Scarlatti composed *The Cat's Fugue* after hearing his cat walk across his harpsichord keyboard. The composer claimed he used the notes struck by his cat's paws in its musical stroll as the basic theme for his fugue.

Igor Stravinsky composed a quartet of melodies dedicated to cats, which were to be rendered vocally by a soprano accompanied instrumentally by clarinets; it would seem a likely blending of sounds to produce a catlike musical quality. There is even an opera with an aria for cats, composed by the French musical genius Maurice Ravel, which is based on a short story by Colette. Other attempts to weave the family *Felidae* into the colorful sound tapestry of music have been made, but mostly without any major musical success. There are, no doubt, symphonies and songs in other countries dedicated to the cat, or in which cats play a definitive part.

To the true Felidaephile the mew, the call, the purr of puss is music enough to the ear. There is no need for great orchestras, string ensembles, sonorous vocalizing, or choral groups to stir the soul with ecstatic sound. For the ailurophile, the limited oral contribution of puss is the music of the spheres.

LITERATURE AND THE CAT

Cats have been more fortunate in their reception in literature than in music and the terpsichorean art. Cat-loving authors, and there are many, have given puss his just due in their writing efforts. On the other hand, there are ailurophobes in our literary society who use the pen as a weapon to castigate the creatures they so dislike. This practice is eminently unfair since cats cannot write back in rebuttal. One rabid ailurophile, who breeds and exhibits fine cats, informed us in all seriousness that if cats wanted to write they could; they simply disdain to express themselves in this mundane manner. The cat lover angrily rejected our suggestion that cats don't write because their spelling is so appalling that they do not choose to be ridiculed on this count.

To get right down to the nitty-kitty of the cat in literature, we must first accept the fact that the domesticated cat is not mentioned at all in the Bible, though the feral big cats are referred to 130 times. To balance this deplorable lack, many celebrated authors have written texts about our feline friends or accorded them mention in their literary efforts (in New Rochelle, New York, there is a bookstore devoted solely to books about cats). Every child confronting his first primer quickly learns that C stands for Cat, and in *Appleton's First Reader,* published almost a century ago, the initial lesson reads: "*a* cat—*the* cat—*my* cat."

When mentioning the cat in literature, the droll travesties of Oliver Herford, *The Rubaiyat of a Persian Kitten* and *A Kitten's Garden of Verses,* immediately come to mind, as does H. Allen Smith's delightful *Rhubarb.* Dickens wove cats into the pages of his wonderful novels as color and character adjuncts to his fascinating personnel, and Charles Darwin, the brilliant amateur scientist who gave the world the controversial *Origin of Species* and *The Descent of Man,* to name but two of his important works, also wrote advocating the use of cats to control the field mice that destroy the combs of bumblebees useful in fertilizing specific varieties of clover and flowering plants. Charles Perrault wrote the ageless fairy tale adventures of *Puss in Boots,* which was illustrated originally by the famous French artist Gustave Doré, and of course every child remembers the Cheshire cat in *Alice in Wonderland* by Lewis Carroll. The charming "Owl and the Pussy Cat" was penned by Edward Lear and subsequently set to music.

Remember "Tyger, Tyger burning bright . . ."? It was written by the esoteric William Blake, who captured the fundamental beauty and

eternal riddle of the cat in his classic poem "The Tyger." Edgar Allan
Poe loved cats—as did Chaucer, La Fontaine, Colette, Paul Gallico,
and T. S. Eliot, who wrote musingly, in *Old Possum's Book of Practical
Cats:* "Macavity, Macavity, there's no one like Macavity, / There never
was a Cat of such deceitfulness and suavity." All of these talented
writers gave puss the benefit of their literary legerdemain. Samuel
Butler, the eminent British writer who loved cats more than he did his
fellow man, once opined that the naming of a kitten is the end proof
of literary skill. Quite possibly Mr. Butler did not have any children.

An evident ailurophile, Pierre Loti wrote of cats with refreshing
insight, and Honoré de Balzac composed the satirical "Peines de Coeur
d'une Chatte Anglaise." Another cat lover, Emile Zola, wrote many
interesting cats into the pages of his novels, and novelist Champfleury
authored a chatty book on cats that was illustrated by Manet.

"The Cat That Walked by Himself" is Rudyard Kipling's delightful
tale of the clever bargain made by a cat with a family of early humans.
Ambrose Bierce, the journalist and short story writer, wrote three
feline fables; and Cervantes told of his heroic but impractical Don
Quixote's misadventure in the castle of the Duke de Villahermosa
when he suffered an invasion of cats in his chambers at midnight.
Quixote, awakening in the dark, of course imagined the cats to be
demons and wizards of stupendous evil. Drawing his sword he chal-
lenged them to combat, sonorously shouting: "Avaunt, malignant en-
chanters! Avaunt, ye witchcraft-working rabble!"—a typical incident
in the life of that extravagantly chivalrous romantic.

We must mention the many books written about cats for cat lovers
concerning breeding, husbandry, feeding, and allied subjects. For example, *Celebrated Cats* was penned by Constantine E. Brooks, and more
recently the psychologist Donald K. Adams wrote the highly informa-
tive *Experimental Studies of Adaptive Behavior in Cats.* Such books, written by individuals who are experienced and knowledgeable in the
feline field, are often good reference books (though generally not complete in all areas) but not literary achievements. There have been a few,
a very few, books about cats written by professional writers that do
have, also, literary value, such as Carl Van Vechten's delightful *Tiger
in the House.* As Pope put it in his *Essay on Criticism:*

> True ease in writing comes from art, not chance,
> As those move easiest who have learn'd to dance.

Some mention of cats is made in Greek and early Persian poetry, and
Lope de Vega, one of Spain's most revered classical dramatists, has
written in rhyme of the cat's inordinate beauty. Early-nineteenth-
century English poet Jane Taylor wrote "I Like Little Pussy"; Robert
Herrick, the English poet, Théophile Gautier, the French poet, critic,

and novelist, and the German lyric and satiric poet and sometime critic and journalist Heinrich Heine all devoted many lines of verse to the wonderful qualities of cats. Saki (H. H. Munro) wrote "The Achievement of the Cat," and Aldous Huxley penned "A Sermon on Cats." Authors of celebrated achievement who were passionate ailurophiles include the Brontë sisters (Anne, Charlotte, and Emily), Sir Walter Scott, Swinburne ("To a Cat"), and in our own time Raymond Chandler, author of the Philip Marlowe "private eye" novels. And that forceful man of American prose Ernest Hemingway was also a practicing ailurophile. Vigorous and extreme in all facets of the life he embraced with such ardor, he consorted with as many as fifty felines in his home at Key West, Florida.

In his inimitable fashion Shakespeare often referred to cats, frequently in connection with the occult, as in *Macbeth:* "Thrice the brindled cat hath mewed." John Gay also leaned toward witchcraft and the occult in his fable "The Old Woman and Her Cats." Keats and Wordsworth gave puss the benefit of their considerable literary talent. Joseph Victor von Scheffel wrote a lengthy poem about a tom cat, and Baudelaire's verse was figuratively alive with feline references. A more contemporary bard, Wallace Stevens, selected the first line of his poem for its title:

> The lion roars at the enraging desert,
> Reddens the sand with his red-colored noise,
> Defies red emptiness to evolve his match.

The fabulous Chilean poet Pablo Neruda has turned his verse to a vast variety of subjects, including a lengthy *Ode to a Cat;* one particular section seems to remain in the mind:

> His is that peerless
> integrity
> neither moonlight nor petal
> repeats
> his contexture*

From the earliest days of the written word to the present, the cat has found a niche in verse, for its rhythmic cadence can express the qualities inherent in the cat: the beauty, passion, slumbering grace in repose, and pulsing power in movement. How often have we heard it said that the cat is poetry in motion?

---

*No hay unidad
como él
no tiene
la luna ni la flor
tal contextura

THE CAT IN PAINTING AND SCULPTURE

The arts are the culmination of mankind's cultural experience, and in the visual art of painting the creation of animal forms is the most ancient of artistic endeavors. In primitive caves, carved during earth's genesis, we find the records of early man's initial attempts to interpret his contemporary world through the art of animal painting. Particularly in France and Spain these remarkable true works of art can be seen on the cave walls, so deep in the grottos that they have been preserved from the destructive elements, a precious gift to us from our ancient ancestors.

Many of our more critical and articulate ailurophiles castigate artists for their lack of ability in representing the feline family. But there is a valid reason for this deficiency. The artist learns basic human anatomy—how the bones and muscles attach and move. He studies perspective, color, light and shadow, the texture of skin, tree bark, soil, water, all the bounties of nature that spring from the soil, and the way in which clothing materials drape and fold. But he does not usually study the anatomy, the individuality, and the movement of animals.

There are few painters, sculptors, and illustrators who devote their craft to the depiction of animals. Two of the better-known animal painters, the English Sir Edwin Landseer, whose animals are more "noble Romans" than beasts, and the famous French artist Rosa Bonheur, whose celebrated *Horse Fair* hangs in the Metropolitan Museum of Art in New York, both gave scant notice to the cat. The truth is that the cat is a very difficult subject to portray accurately because of its many moods and postures.

Egypt in the days of its glory was a kingdom of inspired beauty, ablaze with decorative murals, vast temples, great pyramids, palaces, and statuary of such magnitude that it astounds us even today. In murals depicting events of interest in the life of the great empire, the cat frequently appears, sometimes as a god or goddess, occasionally as a hunting companion, but most often as just a household favorite. Persian artists and sculptors depicted cats with varied degrees of accuracy, and the cat was a popular model in the delicately executed art of China and Japan. Foujita, an early-twentieth-century Japanese artist, painted cats modern in concept but in the ancient tradition of Japanese painting, capturing the feline essence. Roman painting (frescos) and decorative mosaics occasionally depicted the feline form, more often the big predacious cats than the domesticated puss.

In one of the early Last Supper paintings, from the Sienese school of Pietro Lorenzetti in the early fourteenth century, we see a gray tiger cat in the left corner of the room patiently awaiting scraps from the table. In the masterly, flowing sixteenth-century *Last Supper* by the great Tintoretto, a cat drinks from a wine vat in the center foreground. Leonardo da Vinci, genius of the Renaissance, sketched and painted many cats. Two of his early and most interesting drawings were both entitled *Madonna and Child with a Cat.* In his unfinished *Saint Jerome,* a lion lies in the foreground, and the Saint and the great cat seem to find emotional reciprocation.

The famous *Praying Hands* of Albrecht Dürer is a splendid example of the superb draftsmanship he brought to all his works. The master was fascinated by animals, and he rendered a host of realistic sketches and watercolors of all kinds of creatures. In his engraving of *Saint Jerome* the lion lacks authority, for Dürer had never seen a living lion. Later, after studying and sketching a lion in a Netherlands zoo, his king of beasts became far more effective, and in his detailed engraving *The Fall of Man,* etched in 1504, he drew a sleepy but solid domestic cat in the foreground.

Veronese painted cats into several of his important canvases, but with no great conviction. Both Pieter Bruegel and Hieronymus Bosch used felines in many of their active artworks. The chillingly absurd nightmares of Bosch lend his cats an otherworld aura. The techniques and painterly philosophy of both these artists were similar and cause a coupling in the mind when discussing their works. The famous altarpiece by Federico Baroccio, *The Madonna of the Cat (La Madonna del Gatto),* through association lends religious significance to the cat. The swashbuckling swordsman and celebrated Italian goldsmith, autobiographer, and artist Benvenuto Cellini used the cat in at least one of his small but priceless works. The Renaissance genius was a known ailurophile.

The flamboyant Peter Paul Rubens painted lions, tigers, and leopards in his huge action-motivated allegories; he also combined them with his voluptuous and fleshy females. Rubens painted and sketched lions more than any other animal, for he was fascinated by their lithe and graceful power. In his *Daniel in the Lion's Den* there are no less than nine of the huge, maned beasts; this is also one of the few large canvases said to be painted in its entirety by the Flemish master. The Dutch master of shadow and substance, Rembrandt, has left us a rather loosely handled sketch of a *Lion Resting;* and Goya's well-known portrait of the youthful Don Manuel Osorio de Zúñiga includes three large cats hungrily eyeing the child's pet magpie. Again, in his series of eighty etchings entitled *The Caprices (Los Caprichos),* the Spanish genius employed cats, usually associating them with the supernatural, as in the print *The Sleep of Reason Produces Monsters (El Sueño de la Razón Produce Monstruos)*. In New York's Metropolitan Museum of Art you will find a Gainsborough entitled *Child with a Cat*. And Sir Joshua Reynolds painted *Felina*, a portrait of a young girl with a kitten.

Perhaps the finest work by the Spanish master and court painter Diego de Silva Velázquez is the popular *Tapestry Weavers (Las Hilanderas)*, which is known in art circles as *The Fable of Arachne*. In almost the exact center foreground Velázquez has painted a very representative cat. There is an excellently painted puss in a work by William Hogarth depicting the cat eagerly approaching a caged bird. Eugène Delacroix, a true romantic, was fascinated by the big cats and sketched them without skin to realize the quality of their skeletal structure and musculature. These careful studies resulted in a series of canvases of hunting scenes and animal combats. He found precedents in George Stubbs, the French sculptor Antoine Louis Barye, Géricault, and Rubens: as a matter of fact, from Rubens he borrowed both composition and movement for his *Lion Hunt*, painted in 1861. Artists frequently borrow compositional movement and sometimes color usage from the works of an admired master's works.

A white Angora cat plays before his master, the painter Courbet, in a huge allegorical canvas of the artist in his studio, appropriately entitled *The Painter's Studio*. Edouard Manet, whom Zola called the "regenerator," and who was known to his contemporaries as the creator of modern art, frequently painted cats—on the lap of the *Woman in Pink*, in the *Luncheon on the Grass* (the famous *Déjeuner sur l'Herbe*), on notes he wrote to his friends, and in the famous lithograph of two amorous cats on a rooftop, a poster that advertised a book about cats written by his friend Champfleury. This lithograph was but one of several Manet drew to illustrate the text. His black cat in the famous nude *Olympia* hangs in the Louvre.

The Peasant Family, painted with a limited palette in a simple, severe style by the fine draftsman Le Nain, has the family cat in evidence; *The Music Lesson*, by Fragonard, depicts an exceedingly round-skulled puss evidently bored and waiting for the lesson to end; and Paul Gauguin's strong allegorical painting with the pretentious title *Whence Came We? What Are We? Whither Go We?* has two well-realized cats toward the center of the huge composition. Edward Hicks painted several of the big feral cats in his primitive *The Peaceable Kingdom*, illustrating verses from Isaiah: "The wolf shall dwell with the lamb, and the leopard shall lie down with the kid; and the calf and the young lion and the fatling together; and a little child shall lead them. . . ."

Rousseau the naïve primitive and Matisse the sophisticate both used cats large and small in their compositions, and the strange, anthropomorphic cats of Marc Chagall are familiar to all lovers of modern art. The authors' favorite Chagall cat is a happy green puss with a sunrise-hued belly in *The Poet, or Half Past Three*. Paul Klee, Richard Lindner, Fernand Léger, and Fernando Botero all introduced felines into their canvases, and the cats of Picasso are touched with the African primitivism he brought to much of his work. Franz Marc painted animals as life embedded in the totality of creation.

There have been a few artists and illustrators who have dedicated their abilities almost exclusively to portrayals of cats and who have gained some repute in this field. Louis Lambert and Henriette Ronner are two artists who have had some recognition; but Jean Grandville (né Gérard), an illustrator, caught more of the feline essence in his work than either Lambert or Ronner. A Swiss painter, Gottfried Mind, was considered by many critics to be the finest academic delineator of cats in his day. Max Beckmann painted *Friendel Battenberg with Cat*.

Oliver Herford's drawings of Persian kittens enhance his volumes of poetry and are unquestionably enchanting feline "children."

Alexandre Steinlen is an accomplished illustrator of cats, who has evidently studied the feline body in action and who captures the substance of cat kinetics in his work. The Victorian Englishman Randolph Caldecott used line sparingly in his feline illustrations for children's books; and George C. Bingham's *Fur Traders Descending the Missouri* features a black cat in the traders' canoe in this early American genre painting.

Painters linked with the American "ash can" school of painting used cats in their canvases: John Sloan's stretched black cat in *Greenwich Village Backyards* is a memorable example (from a time when the "ash can" school was still a major factor in American art). In Mexico, where a vigorous art movement flourishes, Frido Kahlo has painted a self-portrait with a fine black cat over his left shoulder; and Rufino Tamayo's strong *Horse and Lion* is slightly cubistic. We have also seen a delightful portfolio of drawings, *Cats Themselves*, by the contemporary artist Robert Kuhn.

Though not a painter himself, artistically intuitive Ambroise Vollard—publisher and gallery owner, who possessed the genius to recognize genius in the modern, departural masterpieces of Van Gogh, Bonnard, Gauguin, Cézanne, Matisse, Picasso, Renoir, Vuillard, Chagall, and a host of other fine new-thinking artists—was a lover of cats. He would sit for hours stroking one of his favorites in his cluttered gallery on the Rue Laffitte in Paris; a huge, immobile figure, seemingly absorbed in finding complete and utter relaxation from his feline friend. Most of the ostracized artists whom he espoused painted and sketched him, frequently holding or caressing one of his cats.

Other painters and sculptors who have used cats as models include quite a few of the primitive early American painters, such as Bradley,

Badami, Jennie Novik, Flora Bailey, Cugino, Eisenhauer, Davis, Gorman, and Bartoll. And artists whose talent is internationally recognized who painted cats into their compositions include Watteau and Renoir; Penfield (one of America's finest graphic artists); the Japanese painters Toko and Hiroshiga; Frost, whose black humor in 1894 forged *The Fatal Mistake;* Hérouard, the French illustrator noted for the sensual aura of his work; and the contemporary, staunchly academic painters Norman Rockwell and Andrew Wyeth.

Many of the artists named here will be familiar to the reader, and their work perhaps much admired. To choose among them, to select a favorite animal artist, is exceedingly difficult—yet unconsciously one does make a choice. The senior author of this book is partial to the radiant, sensitive, yet exciting semi-abstract and abstract paintings of Franz Marc, while the junior author favors the strong, colorful, naturalistic animal work of his father—who happens to be the senior author—and that is as it should be.

CHAPTER 5

All Cats: Wild . . .

The word "cat" is used to identify all members of the family *Felidae*, feral or domestic. The "big cats" are distinguished, other than through sheer size, by the manner in which they crouch with their forelegs and feet parallel to each other and extended in front of their bodies. The small cats tuck their feet in when crouching. Of the truly big cats of the world, we count eight; all but two (the cheetah and the ounce) sport the scientific designation *Panthera*. The jaguar and the puma, or mountain lion, enjoy a New World habitat, while the lion, tiger, leopard, clouded leopard, snow leopard, and cheetah are listed as Old World cats. The lion and the tiger are, of course, the giants of the big cat group, and all the family *Felidae*, feral or domestic, are extremely intelligent; in their role of carnivore they necessarily must be, for there is a basic law of nature that predacious animals exhibit greater sagacity than the creatures upon which they prey.

In total there are about thirty-five species of feral cats and many subspecies and closely allied subdivisions, most all of them inhabiting tropical or semitropical climes. These feral feline races are distributed widely on our planet except in Madagascar, Australasia, and Antarctica. No native feral cats prowl these far-flung areas. Most of the species of wild cats are found in Asia, Africa, and South America, and though it is generally thought that cats abhor water, most of these wild felines take advantage of the waters in their habitat area. All but the cheetah are physiologically fashioned to be night hunters; they are also natural opportunists, and if during daylight hours game is close and can be easily taken, they will not allow the occasion to pass without striking.

OLD WORLD BIG CATS

The lion *(Panthera leo)* is an impressive beast that has been closely linked to human history. Initially widespread, the lion has been forced to retreat steadily before civilization's advance, and today can only be found in numerical strength in protected areas in Africa. The great cat has disappeared from the Balkan Peninsula, Greece, and the Near

East. The last Barbary lions were exterminated in the past century in Morocco, Tunisia, and Algeria. A small number of Indian (or Asiatic) lions *(Panthera leo persica)* can still be found in the Gir Forest Sanctuary (Kathiawar) and Rajasthan in India, but the species is endangered.

The lion's tawny body hue is protective coloration mimicking its habitat, but lion cubs, two or three in number in a litter, are born spotted. Their eyes are open when born after a gestation period of approximately 106 days, and they are weaned at 6 months. One of the great thrills of an African safari (camera safari, naturally) is the first sight of a pride of lions in the wild. They are majestic, awe-inspiring, and the most gregarious of the feral cats; they travel in groups known as "prides."

A mature male lion will reach from 39 to 42 inches at the shoulder, stretch approximately 9 feet in length, and weigh 400 to 550 pounds. There are many (and were more) subspecies, but the difference in physical appearance is negligible. In some areas, the males are almost

In certain areas of Africa, lions climb trees to drowse away the hot tropical afternoons.

maneless; in others, they boast heavy manes ranging in color from light yellow to red-browns and black. Lions have a vestigial "claw" concealed in the hair-plume at the end of their tails; it's a strange appendage that seems to have no utilitarian value. Lions are generally night hunters, waiting patiently for their prey—zebra, antelope, giraffe, or any other of the herbivorous *Bovidae*—to come within striking distance. Except for the lone males, the lioness does the stalking and killing for the pride. The lion is the least bloodthirsty of the big cats and is essentially a rather lazy beast, sleeping the hot day away in whatever shade is available on the African plains. A full-maned, big male is an impressive animal worthy of his title "King of Beasts," and his coughing roar can shake the earth—or the African tourist sleeping in a flimsy tent in the bush.

A male tiger, huge, striped, and handsome, is the largest of cats, measuring 40 to 43 inches in height at the shoulders, stretching up to 10 feet in length, weighing over 500 pounds, and displaying fangs 5 inches long. The Siberian tiger, a subspecies, sometimes called the Manchurian tiger, wears a luxuriant coat as thick as an Alaskan bear's, and is the largest and heaviest species. A big male, it has been recently reported, can weigh up to 800 pounds, and that is a lot of cat.

The tiger *(Panthera tigris)* is a forest beast and a nocturnal stalker of game, preying upon deer, wild pig, cattle, oxen, buffalo, and peacock. If game is scarce, it will fish using its paw much as a grizzly bear does; and like a bear, this big cat is very much at home in the water.

In India, many of the aboriginal tribes regard the indigenous striped cat with superstitious awe, often worshipping it as a supernatural and fearsome god. Considering the toll in human lives taken by some of the man-eating tigers of India, one can understand the fear-spawned idolatry accorded the beast. The worst of such incidents known was perpetrated by a family of man-eating tigers in Bhwapur. They killed and ate over four hundred people before the frightened villagers finally fled the area. In mitigation of tigers, however, it should be said that only an estimated three out of every thousand tigers become man-eaters.

The tigress has a gestation period of three months and whelps two or three cubs: unlike the lion's young, the striped cat's kits are born blind, as are domestic kittens. Tiger cubs become independent at about two years of age, if they live that long. Before the age of six months, cubs sometimes fall victim to the voracious appetites of their parents.

The tiger originated in northern Siberia but was pushed south by the ice ages. It dislikes hot weather as fervently as the lion does. Tigers now range from southern Siberia to Korea, from Iran through Pakistan and into Tibet, India, China (where they are almost extinct), Thailand, Indochina, the Malay Peninsula, Sumatra, and Java. Due to such wide distribution, there are many subspecies genetically modified to fit the various environments so that at the extremes there is noticeable variation. Occasionally albino (white) or melanistic (black) specimens are born. A "white" strain of tigers is now being cultivated under human management in India, and they are extremely handsome beasts. A fine group of these rare cats is on exhibition in the Calcutta zoo. Albinism is carried as a recessive genetic characteristic by tigers in this area, for a "white" bred to a normal will often produce some cubs exhibiting recessive albinism. There also exist the rare "tigon" and "liger," the hybrid results of lion and tiger crossbreedings. Incidentally, the tiger's olfactory sense is not very keen.

This handsome felid is an endangered species, its enemy not so much the gun as the chain saw rapaciously chewing through and destroying the forests that are its habitat. Occasionally several tigers will congregate at a kill, so they cannot be considered a completely solitary breed of feral cat.

Strongly resembling the proportions of the domestic cat but much larger, the leopard *(Panthera pardus)* enjoys the most extensive range of all the big cats: Asia to India and the East Indies (where melanistic specimens are found), to southern Siberia, most of Africa, and from Asia Minor to China. The yellowish base color of the leopard's pelage is lavishly decorated with black spots. Implacably ferocious, the leopard is the most efficient killing machine of all the cats. When hunting, it moves with the floating grace of a ballet dancer and is as silent and stealthy as a venomous snake. Completely self-sufficient, it can climb with the agility of a monkey, and pound for pound it is one of the most powerful animals alive. The leopard is a jungle creature and a night hunter, who will not hesitate to kill during daylight hours if game is handy and a quick kill is in the offing. Leopards can also become man-eaters. In *The Times of India,* April 21, 1978, the senior author found an item about "the dreaded maneater of Dogadda" that had been "killed near Bareth village."

After the male leopard mates with the female of the species, he leaves, wanting no part of family life; his duty in perpetuating his species concluded, he feels no other obligation. The gestation period, the number of young, and their condition at birth are similar to the tiger's except that leopards have slightly larger litters.

A subspecies of *Panthera pardus,* the clouded leopard *(Neofelis nebulosa),* is strictly tropical in habitat and likes dense and humid jungle and rain forests: its range embraces eastern India and Malaysia. The base pelt color ranges from olive to almost red, with large, free-form darker areas enclosed by a black border distributed throughout the coat. It prefers to rest high in the treetops and peer down through the foliage surveying its sweltering territory for prey. The beauty of its markings and color lends a particular feral elegance to the clouded leopard. It is medium in size but varies considerably more in dimension than the African species, though in all other life phases they are alike, even to their matching ferocity. The canine teeth of this leopard are comparatively larger than those of the other large feral cats.

Without doubt the most handsome of the big cats is the snow leopard or ounce *(Uncia uncia)*, which is said not to be a true leopard though it is always listed with them because of physical similarity. Its snowy habitat is the high plateaus of Central Asia from the Himalayas to Mongolia. Its pelage is magnificently luxurious, soft and silvery, with smoky-black spots a rich ornamentation. The tail is thickly furred and quite long. Because of its valuable pelt, human predation has reduced its population to endangered status in the Himalayas, particularly in India, from Kashmir to Sikkim. The ounce feeds on domestic ungulates only occasionally, for it avoids areas of human habitation. The Asiatic ibex or Sakin and the other wild sheep and goats that share its dangerous environment are its main diet. The ounce is not often seen in captivity because the difficult terrain in which it lives impedes capture. Zoo keepers declare that the individual character of captured specimens varies greatly, some remaining totally vicious and untrustworthy while others become fairly tame and approachable.

The last of the Old World big cats, the cheetah *(Acinonyx jubatus)*, differs in many ways from its fellow cats. Long in body, high on its legs, small-headed and long-tailed, it is adapted to running down its prey rather than stalking and pouncing. The cheetah is the epitome of elegance and fluid grace when in action, and can run at better than a mile-a-minute pace, which rates it the fastest creature on four legs. This lithe and lovely cat does not climb as do most cats, for its claws are blunt and not completely retractile.

The cheetah's visual perception is not as keen as that of other cats, and it has poor night vision; as a result, it hunts during the day, preferring Thompson's gazelles as its regular diet. At full gallop, the hunting cheetah will reach out with both paws and bring down its running, herbivorous prey, then grasp the neck in its jaws to make the kill. Again unlike the other big cats, the cheetah will only dine on a fresh kill. Jackals often follow these cats, knowing that there will be fresh food left behind. The cheetah's vocal sounds are entirely different from the audio efforts of all other *Felidae*. Indeed, they possess so many uncatlike characteristics that some zoologists question their inclusion in the family *Felidae*.

Since no fossil remains have ever been found in Africa, the genesis of the cheetah is thought to have been in Asia, but the range of this big cat once extended from India westward to Morocco and throughout Africa. Today the species survives only in Africa. The cheetah stands 3 feet high and weighs over 100 pounds. The ground color of its pelt is a tawny yellow with whitish underparts; its entire body is liberally sprinkled with closely spaced black spots. The male cheetah usually leaves the female after breeding, so she must fend for her subsequent litter of about five cubs herself. She must raise and educate them in the ways of survival in the wild. Out of the litter less than half generally survives.

These beautiful cats are easily tamed and trained: the maharajahs in India kept them as hunting cats to run down the fleet black buck. The sixteenth-century emperor Akbar kept a thousand hunting cheetahs that were led around by handlers on a collar and leash. We have seen a film about cheetahs trained by American sportsmen to retrieve ducks from the water. Cheetahs have also been trained to run down and kill coyotes and wolves in the American Southwest. Because of their virtues cheetahs can make good pets, but even when domesticated they can revert to the basic instinct to give chase and bring down any creature that runs away from them, including other domesticated animals and even children. An endangered species, the cheetah has recently been successfully bred in captivity. Of all the big cats, this beauty is our personal favorite.

BIG CATS IN THE NEW WORLD

The duo of big cats of the New World is the jaguar and the native American lion of many names, including puma, cougar, mountain lion, American panther, catamount, panther, and painter. Both the jaguar and mountain lion are excellent climbers, and the jaguar is an excellent swimmer. This latter cat is larger and more powerful than the African leopard, and will fearlessly attack anything that moves.

Named *"el tigre"* in South and Central America where it ranges, the jaguar *(Panthera onca)* is a vicious night hunter, preying upon many species of animal, terrestrial and aquatic: it will even attack alligators, though its preferred menu includes tapirs, peccaries, domestic ruminants, and horses. This feral feline evinces no fear of man and if provoked will attack him as quickly as it will assault the huge Amazonian anaconda.

The jaguar can weigh up to 300 pounds and is capable of quickly and easily killing a fully grown steer, so there is no doubt that an attack upon a human could be lethal. Its yellow coat, adorned with glossy black rosettes stretched over a thick, powerful frame, lends a fierce beauty to this bold killer cat. Jaguars prefer a tree and heavy thicket habitat, but can adapt to a desert or rain-forest environment. Two to four young are born in late spring and remain with their dam until about two years of age.

South American legend tells of a lively character who lived in the steaming hell of the Mato Grosso jungle in South America, Sacha Siemal, named the "Tiger Man" by the Indians. Siemal was of Latvian descent and first appeared in the area about 1918. For fifty years thereafter he hunted the jaguar, and became particularly famous for his hunting prowess with the *zagaya*, a stout spear. His perilous method of hunting was to stalk and provoke the powerful and totally vicious killer cat to charge in attack, then impale the raging beast on the foot-long iron spearhead. For some reason, the Tiger Man's mode of jaguar hunting never became a trend.

Occasionally, a jaguar is acquired by some individual as a pet. Perhaps the person involved wants to investigate the possibility of a one-to-one relationship with a feral cat. Or the beast may be obtained by some *"macho"* idiot on an ego trip. Whatever the reason, it is not based on sound judgment. Either the owner is eventually badly mauled or the cat is declawed and its canine teeth pulled to make the association less hazardous. Under any circumstances the poor animal generally ends up in the nearest zoo. There are some feral cats that can be substantially tamed and there are many that cannot. The jaguar can be considered in the latter category.

The puma *(Felis concolor),* unlike the jaguar, is an exceedingly shy feline, and though in the wild it is a cruel and daring predator, there has never been an authenticated incident of an attack upon a human. This feral cat can sometimes be tamed and, to an extent, domesticated if captured when very young (depending upon individual temperament). The puma, or cougar if you wish, formerly roamed the length and breadth of the American continents, and was at home in the various environments so wide a range offered. But the spread of civilization has eliminated the species in most sections of the two continents, and in North America it can only be found now in remote Southwest forests, the Canadian Rockies, the jungles of Mexico, a limited few in the Eastern United States, and in national parks and reserves where it is protected. In Florida, the puma is an endangered species. Each cat has a territorial range of from 20 to 50 miles, and when one is killed, the puma population in that area is then completely eliminated.

This big tawny cat is arboreal, and, though wary, it is a daring night hunter, feeding on deer (particularly mule deer), elk, and domestic ungulates; it is especially dangerous to sheep, goats, calves, and horse colts, though its territory is seldom close to civilization where man's herbivorous creatures can be found. These felines are loners. Pairs unite to breed for a brief three weeks only. The females produce litters of from one to six blind, spotted kittens, which depend upon their mothers for sustenance and lessons in the arts of living until they are about two years of age. Females must protect the young from their sires and other passing males.

The cougar stakes out its hunting territory and defends it with tooth and nail against interlopers. This big cat's pelage is much the same color as the African lion's coat, but unlike the lion, its head is proportionately small and its powerful body lithe and long. A large male puma can weigh up to 200 pounds and measure 8 feet from nose to long tail tip. It prowls its domain with the silence of drifting smoke. In the Southwest these big felines are hunted with "cat" hounds, who trail and eventually tree the cat, keeping it treed until the hunters arrive. Teddy Roosevelt named the puma "the great horse-killer cat" and gave credence to the myth of its ferocity.

The "big cats" are tremendously interesting animals, perhaps in the aggregate the most interesting of all mammals because they so perfectly fit their destined role as carnivorous predators. They are the kings of their domains, handsome, powerful beyond belief, in action pure savage ballet; and cruel—as cruel and malevolent as the Prince of Darkness. Rudyard Kipling described a majestic black leopard as "black as the pit and terrible as the Demon." The big cats bring fear to the hearts of most men, for there is deep within us a residual ancestral horror of the rending teeth and ripping claws that filled the days and nights of our apelike progenitors with abysmal terror.

OLD WORLD SMALLER WILD CATS

There are a host of smaller feral felines, many of surpassing barbarous beauty, all typical of their family, and all practiced predators. The serval *(Felis serval)* boasts a shoulder height of 18 to 20 inches and can weigh up to 40 pounds. It is a handsomely marked cat, with a tawny yellow, black-spotted coat, a short black-banded tail, and rather large bat ears. A subspecies, the servaline, exhibits smaller spots. Like most cats, the serval is solitary, nocturnal, and generally terrestrial, but it can climb trees after prey when necessary. All-black melanistic specimens are not uncommon, and in their glossy midnight coat are exceedingly comely cats. The serval's distribution is wide in East Africa, and it usually frequents scrub grass areas where its favorite food, guinea fowl, can be found—a true gourmet, this feline. Like the cheetah, this is a long-legged cat, physically molded to chase and catch its prey while running. Over the centuries, African tribal chiefs have used serval pelts as decorative cloaks and chief-symbol mantles.

Another short-tailed African cat is the caracal *(Caracal caracal)*. It wears a sleek, red-brown coat and has long-tufted ears, a peculiarity that has led to its pseudonym, desert lynx. A swift-running graceful feline, the caracal is closely related to the serval and, though not quite as large, hunts bigger game, including the Thompson gazelle. The caracal reaches a shoulder height of 16 to 18 inches, and a length that can vary between 26 and 36 inches. Again like the serval, it is nocturnal, short-tailed, usually terrestrial (though it is a very capable climber), mainly solitary, and its agility is legendary. Caracals were tamed and trained to compete in pigeon-catching contests by Eastern potentates. This interesting feline ranges over a large part of the Dark Continent.

A good-sized, strangely marked wild feline is the golden cat or Temminck's cat *(Felis temmincki)*, which reaches a height at the withers of approximately 16 inches, and a length, including the tail, of 40 inches. In color it is either a lustrous red-brown or gray-brown, fading to white on the underparts. Black spots are confined to the flanks and underbody of the cat. This handsome feline is rather rare: it is solitary, nocturnal, and normally terrestrial. Its habitat embraces Southeast Asia and Africa, including the Ruwenzori range forests and south-western Kigezi in Uganda. Some specimens take readily to domestication and are quick to learn. The fierce marbled cat inhabits the jungles of Southeast Asia.

Among the small, spotted wild cats of the Old World can be listed the fishing cat *(Felis viverrina)* of Southeast Asia and India; the leopard cat *(Felis bengalensis)*, a beautiful, small, leopard-spotted feline that was once the most numerous of the little wild Asiatic cats but is now endangered due to constant exportation as an exotic pet; the shy jungle cat *(Felis chaus)*, with a habitat range from Africa through southern Asia to Indochina, gray-brown with broken markings and a weight of approximately 20 pounds; the small, Asian, Arabian sand cat, pale buff in color, who looks much like a domesticated cat but is actually quite ferocious and untamable; and the Pallas's cat *(Felis manul)*, a striped Asian wild cat who ranges from the Caspian Sea east to Tibet and Mongolia. This last is rather a strange-looking cat, with a low forehead, wide-spaced ears, and a long coat of gray or orange color.

An agile climber, the European lynx *(Lynx lynx)* is identified by its typical tufted ear tips and short tail. All lynxes differ from other wild cats in possessing only twenty-eight teeth. This active and powerful wild cat reaches over large areas of Europe, Siberia, and Mongolia. When game is scarce, it will prey on sheep and goats. The lynx is a handsome fellow in his spotted coat, and the Spanish lynx *(Lynx pardellua)* is the most attractive of the species.

The European wild cat *(Felis silvestris)* claims the forests of Europe as its native heath: the Scottish Highlands, France, and Italy. It is nocturnal, and though rather small is strong and ferocious. It resembles our domestic cat and furthers this disguise by wearing the tabby pattern of stripes and bars. Even the kittens of this wild cat are too feral to be tamed. The Scottish wild cat is a subspecies.

The caffer cat *(Felis lybica),* also known as the African wild cat, comes from Africa, Syria, and Egypt. Like the European wild cat, it strongly resembles the domestic cat but is broader in head and body, with a slightly shorter tail. Its tabby markings are not as distinct as those of the domestic cat. Approximately 9 inches high at the shoulder and 28 to 30 inches long, it is solitary, nocturnal, both terrestrial and arboreal, and will often mate with domestic felines when close to human habitation. The Indian desert cat *(Felis lybica ornata)* is a subspecies of the caffer cat.

The last two, the caffer and the European wild cat, are the most important of wild felines to the dedicated ailurophile, for the domestic cat is thought to have originally evolved from ancestral forms of this duo.

SMALLER WILD CATS IN THE NEW WORLD

There are some extremely interesting small wild cats in the Americas, particularly in tropical and semitropical areas. The great jungle of the Mato Grosso (called "Green Hell" by those who have entered the overgrown, twilight confines of this dangerous area), through which flows the mighty, brown-hued Amazon River, is fertile territory for wild tropical felines, as are the moist tangled forests that border the wild Orinoco River. Large expanses of these regions still have not seen the footprints of modern civilized man, incredible as it may seem when man has stood upon the surface of the Moon and sent mechanical space probes to Mars, Venus, Saturn, and other deep-space planets.

The largest of these wild cats of the Americas is the Canadian lynx *(Lynx canadensis).* It wears a heavier and thicker coat and has larger, broader feet (for walking on snow) than its European counterpart, but in all other respects—bobtail, tufted ears, and large powerful hindquarters—it resembles the European lynx. Its valuable pelt is gray or brownish with indistinct spots, and it can reach a maximum weight of about 40 pounds spread over a muscular 3½-foot frame. Its hindquarters are proportionately larger and higher than those of the long-tailed wild cats in order to supply balance, particularly when climbing. The lynx is an excellent climber and ranges the forests of Canada and Northern United States preying chiefly on hares and rabbits (snowshoe preferred). Subspecies occur in the Canadian Northwest and the Western United States.

The bobcat *(Lynx rufus)*, also called the bay lynx and more simply wildcat, is considerably smaller than the lynx, generally weighing from 15 to 30 pounds, with lesser ear tufts and smaller paws, but in basic fierceness it equals the larger lynx. It is rufus (reddish-brown) in color, with black spots distributed throughout its coat. This cat can be found in most forest areas of the United States and Canada. Due to its excessive stealth and moderate size, it has not been too seriously depleted in numbers though it has been diligently hunted by man. The Catskill Mountains, christened by early Dutch settlers in New York State, were named after the wildcat (Kaatskill). This cat is nocturnal, arboreal, and a practiced predator. It has been known upon occasion to mate with a domestic puss, and the kittens, it is rumored, have made interesting pets. The barred wildcat *(Lynx rufus fasciatus)*, a subspecies, wears bars on its legs accompanying the black spots. There is another subspecies in Nova Scotia *(Lynx rufus gigas)* that reportedly can reach much greater size and weigh in excess of 60 pounds.

One of the most attractive of the lesser felids, the ocelot *(Felis pardalis)*, lives in South America. A skillful predator, arboreal and occasionally aquatic, the ocelot is in appearance much like a small jaguar. Also called the painted leopard, this cat has a handsome spotted coat that has value in the marketplace and makes the ocelot a target for greedy hunters. This feline often lives near native villages where farmyard creatures can be added to its menu. The ocelot weighs about 35 pounds and is about 3 to 4 feet long, including its tail. It is completely harmless to man in the wild (other than feasting upon his domestic food animals, particularly poultry), and if taken when young can be raised as a pet. Several South American friends of ours keep ocelots as home pets. A related species, now quite rare, is the giant ocelot *(Felis chibigouavou)* that inhabits the deepest jungle. Occasionally, specimens almost reach a size that tempts their being listed among the larger feral cats.

Another related species is the margay or American tiger cat *(Felis tigrina)*. Its habits mimic those of the ocelot, but it is smaller, about the size of a domestic puss. It ranges through northern Brazil and from Cayenne to eastern Venezuela. Its large, fine eyes are those of a nocturnal animal, and it is a productive predator. Both the ocelot and the margay emit deep, menacing vocal sounds, much stronger than their size would indicate. The margay cat can also be tamed to pet status if acquired when young, before it is tutored in the ways of the wild by its dam; but like most wild cats, it is not as reliable a companion as any of the domestic breeds. Both the ocelot and margay are endangered species.

An interesting and unusual member of the New World smaller felids is the eyra cat or jaguarundi *(Felis yagouaroundi)*. It is a small cat with a small head and a long, slender, otter-like body and tail, and no resemblance to the handsome jaguar at all. The jaguarundi glides through its jungle abode both on the ground and in the trees; it is lithe and quick enough to catch fish, small animals, and birds, and has been known upon occasion to eat fruit. There are two color phases: one red-brown (eyra) and the other dark gray (jaguarundi). Both types range the same territory from Argentina through Central America to southern Texas. In Brazil, Argentina, and Peru there ranges a gray, reddish-striped feral feline named the Pampas cat, the appellation indicative of its habitat. These small cats are terrestrial, extremely furtive, and very savage predators. They weigh approximately 30 pounds and are said to be completely untamable. Geoffroy's cat inhabits the high Andes of South America.

All of the American feral *Felidae* are solitary cats and only during the mating season do the sexes associate. Two to four cubs are a normal litter, born blind like domestic kittens. Felid females are generally fine mothers and take excellent care of their cubs.

It is quite evident that the feral cats share many characteristics, even though they vary greatly in size. Whatever the species, the members of the genus are phylogenetically very closely related and are similar in appearance. They are cats, and they look and act like cats. They are all generally excellent climbers, lithe, nocturnal, and solitary. They are unsurpassed and puissant predators.

There is one bit of pertinent information about the feral cats that must be stressed—they are *wild cats*, killers and predators by necessity to sustain life, and they should be considered dangerous animals. Though we have mentioned that some species can be tamed and domesticated, they must, for this purpose, be acquired when very young, and should only be owned and handled by those rare individuals who have a rapport with animals in general and cats in particular. Books and films may give the layman the impression that even the largest and most savage of the "big cats" can become friendly with a human and live with him or her in harmony under certain circumstances. To an extent this could be true, but the person would have to be a special individual, the one in a million (or perhaps ten million) who can develop a sympathetic relationship with the beasts, and who would be able to live with the feral cats on their own terms and in their own environment and territory.

Owners of any of the smaller feral felines that can be tamed must be careful never to allow their pet to become involved in a situation, even for a moment, where its basic wild instincts can become suddenly aroused, for though they may think their pet is thoroughly tamed, the veneer of domestication is too often thinner than they realize.

Before we leave this chapter, there is one more item we must mention. You who read this book love cats and can, in the aggregate and possibly singly, exert influence in high places to stem the tide of the hideous fur trade, the massive murder of wild felines (even those on the endangered lists) for their fur. Included in this endangered list and close to extinction are the Chinese tiger, jaguar, ocelot, margay, and many other feral cats. They are linked in their membership in this dread category with the California condor, giant armadillo, giant tortoise, black-footed ferret, and a host of other wild creatures. Several species of whales are also on the endangered list: these mammoth mammals are tracked by radar and other highly sophisticated devices and murdered with explosives (grenades attached to guided harpoons).

In the late 1960s a report was published indicating that approximately 250,000 pelts of ocelots, jaguars, and margays were imported to furriers in the United States within a span of less than two years. Add to this sum the number of skins of other feline species taken, and the number that must have entered other countries, and you have a fair idea of the extent of this assassination of our wild felines and the rape of their habitats. In many instances protective methods have been evolved and preserves allocated for their safety, but poachers know no boundaries and flaunt all laws so long as the demand exists for exotic feline pelts and the payment is high. So the slaughter continues, and every year it lowers the numbers of these precious cats and the young they produce. They must be saved for the future, because extinction is close—and extinction is final and forever.

CHAPTER 6

... And Domestic

Of all domestic animals the cat is the most intelligent, the most comfortable to live with, the cleanest and, excluding the long-haired varieties, the easiest to care for. Adopted by man approximately three thousand years ago, the cat has proven to be worthy of the accolades accorded it as an amenable, loving household pet and, true to its heritage, a rodent eradicator without peer. Puss is self-sufficient, mercurial, affectionate, esoteric, a practiced narcissist, and wholly unique. The domestic cat has a fluidity of movement, an elegance and beauty that are unmatched by any other pet known to man.

These many virtues of the cat can be held comparable to the eight basic notes of the musical scale from which composers have proliferated an endless flow of concertos, operas, cantatas, symphonies, and less exalted musical experiences. In the same way, earnest breeders have noted feline attributes, and have, through assiduous selection for specific genetic traits, molded the many breeds of domestic felines we are about to discuss.

But despite man's manipulation of genetic variables, his keen and intense search for mutations, and the generally eager acceptance of new varieties by the cat fancy, the domestic feline has remained much the same in conformation, size, and temperament throughout the ages —proof of the inherent staunchness of the basic heritage of the family *Felidae.*

The British, inveterate animal lovers that they are, were the first ailurophiles to hold a cat show, thereby granting status to the then-recognized breeds of purebred domestic feline varieties of the nineteenth century. In the decades that followed, many new varieties were introduced to the cat fancy, or fashioned by breeders from the cross-breeding of existing types, and through selection for wanted values. At the moment there are over thirty accepted, distinct breeds, some recognized by several of the registration associations and others not yet given official recognition. We will list and describe also several other pure breeds known as exotics or experimentals that have not yet received authorized acknowledgment as true varieties.

Cats can be roughly divided into two categories: the mixed breeds or general house cats, the result of unplanned and often secret matings; and the purebred cats, the fruit of intentional breeding by people for

The pug face of a Persian cat.

specific and selective conformation and general physical appearance. The purebreds can in turn be segregated into two classes: the short-haired breeds and the long-haired varieties. All purebred felines can also be partitioned into two other subdivisions: those with traits conforming so closely to their variety's standard that they can be successfully exhibited in competition at cat shows and used as breeding animals; and those that, though pedigreed and registered, are not without faults that would eliminate them from show competition. Such cats must fulfill their destiny as beloved household pets and companions, a fate much to be desired by most cats. Breeders of fine cats tend to specialize and dedicate all their efforts to the production of excellent specimens of one or a selected few special breeds. But all cats belong to the same species—*Felis catus.*

Before we delve into the physical and mental characteristics of the divers varieties, it is essential that we understand and identify the colors and patterns of color to which the domestic puss is heir. At the moment we will merely indulge in color classification, but more about color, relative to inheritance, will be found in Chapter 10, on cat genetics. Both short- and long-haired felines flaunt the same colors and markings, with the exception of spotting which, at present, is confined to the short-hairs.

We will begin color and pattern recognition with the tabby effect, which is the basic color arrangement inherited from what we assume were the domestic feline's prototypical ancestors. The word "tabby" is the English borrowing of *attabi,* an old Arabic word used to identify a wavy, watered silk, taffeta cloth. There are four basic types of tabby markings: a medium-wide, fairly clean-edged, black-striped effect; the Abyssinian, or ticked (not always considered a true tabby); a narrow-striped effect, with close, clearly defined narrow bands of dark stripes (mackerel tabby); and the classic blotched tabby markings, consisting of a few wide bands that are broken in design. The last effect, brought to an extreme, becomes the spotted cat. Tabbies can be russet brown, orange (with deep reddish-orange stripes), gray, blue, cream, or silver. The tabby pattern in all varieties must never be caliginous: it must always be sharp and well defined. Finally, it must be noted that domestic cats which have become feral produce offspring that after several generations of breeding in the wild generally revert to the basic tabby color, regardless of the pigmentation of their original domestic ancestors.

White cats can be listed in three categories: (1) the all-white with pigmented eyes (blue, green, copper, orange, or with each eye a different color); (2) the pink-eyed white, a true albino with a complete absence of color; and (3) the white-spotted cat, exhibiting the white element through large pied areas over the body and accompanied by blotches of color, or the confined white pattern (bicolor) that embraces the chest, feet, legs, tail, and face. There is also a white variety of Siamese cat that does not exhibit the pink eyes of the recessive albino factor.

Black needs no description. A black cat is very simply a black cat, and if one crosses your path it can bring you good luck or bad luck, according to how coordinated or accident-prone you are. Incidentally, in the world of cats a tiny white spot on the chest of an otherwise black cat is called a locket. The blue color (also referred to as "Maltese") is a dilute phase of black and can be light to medium in color value. Orange is familiar to everyone, and the color cream should be a rich cream, for it is genetically a dilute orange. Smoke-colored cats are basically silvers that lack the tabby-producing gene. Short-haired cats do not exhibit the smoke hue to its fullest extent, but the blending produced by the coats of long-hairs achieves a lovely smoky effect.

Chinchilla exhibits silver ticking that lends a sprightly sparkle to the pelage. Red is a deeper, more bricklike hue than orange, and the color should be rich and full: when tabby-marked, the striping should be a deep mahogany shade. Blue-creams display either a soft blending (in England), or a patching effect (in the United States) of blue and cream hues.

Tortoiseshell is a distinct combination of black and light and dark red, like a Matisse *découpage*. Add white in discreet measure and you have the calico cat. If the tortie carries the gene for dilution, it becomes blue and cream if solidly colored or it can exhibit white markings. The term "calico" was borrowed from a cloth imported from India that is printed in multicolored designs. A bicolor is a feline demonstrating two clearly defined colors; black and white, blue and white, et cetera. A self is a cat with a single, solid color completely covering its entire body.

The Siamese color, whether carried by the true Siamese or by other varieties that indicate genetic linkage to the Siamese, is a distinct pattern of light and dark, or light and dilute. The darker areas are confined to the head area, the feet and lower section of the legs, and the tail. Body color varies in tone to conform with the color density of the points: richer when the points are dark, and paler when the points are lighter and display the effects of a dilution factor.

The seal-pointed Siamese possesses deep, rich seal-brown points and a fawn-hued body, shading to a deeper fawn from the withers back toward the seal-shaded tail. The blue-point has gray-blue, rather frosty points, and a pale, somewhat cold-hued body shade. The pelage of the chocolate-point is a pale ivory accompanied by rich, milk-chocolate points; and the frost-point Siamese displays an overall pale body tone with points of pale blue-gray carrying a subtle overtone of pink. The red-point reveals the red extremities against a light body coat. The lilac-point exhibits a rather cold, white body color against delicate, grayish-lilac points; and the lynx-point, or tabby, has a pale body hue with tabby striping confined to the point areas. Tortoiseshell-point Siamese exhibit tortie markings in the usual restricted Siamese point areas, and these can be seal, chocolate, blue, or lilac tortoiseshell points. Cream-point and red and cream tabby-points have also been bred.

A ticked (banded or agouti hair), ruddy-colored coat (ruddy-brown ticked with black) is worn by the Abyssinian cat in the normal phase, but the shade of the red Abyssinian is copper-red with darker (chocolate) ticking. The same colors are displayed by the longer-coated Somali.

The original Burmese pigment is a solid seal brown, paling slightly on the underbelly and chest areas. Cameo is a color variation developed in this country that presents a ticked or shaded pelt and is associated with Persians. Shell cameo is very pale cream with red hair-tipping and white ear tufts, chin and chest; shaded cameo displays much more red coloring than the shell cameo, with graded red shading on the tail, sides, and face merging to pale ivory on the underside of the tail and body and on the chest. Presenting a rich, red-beige fur, the smoke cameo reveals an ivory to white undercoat when moving; and the tabby cameo boasts a soft cream pelt enhanced by a red or beige tabby design.

Marmalade is a ginger or orange shade usually accompanied by a tabby pattern. This tasty preserve shade is generally worn by a non-purebred variety of felines that are usually males, so we may assume that it is a color correlated with a sex-linked characteristic. Bronze (as in the Egyptian mau) presents a warm fawn body color with chestnut-hued markings.

The foregoing paragraphs on color and the nomenclature used for the various coat pigments are evidence that ailurophiles possess a distinct artistic feeling for the niceties of shades, colors, and markings worn by our feline companions.

THE VARIETIES OF SHORT-HAIRED DOMESTIC CATS

Each variety of purebred cat is accorded a specific, written standard predicated upon a point system that allots a certain number of points to various areas of conformation and that adds up finally to a total of 100 points for a perfect specimen—a goal much to be desired but seldom, if ever, achieved.

In discussing the desired attributes of the many feline breeds we will, for clarification, include the written standard and point system accorded to four of the most prominent breeds: the domestic short-hair and the Siamese as representatives of the short-haired varieties, and the Persian and Himalayan as examples of the long-haired breeds. You will note the difference in the allocation of points to give emphasis to individual breed requirements. In the interest of brevity, all other varieties will be informally discussed with emphasis upon the most pertinent features their standards stress.

The Domestic Short-Hair (or American short-hair)

This breed is actually the feline that was labeled "just plain cat," the variety whose ancestors came from Europe with Columbus and from England with the Pilgrims. Fairly recently, aware of the many virtues possessed by these unpedigreed cats, intrepid breeders decided upon a show standard, bred the domestic short-hair (the name they christened this deserving puss) to fit their ideal of breed perfection, and thereby gave it equal status in the family of felines. Basically, the domestic short-hair wears a short, thick coat, is cobby (short in body and strong), powerful, and lithe, with a typical round (not elongated) feline head. It can be found in the full range of cat colors.

The *mackerel-striped tabby short-hair* is a variety very similar to the domestic short-hair. This breed is claimed by its proponents to be the original domestic cat. In color and design, the mackerel's plentiful tabby rings spring vertically from the backline and are narrow and sharply defined against the body shade. A new wire-haired mutation has appeared with a coat similar to that sported by the wire-haired fox terrier, if the authors may make so bold as to mention a dog in a book about cats.

In temperament, the domestic short-hair is sweet and lovable, easy to live with, intelligent, and a well-mannered, pleasant member of the cat family. The standard and scale of points for this breed is as follows:

STANDARD	*Domestic Short-Hair*	POINTS
BODY COLOR: Same as for long-haired cats. Standard markings.		25 points
COAT: Short, thick, lustrous, good texture, slightly thicker in winter months.		15 points
BODY TYPE AND SHAPE: Well knit, powerful, good depth and full chest, ranging from medium to large in size. Neck medium short, strong, in proportion to body.		15 points
HEAD: Broad between the ears, cheeks well developed, especially in studs. Nose and face medium short with eyes set wide apart, muzzle presenting a squarish look but not as short as long-hairs. Chin well developed.		10 points
EARS: Medium in size, wide-set, rounded tips, not too large at base.		5 points
EYES: Round, full, set to show breadth of nose.		5 points
EYE COLOR: Conforming to coat color.		5 points
LEGS AND FEET: In proportion to body; legs of good substance; feet neat and well rounded, five toes in front, four behind.		10 points
TAIL: Slightly heavy at base, proportionate to body, tapering to abrupt end.		5 points
CONDITION: Hard and muscular, general appearance one of strength, vigor, and balance.		5 points
		100 points

UNDESIRABLE: Too high on the legs, receding chin, snub nose or "Pekingese" face, coat fluffy or too fine, wedge-shaped head and long nose, ears set too close and long and pointed, slanting, narrow eyes or Oriental look, neck too long and slender, or too short and thick, tail short and whiplike. Not to resemble Siamese in any manner.

The Siamese Cat

The exotic, aristocratic Siamese is the legendary sacred temple cat of Thailand, and the most popular and widely recognized, even by the neophyte, of all purebred short-haired cats. The breed was originally introduced to the British Isles in 1884 and reached ailurophiles in the United States ten years later. Its "foreign" appearance, unusual color and color pattern, linked to its attractive disposition, made the Siamese an instant hit wherever it was seen by cat lovers. The Siamese quickly became a prominent breed. The singular color arrangement dictates that the darker areas (designated as "points") be confined to the ears, face mask, feet and legs, and the long tail, lending lovely contrast to the much lighter shades of the sleek, slender body.

The color varieties are: seal-point, a dark, rich brown accompanied by a cream and tan body hue; chocolate-point, milk-chocolate color points with an ivory body color; blue-point, as contrast to a bluish-white and oyster (perhaps this word should not be used with the blue-point) body; frost-point, a dilute of blue-point exhibiting a frosty-white body color, a delightfully delicate combination; lilac-point, displaying lavender points and a white body with a faint overlay of pinkish pastel; red-point (also called flame concha), dark red points and a warm whitish body; and tabby-point (or lynx-point) and tortoise-shell-point, both of which describe themselves.

Brilliant blue Oriental eyes are characteristic of all Siamese, varying slightly in color depth with the overall pigmentation of the point variety. Some unfortunate individuals display crossed eyes (strabismus or "squint"), and some a knot or bend in their tails. The nose-leather and footpad color of kittens are sometimes used by breeders to predict the mature color of some of the varieties, particularly the blue- and frost-point Siamese. The pelt is sleek and short, the longish body slopes slightly upward from shoulder to pelvis, and the head is long, lean, and wedge-shaped.

This charming breed is extremely intelligent, active, sensitive, and affectionate. The cleverness and devotion of the Siamese and its ability to absorb training are legendary. It has a need to love and to be loved and can be quite demanding in its affection. Its devotion to master or mistress is almost doglike in intensity. Generally vociferous, the Siamese has a loud and distinctive voice, and the "calling" of the female when in heat is cacophonous—true caterwauling.

STANDARD	*Siamese*	POINTS

BODY COLOR: Should be even, shading to lighter hue on underbody and chest. Older cats tend to darken with age. — 15 points

POINTS: Dense and clearly defined on mask, ears, legs, feet, and tail, and all points of the same shade. Mask should be connected to ears by tracings, except in kittens. — 10 points

COAT: Short, fine in texture, lying close to the body. Satiny short and sleek. — 10 points

BODY TYPE AND SHAPE: Medium in size, dainty, long and svelte. Neck long and slender. Legs proportionately long and slim. Hind legs slightly higher than front. Body should exhibit some tuck-up in belly. Feet oval in shape and dainty. Tail long in proportion to body, tapering with no visible kinks. Males to be proportionally larger than females. — 20 points

HEAD AND EARS: Head long, tapering in straight lines from ears to narrow muzzle with no break. Shaped like a fine wedge. A receding chin caused by improper occlusion of the teeth is a serious fault. The skull is flat and in profile exhibits a straight line from center of forehead to tip of nose. Allowance to be made for the jowls of a stud cat. Between the eyes there should be the width of one eye. Ears rather wide, large and pricked, wide at base. — 20 points

EYES: Clear and of a vivid deep blue. Eye aperture almond in shape and slanting toward the nose in true Oriental fashion. — 20 points

CONDITION: Good physical condition, not fat; inclined to muscle. Judges to penalize for emaciation. Should be in athletic condition. — 5 points

_____

100 points

UNDESIRABLE: Rounded head, rough, shaggy, dull coat, fat, short-necked, thickest, or cobby specimens. Crossed eyes, odd eye color: gray or yellow tinge marring eye color. Belly and/or hip spots. Light hairs in the points. White on toes. Receding chin. Tail kink, obvious or invisible. Tabby or ticked markings (exception, the lynx-point). Hood: an extension of point coloring over top of head, sides, and under throat, giving appearance of hood tied around head.

Some of the newer varieties of Siamese named here have not yet been given official recognition by all the cat associations, but are instead called colorpoint short-hairs. Among the breeds to follow you will find many that were fashioned wholly or in part from Siamese heritage. The cat from Siam, like the Arabian horse among equines, has been the fountainhead from which has flowed a plethora of new cat breeds and improvement to many other varieties.

The Exotic Short-Hair

A fairly new breed developed in the United States, the exotic short-hair is the epitome of everything the Siamese isn't. Here in America the products of short- to long-hair breedings have been *persona non grata* on the show bench, but the exotic short-hair—a hybrid produced by crossing the American short-hair, or the Burmese, to the long-hair Persian—has broken the ethnic barrier and achieved association recognition. Since short hair is dominant over long hair, the breed was not difficult to establish in the short-hair category. The exotic short-hair is sturdy in bone, has a massive, round head with a wide skull, and a cobby, low-set body. In all details of conformation it follows the Persian standard, but without the nose break and with a soft, medium-length hair coat. Color classifications ape that of the Persian. Strong, affectionate, and healthy, the exotic short-hair makes an ideal exhibition and house cat.

The Burmese Cat

Solidly built, dark brown felines, called *zibelines* in France, where they are said to have originated, the Burmese were purported to be the darlings of the ancient aristocracy and priests of Burma, where each cat had its human servant. The Burmese cat, however, actually developed in the United States, and it owes much of its modern heritage to the Siamese. In conformation it is greatly similar to the Siamese, possessing the same slanting-eyed, Oriental appearance but with a wider, shorter jaw and shorter ears. It is affectionate and intelligent, but not as raucous or as demanding as the Siamese. In color the Burmese is a deep, solid seal brown with lighter shading on the chest and underbody. A blue variety is also extant, probably the effect of the same recessive dilution factor that produced the blue-point Siamese. Other colors departing from the normal Burmese brown hue are the red, tortie, platinum (or lilac), cream, blue-cream, and champagne (chocolate). Eye color ranges from yellow to gold but never green. The

Burmese is a fearless, active cat. Its beguiling personality makes it an excellent house pet and companion.

The Abyssinian Cat

Of obvious foreign type, slender, medium in size and graceful, the Aby is an anomaly in the domestic cat family because it obviously enjoys water and frequently finds amusement playing in it. In 1868 a British military expedition to Abyssinia brought back to England the first Abyssinian, and crosses to this cat established the breed in the British Isles. The Aby is a sensitive puss and must be treated with kindness and consideration in order to touch its inner core of devotion. Thought to be linked genetically (in its original form) to the sacred cats of ancient Egypt, the Aby wears a distinctive coat of banded (agouti) hairs, which fuse to a rather solid ruddy brown tipped with black, with a darker hue accenting the spine. The underbody and the insides of the legs are lighter and touched with an orange tone. The back is quite level and straight, accompanying a lithe, rather long body, and a long neck with large ears adorning a head that is a modified wedge. The Aby has a definite feral appearance but is actually a friendly, intelligent feline with an individual personality. An ideal cat for the country, it is very active and must be allowed a good deal of exercise. The Aby was accorded breed status in the United States after the turn of the century.

Three other colors of this interesting breed are also available: the silver; red (a lovely warm tint devoid of black ticking and with tile-red nose leather); and the most recent hue to appear, the cream Abyssinian. The wide-set almond eyes can be green, yellow, or glowing hazel. As a breeding cat, the Aby is not as prolific as most other feline varieties.

The Havana Brown Cat

Manufactured by both English and American ailurophiles through the canny crossing of seal-point Siamese and Russian blues, the Havana brown was eventually achieved by intense selection for the wanted color, a rich mahogany brown. Cats of similar shade were earlier known in Europe as Swiss mountain cats. Smokes were not used in its genesis despite the fact that the name Havana brown sounds more like a cigar than a lovely variety of feline. In England, the Havana (formerly called the chestnut brown foreign) retains the long, lithe conformation of the Siamese, which, combined with that pervasive breed's head and eye shape, lend it an exotic, Oriental appearance. Actually, the Havana brown is a self-colored chocolate Siamese with emerald green eyes. The American standard calls for a definite stop between the skull and muzzle when the head is viewed in profile. Affectionate, very intelligent, and possessed of quiet vocal tones, the Havana brown makes a charming member of any household.

The Russian Blue Cat
(also called foreign blue and Maltese)

Initially named the Archangel cat because of its supposed origin in Archangel, Russia, this variety is probably the result of a dilution factor affecting the color genes of a strain of black cats. Bright, solid blue, the plush double coat of the Russian blue does not lie flat as in most short-hairs, causing an appearance of greater bulk than the cat actually has. The eyes of the kittens are yellow and change to brilliant green with maturity. Any alteration of the solid blue body hue, such as tabby markings or white hairs, is not permissible, but light silver tipping is typically seen in cold weather. Gentle but fearless, the Russian blue is an alert but exceptionally quiet cat. It is rather fine in bone, with small feet, wedge-shaped head, slightly flat skull, and well-endowed vibrasse (whiskers). The skin of this feline is also blue.

The Manx Cat

Tailless, and with large, powerful hindquarters to give it the balance its tailed relatives possess, the Manx actually displays a distinct depression where the caudal appendage would normally begin. This hollow area is necessary for the exhibition cat, but many Manx kittens are born with varying tail lengths. The lack of a tail, accompanied by a rounded rump and long powerful hind legs, results in a strange, rabbit-like mode of locomotion.

Originating on the Isle of Man in the Irish Sea between England, Ireland, and Scotland, the breed has an early history that is shrouded in myth and legend. One persistent tale has it that a ship of the flamboyant Spanish Armada, sunk near Port Erin, had several ship's cats aboard, two of whom survived the sinking and the angry seas, reached shore looking like drowned cats, and became the progenitors of the Isle of Man's Manx cats.

The Manx wears a double coat consisting of medium-length guard hairs and a dense undercoat. It displays a proportionately large and rounded head, while the pelage is soft and silky to the touch. In color and pattern of coat, the Manx is generously endowed with all the hues and patterns acceptable, and with eye color that best blends with body tone. Soft-voiced, affectionate, swift, a good mouser, rather on the small side (except for some male tabby-striped individuals who seem to attain greater growth), the Manx makes an exceptionally fine pet. But be certain, if your fancy runs to Manx kittens, that you are not sold an ordinary puss that some unprincipled scoundrel has "manxed" with a scissors. Recently, islanders on the Isle of Man have built a municipal cattery where pure Manx cats are being bred under supervision to keep the breed unsullied and assure its continued existence as a specific variety.

The Rex Cat (Cornish rex)

Cats with curly or rippled coats have been reported in many parts of the world, notably in England, Germany, and the United States. The Cornish rex originated in Cornwall, England, and is the result (as are the other rex breeds) of a spontaneous coat mutation that occurred in a litter of normal short-hairs. Through intensive inbreeding the rex was established as a new variety. The mutant coat is short, plush, silky, with curls, waves, or kinks, and it is devoid of guard hairs. The fact that the rex is sometimes called the "poodle" cat gives an excellent idea of its coat quality. The typical rex head is longer than it is wide, and the ears are large, thin, and very finely furred. The breed is slender and long in body, and is said not to shed (the hair is short and any loose hair is held in the coat)—a plus characteristic for any house cat.

The Devon Rex

With no known ancestry common to the Cornish rex, a similar mutation occurred in Devon, England. (The species has not been given separate recognition in the United States, but has in its native country.) The Cornish rex is a cobbier cat and has normal vibrasse, while the Devon's whiskers are short and display a break or curl. The Devon's coat, though appearing rather similar, in fact differs from that of the Cornish, being firm, wavy, and soft—while the Cornish is thick and plush. The Devon displays particularly large, low-set ears, and the head in profile reveals a very strongly marked stop between skull and muzzle. Both rex breeds enjoy a full range of cat colors. Both also share an outgoing nature, low vocal tones, intelligence, and devotion to their owners. The name "rex" is not used in the Latin sense to mean king but is borrowed from the rex rabbit, who wears a similar coat. There is also a German rex and we have heard of an Oregon rex. Both these breeds are again the results of separate coat mutations.

The Korat (or si-sawat)

In Thailand the korat is a breed cherished for its intelligence, devotion, and tranquility. The word *"korat"* in the Thai vocabulary means silver; in this case it indicates that the guard hairs of the coat are tipped with silver, lending a shimmering silver sheen to the handsome pelt. Large, luminous green-gold eyes complement the body hue. In its native land, the korat is renowned for its fighting ability, and it is said that in jungle villages they act as "watch-cats," giving warning at the approach of strangers. Slender in structure, with a roached back, medium size, and a heart-shaped head, the korat is a striking and unique feline breed.

The Foreign Lilac (or lavender)

Again, the Siamese indicates its genetic vigor in the foreign lilac, a variety that exhibits complete Siamese type but is self-colored, showing no points, and has green eyes. The light lavender coat resembles velvet in appearance. The foreign lilac's voice, unlike that of its relative from Siam, is soft. This uniquely colored cat is a gentle, dainty, persistently affectionate puss.

The Foreign White Short-Hair

The pure white, close pelt of this rather recently introduced breed gives it a ghostlike aura. Slim and elegant, the foreign white's golden or brilliant blue, almond-shaped eyes add a nice touch of color to its virgin, frosty appearance. It exhibits the slim "foreign" look in conformation. Actually, this feline is a totally white Siamese of extremely exotic type.

The Egyptian Mau (also called ocicat)

The shape of *Scarabaeus sacer,* the sacred scarab beetle of ancient Egypt, marks the forehead of this interesting breed of domestic cat. In this country, the mau (the Egyptian word for cat) was developed from a pair of felines from Cairo; in England during the development of the tabby-pointed Siamese, stock appeared that was quite similar to the Egyptian mau, and from this stock the breed was evolved in Britain.

The ears of the mau are large and tufted, the muzzle long, and the eyes slanted and colored yellow, amber, to light green. The pelage is thick but silky; in color black tabby markings on a silver base hue (silver), and bronze, with a dark brown pattern of tabby markings on a light bronze pelt base. In England the standard accepts both a spotted design and mackerel tabby markings. There must be a minimum of two bands of clear ticking with strong bands of rings on the legs and tail. The mau follows exactly the conformation standard of the Siamese and also exhibits the Siamese character, but its voice is not raucous. Devoted and loving to its human family, the mau is well worth the attention of the cat fancy.

The Japanese Bobtail

A medium-sized feline introduced to this country via Japan, where it has been in existence as a distinct breed for centuries, the bobtail wears a coat that is slightly longer than that of other short-hair breeds. Its most distinctive anatomical feature is, of course, the bobtail that flaunts stand-off hairs and gives it the appearance of an undecided pompom, or a shaving brush gone berserk. The bobbie can be self-colored in white, red, or black; bicolored; tortoiseshell; or it can display the ancient, most wanted hue, in Japan called *"me-ke,"* the traditional tricolored—red, black, and white. Like the Manx (to which it has no genetic linkage), the bobtail possesses strong hindquarters to compensate for its lack of balancing tail length. The head and eyes of this interesting breed indicate its Oriental heritage. It is a quiet feline, sweet and mannerly. So far, it has not been exported from its native soil to the United States in the overpowering numbers of most Japanese merchandise.

Bobtailed cats can also be found in Thailand. The senior author saw several in the stilt houses that line the *klongs* (canals) of Bangkok, and was told they were "Thai cats." They were of several colors with white predominating, and were of exotic conformation. The natural bobtail was about one-half normal length.

The Tonkinese Cat

The basic genetic stock utilized in fashioning this medium-sized, short-haired breed in Great Britain has been Burmese and Siamese. It is an attractive feline, emitting vocal sounds of much lower volume than the Siamese, and it is intelligent and appealing. The breed has not, as yet, attracted many fanciers in the United States, probably because the Tonkinese is genetically almost impossible to breed true to color and type.

The Scottish Fold

An oddity in catdom, the Scottish fold has ears that lop or fold downward instead of reaching upright in the perky manner expected of a cat's ears. Evidently the result of a natural mutation, the breed was established by selection for this wanted trait. The fold is short-haired, and can be found in the multitude of colors and patterns to which the cat is heir.

The Chartreux

This is a breed that had its genesis in Africa and was brought to France by the Chartreux monks, hence its name. It is the only known breed of felines that is mute. The Chartreux is a handsome blue cat, similar in color and conformation to the British blue, but the coat is less clear blue in hue, more of a gray-blue, and the Chartreux is a larger, more massive cat than its English cousin, though these differences have tended to become less definite over the years and the standards have grown more alike. Weighing up to 18 pounds, the Chartreux has huge, brilliant, copper-hued eyes, and a soft, dense, and plushy pelage. This French cat is an intelligent, gentle feline and an excellent companion.

The Sphinx (or Canadian hairless cat)

The hairless sphinx originated in Canada in the 1960s and was adopted by breeders who were drawn to it because of its novelty and its outgoing and extremely affectionate nature. Accompanying its hairless condition is a complete lack of vibrasse—an absence that is a distinct disadvantage to a cat since whiskers are important sensory organs. The face, backs of the ears, and lobes should display very short, suedelike hair, and short hair should also be in evidence from paws to wrists. The longest hair on the sphinx covers the male's scrotum. There is sparse pelage on the tail tip and just an indication of velvet down on the back. The front legs are slightly bowed, and the naked structure appears to be fine in bone. Though the general appearance is one of strength, the lack of normal pelting lends a look of refinement to the breed. The eyes, large and slightly slanted, are deep gold in tone.

In Mexico, a strain of hairless felines has been established that are not unlike the Mexican hairless dogs (Xoloizcuintle) whose origin is said to be Chinese. In both cases the animals are not completely hairless since they generally show a few fuzzy hairs on the skull. Hairlessness can be the result of mutation or a masked recessive. It is not a desirable condition in any animal species (especially on the scalp in the primate man, as the senior author can testify), and certainly not in the *Felidae* when the hair coat is very often a protection against the elements and a form of protective coloration, as well as their crowning glory.

The Polydactyl Cat

Polydactylism is simply the possession of more than the normal number of digits. Since the characteristic is determined by a dominant gene, it is quite a common occurrence in domestic cats. Some breeders have made a fetish of producing felines with extra digits and have named them polydactyls, a name that is certainly accurate and to the point. This multiple-digit characteristic can affect both short- and long-haired cats.

The British Short-Hairs

The Romans, though tyrannical masters and plundering, rapacious conquerors, brought the first cats to early England accompanied by war, mankind's maximum madness. Puss was subsequently enveloped in the warmth and understanding the English bestow upon all the so-called lower forms of animal life, and the cat became a hugely popular pet in the British Isles.

British short-hairs are clothed in many fascinating colors, and each shade is favored with separate status. In all physical aspects except color, the varieties are much the same, their standards of perfection depicting a strong, proud feline of excellent quality, very close (except in coat) to the Persian long-hair type, with a powerful, deep, full-chested, well-balanced body, the legs well boned and terminating in neat, well-rounded paws. The tail should be well set, thick at the base and in balance with the body in length. The head should be broad between the ears, the cheeks strong and well developed, the nose and face short, and the ears slightly rounded at the tops with not too large a base, and proportionately small in height. The eyes (mirrors of the soul, we are told—if one can believe in an occasional bloodshot soul) must be large, round, and luminous. The coat lies close to the body and should be short, fine in texture, and lustrous. The cat's physical condition should be hard and muscular like a trained athlete, and it should indicate this animal's active, outgoing character.

In relation to its American counterpart, the domestic short-hair, the British short-hair is a slightly smaller, more compact and cobby cat, with a stronger headpiece. These handsome cats make excellent and intelligent companions.

The following are varieties of the British short-hair:

British short-haired black. This is a comely feline. The well-opened eyes should be of a deep copper or shining orange color. There must be no hint of any other color to mar the shining jet coat.

British short-haired bicolor. This breed includes any solid color combined with white. The color patches must be clear, well edged, and evenly distributed. No more than two-thirds of the pelage should be colored, and not more than one-half of the body display white. The face should show patching, the eyes must not be green, and there must be no indication of tabby pattern.

British blue-cream. This is a rather rare variety that has been perpetuated without recourse to constant outcrossing. The coat is quite fine in texture, the blue and cream intermingling and devoid of patching. By contrast, here in America, the American and exotic blue-cream short-haired standards specify that the two hues appear in visibly defined patches.

British blue. This cat was crossbred to long-hairs (Persians) to retain the desired type. The British blue and the French Chartreux are rather similar in general appearance. This is a handsome, strongly made cat, its lovely coat of light to medium solid blue decoratively enhanced by the glowing copper or orange-hued eyes. It is a popular variety in England, noted for its sagacity, affectionate nature, and quiet manner.

British short-haired cream. This cat flaunts a rich cream pelt, free from white or barring. Kittens exhibit some striping, as do those of many other varieties, but the blemishes disappear as the kitten matures.

Spotted British short-hair. This breed bears a distinctive pattern that is as ancient as the feline species. The design is an aberrant tabby-marking broken on the body to form clear spots, which can be round (as in the cheetah), oblong, or rosette-shaped (like a jaguar's). Colors are silver with brown spots, red, cream, and blue, with dark complementary spots. Other hues will probably make their appearance as time passes and more of these handsome cats are bred. Their dappled coat seems to lend them a closer kinship to the feral spotted species of felines.

British short-hair brown tabby, red tabby, and silver tabby. These should all display the butterfly marking (or saddle) as part of their tabby design. The tabby pattern must be distinct and clean, and the tail and legs must be ringed throughout their length. The brown tabby should sport oyster pattern swirls on its flanks, and its chin must be brown or cream but never white. Two necklaces (mayoral chains) should adorn the chest, and the red tabby should reveal oyster patterns on its sides and three dark red stripes ornamenting its back. The tail should show a darker color density. The silver is a beautiful feline with jet black tabby markings etched upon the silver body hue. Its neck rings should completely join, to add a decidedly decorative touch.

Tortoiseshell. This is a many-splendored thing, displaying three rich colors—black, and light and dark red—distributed in clean, separate patches over the pelt, with tail and each paw sharing the trio of tints. The large eyes can be a bright hazel, orange, or deep copper. In the tortoiseshell and white variety, the colored and white areas are evenly distributed. Such cats were also known as "Spanish cats," and are called calicos in this country. The tortie inhabits a matriarchal society with the numerical balance in the female's favor. The few male torties extant are sterile, but there are a few (a *very* few) tortie toms who have proven their fertility by producing progeny. Torties are healthy, playful, and intelligent.

White British short-hair. Wrapped in its pristine coat, this is an ethereal puss, unmarked by color other than the orange or blue of its big, glowing round eyes. Those beautiful blue eyes can indicate deafness in some individuals if they remain blue after the kitten is about ten weeks old. Odd eyes—one blue and one orange—are acceptable.

In British shows, there is a class labeled Any Other Variety for feline breeds that do not fit established standards. These are experimental varieties, often the result of genetic mutation; sometimes they are due to thoughtful crossbreeding of established breeds by earnest breeders attempting to establish new varieties. From this class can emerge a popular breed of the future.

THE LONG-HAIRED CATS

Long-haired cats are the pampered aristocrats of domestic felines. The exact origin of the long-hairs is not known, but it is a generally accepted fact that they came into being in the Orient several hundreds of years ago. In that huge area that we label the fabulous East, the long-hair probably appeared as a mutation, and its worth and beauty were recognized and cherished by races of people about whom we know little more than we do of the genesis of the cats they treasured.

Turkestan, Persia, China, Mongolia, Afghanistan—vast, colorful lands of pagan pageantry, unknown gods, and camel caravans that conjure up visions from the Arabian Nights and perhaps private, inner glimpses from the timeless words of that eminent teller of tales, Rudyard Kipling. This is where the long-haired lovelies (meaning cats, of course) came from. And from those exotic lands they journeyed to Europe and the British Isles in the ships of bold and adventurous traders, and with returning Crusaders in the eleventh, twelfth, and thirteenth centuries as part of the plunder of war. We of the twentieth century can forget the circumstances that brought those felines to us and only be thankful that they came, exquisite creatures that fill the eyes with their elegance and the heart with their charm.

The Persian Cat

The first long-haired cats to arrive on the Continent probably had their origin in Turkey. Later those early aliens were joined by Persian long-hairs, which, through crossbreeding and extensive selective breeding for desired virtues, produced over the course of many long years the beautiful, princely Persian of today.

In England the breed is not technically termed "Persian"; it is simply called a long-hair, with emphasis upon color and pattern—black long-hair, blue long-hair, bicolored long-hair, colorpoint long-hair (the Himalayan), tabby (in various coat colors), red self-long-hair, tortoiseshell long-hair, smoke long-hair, and so on. Each color variety is given separate classification as in the British short-hairs.

It has been rumored that close to the Caucasus, in areas touched by the Caspian Sea, there exists a breed of feral felines from which the Persian descended. But it is difficult to imagine the gorgeous, patrician, sweet Persian living concurrently with a wild ancestor.

When examining a Persian, our eyes are trapped initially by the massive head, the luxuriant coat, and the exquisite, wide range of colors and tone combinations that are complemented by the varied, vivid eye hues. The Persian demonstrates every known cat color and pattern, the long body hair blending the more subtle shades and lending them a soft elegance unmatched in the feline world. The pelage is long, flowing, and full, and must be given daily care. The tail, or "brush," is rather short in appearance and thick, with hair forming a flowing plume, and the ears are furred both inside and out. Between-the-toes puffs of hair are desirable, and the cat should flaunt a full ruff and frill, not unlike the mane of a lion, that fully frames the imposing, haughty head.

This most popular of long-hairs is a living monument to man's ability to mold genetic material into true, classic beauty, for it was the arduous work of breeders over a long period of time that finally produced the Persian of today. A labor of love undoubtedly, but linked to a touch of genius.

In type and conformation the ideal Persian should be endowed with a massive, wide, round-skulled head, an exceedingly short nose, and a cobby, deep-chested middlepiece. It should have strong, heavily boned legs ending in fairly large but compact paws to support the sturdy body. The large eyes should be widely spaced, round and brilliant, and the color of burnished copper, except in the silver tabby, shaded silver, and chinchilla, when the eyes should be green or hazel, and in the white Persian, which has blue or copper eyes, or sometimes one eye of each color.

Today the peke-faced Persian is fairly popular with some fanciers since it is obviously the ultimate of the short-nosed Persian type. The head and muzzle areas of the peke-faced resemble those of the Pekinese dog, with a nose pushed well back into the face and a domed forehead causing a frowning effect between the eyes. This complete altering of the feline head and facial structure is a breakthrough in genetic change that had not previously been accomplished in the family *Felidae*. The innovation will undoubtedly be accompanied by nasal and mouth anomalies and other troubles. In *Man and His Works,* Melville Herskovits makes a pertinent observation applicable to the peke-faced Persian: "The universality of the drive to embellish useful objects, often so elaborately that the utility . . . is lessened in the process, has posed questions that seriously embarrass those who have interpreted human experience in strict rationalistic terms."

Its fabulous coat makes the Persian appear much larger and heavier than it actually is. Be certain if you purchase a Persian that it will submit gracefully to grooming. Persians generally love to be pampered and they accept all favors as though to the manner born. They are decidedly *not* a farm or barn cat, but an indolent aristocrat. Sweet in disposition, affectionate but haughty, the Persian is not a very active cat. The softly modulated voice and dignified bearing speak more insistently than words of the Persian's distinguished heritage.

STANDARD	*Persian*	POINTS
BODY COLOR: According to the standard (colors listed below). Allow 10 points for color and 15 for pattern in tabbies and torties.		25 points
COAT: Finely textured, soft, glossy, full of life, standing off from the body. Huge ruff and frill (between front legs). Brush full. Curved ear tufts. Long toe tufts.		15 points
BODY TYPE AND SHAPE: Cobby body, low on legs, deep in chest, massive over shoulders and rump, short well-rounded middle-piece. Uncurved, short tail. Overall large or medium in size.		20 points
HEAD: Round and massive, with great breadth of skull. Well set on a rather short neck. Eyes round, full, brilliant, of proper color to conform to coat. Ears set wide apart, round-tipped and small. Nose very short and broad, cheeks full, jaws broad and powerful.		30 points
CONDITION: Hard and healthy. Condition mirrored in the lively, glossy coat.		10 points
		100 points

UNDESIRABLE: Rangy, lack of bone, long-tailed, long-nosed, large ears, close-set eyes not full and round, slant eyes, Roman nose, receding chin, narrow face and head, flat coat lacking length and body.

PERSIAN COLORS: Black, white, blue, red, bicolor, cream, chinchilla, brown, shaded silver, smoke, silver tabby, brown tabby, blue tabby, red tabby, tortoiseshell, calico, blue-cream, shell cameo, shaded cameo, red smoke (smoke cameo), tabby cameo, tortoiseshell cameo, cream cameo, cream tabby, self-chocolate, self-lilac.

The Himalayan Cat (or color-point long-hair)

One of the most popular breeds of today, the Himalayan was granted recognition by American cat associations by the latter part of the 1950s and its rise to eminence has been deservedly rapid. This handsome breed combines the color points of the Siamese with the coat and conformation of the Persian. A gorgeous puss, the Himmie was established through long and detailed interbreeding of the Siamese and Persian, with intense selection for desired merit. The initial genetic crossings and development of this exquisite breed can be credited to Richard Cobb of California, and Dr.

STANDARD	*Himalayan*	POINTS

Note: The standard for the Himalayan is exactly parallel to that of the Persian; see Persian standard for more detailed conformation description.

BODY COLOR: Free of barring, even, shading contrast between body hue and points, points clearly defined, correct mask. Allowance to be made for darker tone in older cats. — 10 points

POINTS: Density on mask, ears, legs, feet, tail. Definition of points. — 10 points

COAT: Length, texture, ruff and frill, ear and toe tufts, and brush. — 10 points

BODY TYPE AND SHAPE: Including shape, size, bone, and tail length. — 20 points

HEAD: Including size and shape of eyes, ears, and ear set. — 30 points

EYES AND EYE COLOR: Large and round; a deep and electric blue — 10 points

CONDITION: Physical fitness and musculature. — 10 points

100 points

UNDESIRABLE: Locket or button markings. Abnormal or kinked tail. Crossed eyes. Incorrect number of toes (polydactylism). White toes. Eye color other than blue.

HIMALAYAN COLORS: Seal-point, chocolate-point, blue-point, lilac-point, flame-point, tortie-point, blue cream-point, cream-point, frost-point.

Tjebbes of Sweden. The geneticist Dr. Clyde Keeler and Mrs. Virginia Cobb did Trojan work for the breed, producing a seal-point Himalayan in 1932. Brian Sterling-Webb of England and Mrs. Marguerita Goforth in the United States continued the experiments, while in Canada Mr. and Mrs. Borrett launched an ambitious program of their own. Eventually, in late 1957, the first colorpoint long-hairs were exhibited in the United States. Today the Himalayan (christened by Mrs. Goforth) is one of the most celebrated feline varieties in the world.

The Himalayan sports the same colors and points as the Siamese; but here the similarity ceases, for it must never mirror Siamese type or the occasional crossed eyes and kinked tail of the Siamese. In color, the kittens mimic those of the Siamese since they are born with pale coloration; the point shades appear with more authority as the cat matures. The eyes of the Himalayan are large and round like the Persian's, but in hue they are the deep, electric blue of the Siamese. In conformation the Himmie is an exact duplicate of its sybaritic Persian ancestor. The Himalayan is gentle, intelligent, graceful, and charming, and is certainly one of the most beautiful felines ever to grace the home or show bench.

The Angora Cat

All long-haired cats were once (before the advent of the Persian) called Angoras. There are some ailurophiles who declare that the Angora, as a true breed, no longer exists and that it has been merged and assimilated into the Persian breed. They originated long ago in the capital city of Turkey, Ankara, where today a zoo perpetuates the pure breed (all whites) through a supervised breeding program.

In comparison with the Persian the Angora is longer in body, has longer legs and head shape, and shows no evidence of the peke-faced influence. It is a fine-boned cat, displaying none of the Persian massiveness in body or head. It flaunts a tapered tail, and the fine, silky coat (sometimes wavy) is medium in length. Though on the Continent sometimes other colors appear, pure white is the accepted pigment. The breed displays round to almond-shaped eyes, blue or amber in hue, or an unmatched pair of these colors (odd-eyed). Breeders and owners boast of the Angora's delightful temperament, intelligence, and individual personality.

The Turkish Cat (or Van cat)

Very similar to the original Angora type but sturdier in basic physical aspect, this handsome cat comes from the Lake Van area in Turkey. Unlike the Angora, its fur is thick, long, and silky, and it is cherished for its decorative markings, which uniquely affect only the skull and tail. The Van's face, ears, and body are white, with auburn identifying markings, divided by a white blaze on the face and revealing slightly darker auburn rings on the tinted, full-brush tail. The Turk's eyes are round with pink rims and are light amber in color. These interesting felines have another peculiarity other than their color design—they love water, and like many of their feral cousins, are excellent swimmers. They are good "keepers" (they eat well and stay in good health), strong and adaptable to varied conditions of climate, and are very affectionate toward their human family.

The Maine 'Coon Cat
(also called 'coon cat or Maine cat)

Endowed with a rather lesser undercoat then most long-hairs, this large cat is still amply covered to withstand the vigors of a Maine winter. Unlike the Persian and other long-haired beauties, the Maine 'coon is a utilitarian puss often found on farms as a rodent eliminator, a task for which it is quite fit. Though legend would have us believe it originated from a cross between the big Maine raccoons and the local domestic cats, the genetic connotations of such a tall tale are enough to make Gregor Mendel whirl in his grave.

In all probability the 'coon cat is the result of crossbreeding between long-haired cats from Turkey, Russia, or Asia brought by intrepid early sailors to the New England coast, and domestic cats owned by the early settlers of the region. Natural selection for a long coat, combined with vigor and hardiness to match the climate and environment, resulted in the Maine 'coon cat in which polydactylism is often a factor. Breeders at one time wanted to include polydactylism in their standard, but eventually they wisely decided against it.

Smart, gentle, extremely hardy, and well able to fend for itself, the 'coon is a large (up to 30 pounds), sturdy, and powerful cat, with a dense but silky and flowing outer coat, a medium-long and broad face, and a quiet disposition. The tail is heavily furred, broad at the base and tapering toward the end. The body is cobby, the neck muscular and short, and the legs wide and well boned, terminating in large, round, tufted feet. The back is level or slightly sloped toward the rump, which has a definite look of squareness. Coat colors run the gamut of hues ordained for felines, but tabby striping with white trimming adding to its attractiveness seems to be most popular.

The Balinese (or long-hair Siamese)

This interesting addition to the domestic feline roster is a product of our own country. Kittens with longish coats appeared in litters produced by purebred Siamese in about 1952, and were adopted by two far-sighted California breeders, who bred them to produce the long coat and christened them long-haired Siamese. The long-haired mutation bred true, and a new and interesting breed was born. Normal Siamese breeders objected to calling this new variety long-haired Siamese, so in a flash of inspiration supporters of the new breed christened it with the exotic cognomen Balinese.

In every way other than coat length, the Balinese mimics the Siamese, so perusal of the Siamese standard will introduce you to the type wanted in the Balinese: eyes, points, body colors, and physical conformation are all Siamese. The nose leather should always be completely pigmented and should match the point colors, which must be dense and definite. Add to this vision of the Siamese a long, fine, silky coat and *voilà*—you have the Balinese. Unlike the Persian, the fur of the Balinese seldom mats, so it needs a minimum of care. A svelte, lithe, and dainty puss, the Balinese makes a gentle, discerning, lovable pet.

The Birman Cat (the sacred cat of Burma)

Though the Birman had its genesis in Burma, there is no evidence of a genetic link with the Burmese cat who came to us originally from that same country. In 1919 the Birman first appeared in France where, due to divers circumstances, it took quite a few years to become established. In the 1960s it reached England, and was recognized by the Cat Fanciers' Association, Inc., in the United States in 1967.

The body color of the Birman is cream, but with golden tints lending the cat a precious appearance. The pelage is long, silky, with a tendency to curl on the underbody. The points on head, legs, feet, and tail are rich and in dark contrast to the body hue, and they conform to the typical point distribution of the Siamese. But, unlike other breeds that bear the Siamese points and contrasting body color, a characteristic that divorces the Birman from complete similarity are its four pure white paws. American fanciers sometimes refer to the rear white stockings as "laces," but in Britain they are known as "gauntlets" because of their shape, which ends in a point up the hock.

Said to have once been the darling of temple priests in Burma (so often it is claimed that cat breeds were associates of ancient priests and monks—perhaps because they are creatures of habit?), the Birman's standard calls for a strong, rather cobby body, bearing a round, full-cheeked head decorated with round, deep blue eyes (almost violet except in the blue- and lilac-point phases, when the eyes can be a lighter blue). At the other end a full-coated tail is wanted and pink footpads are to be expected. The Birman displays a majestic bearing, and its sweet disposition makes it a delight to handle and to own.

The Khmer Cat

Legend has it that the Asiatic Khmer people erected a temple many hundreds of years ago to Tsun-Kyan-Kse, the blue-eyed, golden goddess. One terrible night bandits raided the temple and the head priest was killed, but the coarse and sacrilegious brigands fled in fear before the icy-blue angry eyes of the goddess. All night the white temple cats kept vigil over the body of the slain priest, and as the morning sun entered the temple and gently caressed the goddess, the golden reflection from her body reached out and touched the white temple cats, turning their bodies golden and their yellow eyes to the blue of her eyes. Her will painted their faces, legs, and tails with the color of the good, brown earth; only their four paws remained virgin white as a symbol of their purity. In Asia one finds many thousands of temples and shrines dedicated to all manner of gods and goddesses, and as many legends associated with the temples, so there is no reason not to believe this tale if it pleases you to do so.

A long-haired European cat, the Khmer had its genesis in Asia and is named for the Khmer people who occupy the territory from which it came. The Khmer are members of the Cambodian nation who forged an important civilization in Indochina during the Middle Ages. In the Khmer we see again the color and point influence of the ubiquitous Siamese, but in this case it also resembles the Birman, for the Khmer cat and the Birman come from the same area in Asia and are very similar in many respects—except that the Khmer does not display the white paws that give the Birman so piquant an appearance. The long coat should be cream, with richly colored brown points.

The Somali Cat

The Somali is simply a long-haired variety of the lithe Abyssinian. Occasionally a recessive gene for long hair expressed itself in a litter of Abyssinians and resulted in a long-haired kitten. A few breeders cherished these pretty mutants and through selection for the long-hair trait established the Somali variety. The coat is silky and the tail bushy: when linked to the type and warm red and glowing ruddy hues of the Abyssinian, the result is an exceedingly lovely breed. The coat of this large cat is so soft that it seldom mats. It is an alert, curious, but quiet breed.

The Ragdoll

This is another Siamese-tinted variety, confined to either seal- or frost-points (at the moment) as definitive accents to the light tan body hue. The eyes are blue, the tail plumed, and the underbody white. The ragdoll is a rather recent variety offered to the cat fancy, but it should become popular due to its wonderful disposition and devoted character. It is said never to panic or scratch, and can be handled by anyone, without an angry or fearful reaction. Alert, loving, and playful, the ragdoll makes a delightful friend.

Breeders are ever alert to the possibility of new mutations in fur, shade, pattern, or type in existing and established breeds from which they can, by judicious breeding experiment and selection, create new domestic feline varieties that will breed true and eventually become worthy of recognized status. Most of the breeds delineated here have reached official recognition, though some are not recognized by all the cat registries, others are accepted by some of the national associations, and still others have been embraced by foreign registries.

There are further exotic and experimental breeds that have not been given official sanction, or that are not seen here, in England, or on the Continent, except in very small numbers, and so these have not been listed or described in this book. Included in this category are felines such as the delicate Australian cat (said now to be extinct); the Chinese long-hair, with pendant ears and a long, silky coat; the Bombay cat; the honey bear cat; and other new experimentals. There are long-haired brown cats called himber cats that are a cross between a Himalayan and a Burmese, and a short-haired, striped or spotted feline that sometimes sports a copper coat and is called the Bristol cat, developed in southern California. We have heard of a breed of domestic cats in the Mombasa area of Africa with very short-haired coats to fit the hot climate, and of a kimono cat bred in Japan that wears a short black and white pelt with the appearance of a kimono, and there is a feline native to Cyprus called the striped Cyprian cat. The senior author has seen the Mombasa cat in Kenya, as well as a slim, very small cat, quite long in body, that is native to Paraguay, South America.

It is a big world and there are undoubtedly many other unknown varieties of cats in various areas of the globe. Perhaps as time passes and more people travel to unfamiliar places a few cat lovers among them will find and return with specimens of those breeds as yet unknown to American fanciers.

A two-week-old red tabby female exotic short-hair,
Bams Sorrowful Sal. Owned and bred by
Arlene and Bruce Silvers.

A trio of ragdolls. From left to right:
R. Andy IV, owned by Louise Reggie;
Rita, owned by Ann Baker;
Bunny, owned by Mrs. Randy.
(Photo supplied by Ann Baker)

This copper-eyed white female Manx is the result of seven generations
of controlled breeding. She is the grand champion Kelsha Angele I,
owned and bred by Kelly Shaw. Manx walk normally,
and hop only when running.

Three four-month-old Chartreux kittens. From left to right: Gamonal Luciole, Gamonal Lutteur, and Gamonal Luron. Owned and bred by Helen Gamon.

Champion Taquin de St. Pierre, a six-year-old male Chartreux. Bred by Mme S. Bastide and owned by Helen Gamon. (Photo by Portrait World)

This picture of the Abyssinian champion Sherwood Beni Hassan shows the long body typical of the breed.

A blue-point Himalayan, triple grand champion Tunxis Valley Cameron Clings—best all-American long-hair, third best all-American cat, the first Himalayan ever to achieve such rank. Bred by Marianne Fischer, owned by Pat Renninger.

A champion Japanese bobtail, Arlynn Shimon of Mi-Ho. Owned by Mike and Barbara Hodits.

Merchant's Adair's Blue Angel is a blue Persian
owned by Mr. and Mrs. Ralph Adair.

Champion Bams Reuben, a cream exotic short-hair tom.
Owned and bred by Arlene and Bruce Silvers.

Above: Two korat kittens of Solna, Ratchasie-Mae (female) and Valborg (male), at twelve weeks—best Southwest regional korats and second best regional korats in 1977. Owned and bred by Sonia Anderson.

Right: A silver-blue quadruple grand champion korat male, Jesilieu's Pong To Ko of Solna—all-American cat of the year, 1978. Bred by Jessalee Mallalieu, owned by Sonia Anderson. (Photo by MikRon Photos)

An Asiatic tiger (now on the endangered species list) cooling off in the water. (Photo courtesy of Busch Gardens, Tampa, Florida)

All the various domestic cat breeds find favor with a certain number of fanciers and breeders. The selection of color, coat, conformation, and character is the prerogative of the individual ailurophile. All cats are wonderful to cat lovers because they fill the varied needs of a multitude of people throughout this uneasy planet who look for love, beauty, companionship, and many characteristic qualities that only a cat can supply.

CHAPTER 7

Acquiring a Cat

WHY ACQUIRE A CAT?

The reason for acquiring a cat is simply stated: You like cats. Possibly you love them, and you want one to share your life with you and your family. Or perhaps you live alone and need a cat for companionship, or to come home to after a long day's work. If you are lonely, remember that loneliness flees from a dwelling in which a cat lives. There are many valid reasons for acquiring a cat. They are not excuses. One need never make excuses for owning, or wanting to own, a cat.

There is probably also a more basic and little-realized reason for the upsurge in pet popularity, particularly the wide acceptance of the cat as a favored pet in our time. It lies in the pet's therapeutic value; in our need to find inner peace through association with another, less complex creature, and to find solace in the simple acts of caring, loving, and understanding our pet.

Modern man cannot reach a rapport with the impossibly complex environment that is the civilized world of today. He becomes lost spiritually, his individuality obliterated by the gross shadow of the monstrous, intangible machine of commercial and technological tyranny. So, instead of screaming at the sky, he reaches out to another species. What better pet than a cat can anyone imagine to help an individual reach inner tranquility?

The domestic cat is certainly one of the cleanest and most fastidious of all creatures, and the care it needs is minimal. By its very attitudes, its complete repose when at rest, its winsome sport with simple things such as a spool, a string, an errant sunbeam dancing on the floor, it brings quiet, uncomplicated pleasure to its owners.

The domestic puss is a creature of unparalleled grace, its every movement a study in gliding elegance. Cats are dignified, yet they possess a definite sense of humor; they are independent but loving, proud but playful, and completely unself-conscious. Your life will form a new and better pattern if you take the time to understand and appreciate the many values your cat can impart. "Relax! Enjoy!" he seems to say, "I bring you the benediction of peace on earth, good will to cats!" And the soft warmth of the cat, his purr of quiet contentment, will soothe your soul and bring you inner repose. A Bronx sage once said, "If you have a million dollars and a good cat, you should consider yourself well off."

The "why?" of owning a *feral* cat is a slightly different matter. Too often acquisition of such a pet is based upon an ego trip, and the result can be disaster. But if you earnestly wish to attempt to reach rapport with a predatory wild feline, the experiment could be valid. It will still be a dangerous undertaking with most of the feral cats and we do not generally recommend it. If the desired pet is one of the "big cats," we suggest you check your insurance and hospital coverage.

WHERE TO ACQUIRE A CAT

You can acquire a cat in numerous ways. The simplest is to have one follow you home, or to find one on your doorstep looking at you in the most charming manner and reaching out to you with a plaintive, questioning meouw: "Do you want me? I think you and I could make it." Or you can query your friends and through them find someone who owns a female cat who has just littered and who will be only too happy to make you a gift of a kitten.

Under the "pet column" heading in your local newspaper you will usually find notices of cats and kittens to be sold or given away. Felines young or mature from purebred pedigreed stock usually command a decent price, but common cats with no pretensions to illustrious backgrounds are generally free. Frequently older cats, housebroken and trained to be good citizens, are given away by folks who are moving from the area, possibly to an apartment or condominium where pets are not welcomed.

Another way to acquire a cat is to chat with your local veterinarian, who will know who has the kind of cat you are looking for; or you may inquire at the local humane society and examine the kittens they have. Pet shops are also a source for cute kittens, common or purebred. But if your desire is a fine, purebred, registered feline, it is best to purchase it from a breeder or cattery that has registered stock of the breed you are considering.

We have mentioned before that purebred catlings are not inexpensive, but if you spread the initial cost over the animal's lifespan, the purchase price is rather negligible. At a breeder's cattery you will have the opportunity of seeing the dam and possibly the sire of the kittens, and maybe older stock of the same genetic background as the catlings offered for sale. You will also, in all probability, have several kittens of various ages to choose from. Viewing all the related stock will allow you to form a fairly comprehensive picture of what to expect in character, coat, color, and type from a kitten of like bloodlines.

But before you pick a definite breed or variety, learn as much as you can through specific literature about all the varieties of cats. Then familiarize yourself with the standard of the breed of your choice and immerse yourself in the lore and special characteristics of that variety. Attend a local cat show if at all possible. There you will find fine specimens of the many breeds of domestic felines, and you will add a visual dimension to the written words you have absorbed. Chat with the exhibitors; gather information and business cards. Observe the authoritative mystique of judging: listen to the judge's comments, and in general absorb the unique aura of a cat show.

Soon you will realize that you have entered a special world completely divorced from any activity to which you have formerly been exposed—a microcosm, with its own language and distinctive character and motivation, which embraces an exciting competitiveness and an intense absorption in the cult of the cat. File away every bit of information in the recesses of your mind to bring forth later for leisurely examination and critical appraisal when you are alone. After this has been accomplished, you will know exactly what breed of cat you want and where to find it.

If your fancy leads you to the acquisition of a feral cat, you will find it necessary to contact an importer of wild animals and make your wants known to him. He will probably favor you with a jaundiced stare and, if he is a man of honesty and integrity, he will question your motives for such a choice, as well as the depth of your knowledge as to the environment, feeding, care, and training necessary for the health and well-being of your feral friend. He should also mention the risk to you that is involved in such a purchase. But this is to dream! Actually, the importer will name a purchase price (quite a large one) and an appropriate time for delivery. Let us hope that he does not have the wild cat of your choice readily available so that you will have a longer period of time for second thoughts. If you do purchase or fall heir to a wild feline, it should be obtained when quite young and be neutered.

The legality of owning a big cat varies from state to state (sometimes, even from county to county). In some states a special license can be obtained from the state's Game and Fish Commission. In many states, owning a wild cat is not allowed; other states will not allow them to cross state lines in transit.

Many big cats are, of course, on the endangered list and therefore not available at all. Or they are extremely expensive. Ocelots, for example, will sell for from two thousand to three thousand dollars— if you can find one.

HOW TO ACQUIRE A CAT

Here we will examine the mechanics of the actual cat purchase. We assume you have reached a decision as to the breed you wish to acquire and that it fits your requirements exactly. If the kitten or cat is a "freebie" or gift of an inexpensive nonpedigreed, common cat (we are aware that to an ailurophile there is no such thing as a "common" cat; we merely use the term as discreet identification), you must accept your new acquisition with thanks and query diffidently whether it has been wormed or had any protective vaccinations. You will probably find that it hasn't been medically protected in any way from anything, and the attitude (in words or thoughts) of the giver will doubtless be: "What do you want for nothing, a Kentucky Derby winner?" So you smile shakily, withdraw discreetly cuddling your new pet in your arms, and drive immediately to a veterinarian. That worthy doctor will do everything necessary to protect puss and to keep him healthy, and will arrange a program of vaccinations to shield him from the various ailments to which cats are heir.

Your veterinarian will also recommend that you have your non-pure-bred puss neutered. If it is an unneutered male, it will, at the appropriate time, hear the siren song of sex and begin "spraying," causing your home to become permeated with a nauseous odor calculated to cause friends and acquaintances to stay away from the premises in droves. Your cat will also take every opportunity to escape from the house to go "tom-catting," and will return home scratched, bitten, wounded, and in need of care and possibly even professional attention. The course of true love does not run smoothly in the night world of cats.

The nonpedigreed female should also be altered, for she too, when in season, will attempt to escape so that nature can take its course. Successful escape results in litter after litter of unwanted kittens. Male cats can be neutered from six months on, and females may be spayed at any age after six months. Neutering your cat will not drastically change its deportment except for the better. Psychologists agree that the androgynous personality of the neutered cat allows it to be tender and independent, assertive and yielding, and that neutering often expands the behavioral range of the affected animal to a remarkable extent.

The sex of a cat can be determined quite simply. A female cat displays an upside-down exclamation point directly below her tail, while the tom, or male cat, displays two dots that resemble a colon below his tail. The vagina and the rectum of the female come through the pelvis together; the vulva (termination of the vagina) and the anus (end of the rectum) are therefore in very close visual proximity. The anus and testicles of the male cat show a much greater separation: in the mature tom cat, the swelling of the testicles in the scrotum can be seen and felt.

After carefully considering the information encountered in the first section here ("Where to Acquire a Cat"), let us assume that you have decided upon a specific breed of pedigreed, purebred feline. Your attitude, under these circumstances, should be in drastic contrast to that of the individual who has been given a cat for free. You are about to pay a decent sum of money for a cat, and so you can be a bit sassy in asking questions and making certain that you receive everything you are paying for.

If the kitten (or cat) you consider purchasing is in a pet shop, a breeder's home, or a cattery, use both your eyes and nose to measure the cleanliness of the surroundings. If the place is not clean, don't buy. Find another place that *is* clean. We recommend that it be a cattery which specializes in the breed of cat you have selected and which has had success in the show ring.

Let us again assume that by now you have learned enough to have selected a knowledgeable breeder (whom you have been advised is honest), who consistently produces fine specimens with typical temperament, in quarters that are clean and sanitary. If you are wise, you will ask the aid of the breeder in picking a kitten from a litter. Breeders are aware of the variables that exist in the particular lines or strains they produce and can therefore select a better kitten from any given litter than you can. The final choice is of course up to you.

Select a kitten (or cat) that displays the physical characteristics wanted in the breed of your choice. But above all be certain that it is healthy and of good temperament. The coat should be soft and glossy with no patchy, uneven areas, the skin loose, pliable, and displaying no signs of a skin affliction. Examine the eyes, nose, and mouth. The eyes should be bright and clear, the nose leather slightly moist, and neither eyes nor nose should display any signs of mucus discharge. The mouth, lips, and gums should be free of infection, the teeth white and even, meeting in the required manner (neither over- or undershot). Try to ascertain, if you buy from a cattery, that the kitten does not carry leukemia. A laboratory test can give you as high as 95 percent accuracy. Tests can also indicate the presence of infectious peritonitis and several other diseases. If you contemplate ever using your new puss for breeding or as a foundation cat on which to build a future strain, then, rather than spending the rest of your hobby time in the future battling such pernicious maladies in your breeding, it is best to have the tests made to eliminate the possibility of introducing diseases into your stock.

Kittens will be playful and filled with the verve of carefree existence, but both cats and kits should give evidence of vitality, with no indication of debility or sluggishness. Avoid the cat or kitten that sits huddled in a corner evincing no interest in its surroundings. It is either a misfit (there is at least one in every family, feline and human), is ill, stupid (there is one of these also in almost every family, human and feline), or it lacks the outgoing nature to become a pleasant pet or a good breeding animal if this should be your eventual desire.

If your choice is a white puss with blue eyes, test its hearing ability —it could be deaf: a fact first reported by Charles Darwin. Other British scientists later confirmed the phenomenon but found that white, blue-eyed kittens when quite young have normal hearing though, as they mature, 75 percent become deaf. If your fancy leans toward a long-haired cat, learn whether the kitten's parents permit or resent grooming. If the parents are docile during grooming, chances are their offspring will also be submissive, provided that the initial brush and comb ministrations are handled delicately and with solicitude.

Ask the breeder for a health certificate and a written list of the medical protection the cat has had, such as when the animal was wormed and what immunization has been supplied, with the dates medication and vaccines were administered. Insist that a clause be inserted in the sales contract allowing you forty-eight hours in which to have your new purchase examined by your own veterinarian, so that if he should find it to be in less than excellent health the cat can be returned to the seller and the full purchase price refunded. You should expect a purebred kitten or cat to have been registered, or to be eligible for registration, with one of the major cat associations. If you acquire a cat that has been registered in the former owner's name, a transfer certificate will enable it to be registered in your name. A pedigree, which is simply the recorded ancestry of the cat or kitten, should also be supplied to you. If the cat is to be used for breeding, the pedigree is an important geneological record. You will find more about registration associations in Chapter 14, which is on cat shows.

In the selection of an ordinary house cat (one *sans* pedigree and registration but loaded with charisma), the same yardstick of worth should be applied but in a more casual manner, particularly if the animal is to be a gift. In a last analysis one generally selects a kitten or cat because it "sends" one, because that particular puss reaches out and captivates your heart and you both seem to meet on some common ground. When this occurs, try to retain your cool long enough to use your head as well as your heart and select wisely, utilizing the advice given here.

The price of kittens and cats varies greatly, from nothing (a deal you can't refuse) to a three-figure price for a fine specimen of one of the more popular purebreds or rare new exotics. Your taste and bankbook must be the measure of your selection. Just remember that should you not be able to afford the breed of your choice, any cat is better than no cat at all. Many talented and important people have not cared a whit whether their feline friends were purebred or not, so long as they were cats, so you can consider yourself in excellent company should your final acquisition be just an uncommon common cat with no pretensions to pedigree but possessing all the wonderful qualities—and charisma—that are shared by every cat, aristocrat or commoner.

The age of your kitten or cat is important. A kitten should be no less than seven weeks of age when obtained. If its teeth have not yet pierced the gums, it is too young to be taken from its mother. Kittens of either sex and any breed are easily molded to fit your lifestyle. If you live alone or are one of a childless couple, a kitten can be trained to fit your design for living. If you have small children, the kitten can adapt to the sound level and the rather frenetic conditions that little children generally introduce to the household. An older cat, from a quiet environment, sensitive to the decibel level and avalanche-like activity of children, may resent the cacophony of its new habitat, become noticeably nervous and unhappy, and possibly leave without notice at the first opportunity.

Playtime for kittens and cats and children together should be supervised by an adult to avoid injury to either species. Little children have no inhibitions and have not yet reached the age of discipline and so, like healthy young animals, they play too hard and can severely injure a small kitten. The young humans in your home must be taught that a tiny kitten is not a toy and that it can be easily hurt just as they can. Once this simple philosophy is imparted to your child, owning a kitten and watching it grow can be a most rewarding and happy experience for a youngster.

A new kitten in the home must be trained to a completely new environment, one with which it has had no previous experience; but kittens are smart and soon learn the ABCs of their new life. A grown cat will, in a very short time, cope and adapt completely to its new abode, particularly if the atmosphere is not too alien from its past experience. The mature cat, housebroken and familiar with the routine of home living, is less trouble initially than the kitten.

The newly acquired kitten or cat should be taken to its new home in a cat carrier. This enclosure gives the cat, especially if young, a feeling of security and keeps it from dashing about in a moving vehicle if it has to be transported any distance. If puss is loose, you could encounter some very disturbing moments during the drive home, with a frightened cat clinging to your scalp at a bad traffic corner.

Cats are very special individuals and the adoption of one, whether young or mature, must be approached with sincerity and deliberation. Beauty, devotion, companionship, and love are what you obtain when you bring home a cat. It can teach you a great deal about the art of living and of shedding the stress of a society and era that has outdistanced the ability of its citizens to cope.

So look to the cat, and imitate its utter repose, infinite patience, calm dignity, and tranquil independence. Remember, cats inhabited this planet long before man was spawned from ape, and during those protracted millennia the cat probably learned some archaic wisdom that mankind has never been granted.

CHAPTER 8

Caring for Cats

FEEDING

Proper diet is the most important item one can list under the heading of general care and husbandry for kittens and cats. Lack of the necessary food essentials in the kitten's diet can produce drastic detrimental results in bone growth and formation, size and coat. It can cause mental retardation, and it can affect the nervous and sensory systems.

To support the life processes of our feline friends, it is necessary to supply the nutrients that foster growth and health. Nutritional support begins *in utero* with correct feeding of the pregnant queen (as the mother is termed). After birth, the kitten depends upon its mother's milk for sustenance until it is weaned. In the wild, the feral cat soon begins a period of schooling in the art of hunting while being fed meat from the prey killed by its carnivorous dam. The domestic kitten, after weaning, needs to be fed the correct nutrients by its human benefactor.

We need not experiment to arrive at the proper dietary requirements for kittens and cats. In the last two decades such investigation has been accomplished for us by the manufacturers of cat foods as well as by university research laboratories that have delved into feline dietary needs. We are aware that the cat is a predator (under natural conditions) and therefore carnivorous. But when felines (feral and domestic) make a kill, they consume the entire animal, including the bones and bone marrow, blood, heart, liver, lungs, spleen, glands, stomach, and the fat-encrusted intestines that are filled with predigested vegetable matter. The cat, it is evident, does not live on muscle meat alone.

The *Felidae* that became the ancestors of the domestic cat originated in arid, subtropical areas and can therefore be considered desert-type animals. They definitely need water, but have a minimal intake compared to many other mammals. Feral felines recover fluid from their living prey, which contains about 70 percent water. The cat, like other desert creatures, retains water through its capacity to concentrate its urinary output. An appreciable amount of fat rich in vitamin A is found in the cat's kidney rather than the liver, and aids in the conservation of water. Through the agency of a specific amino acid (felinine) in the kidneys, excess sulfate, phosphate, and nitrogen (the result of a high-protein diet) are excreted through the urine.

Cats are considered occasional rather than continuous feeders, but they have a relatively high protein need, much beyond what one would predict from their size (the percentage of protein calories needed is almost twice that of a dog). The cat at times appears to be a lethargic creature, but its large protein requirement is essential to produce the sheer energy necessary to a feline predator. Its protein requirement is not determined by its rate of growth or its metabolic needs.

Kittens must ingest protein of high biological value, particularly for growth. Fats are important, because they supply about 60 percent of the cat's dietary calories and lend palatability to the diet. Vitamins and essential minerals must also be supplied in necessary amounts. Cats need a comparatively large amount of vitamin A in supplied foods since they do not manufacture it within themselves. In the feral state they are dependent upon the vitamin A stored in the livers of their prey. Unlike humans, cats manufacture their own vitamin C (ascorbic acid). Kittens and pregnant or nursing queens need extra calcium and phosphorus for bone growth. These elements are badly lacking in muscle meat.

Several facts pertinent to the feeding of cats can be set forth: they thrive best on a high protein, high fat diet, with fish, fowl, eggs, meat, and vegetables as necessary ingredients; grains and starches must be crushed or cooked to be easily assimilated because a cat (unlike man) gulps rather than chews its food, and the pancreatic enzyme (amylase) cannot effectively dissolve compact lumps of starchy material in the cat's digestive system.

Cats need water, but they do not need milk, which many cats find difficult to digest; they derive nutritional gain from it only until the age of eight or ten weeks. Felines do best on a moist diet, and palatability can be added to their food through fats and fish liver oils (which contain a high percentage of unsaturated fatty acids, of which 95 percent are digestible). Fats are also carriers of fat-soluble vitamins A, D, E, and K. Since cats are basically predators who consume warm kills, all their food should be offered at no less than room temperature—never cold or directly from the refrigerator.

All food elements in the feline's diet should be easily digestible since the length of the cat's small intestine is relatively short and food moves through it rather rapidly. Foods that cats do not chew, such as vegetables, are digested with greater ease when cooked, but meats and fish, whether raw or cooked, are easily assimilated by them. Felines allowed outdoor freedom to roam country fields and woods necessarily need more energy-producing foods than those restricted to an indoor house or apartment lifestyle. Of course, unless belled, the outdoor cat will almost certainly add living prey to its diet.

Basic Nutritional Essentials

Any substance can be designated as food if it can be used by the cat as a source of energy, a body-building substance, or as a regulator of body activity. The following list indicates the basic dietary essentials and their natural sources:

Protein: meat (beef, lamb, chicken, rabbit, fish, etc.), eggs, dairy products, soybeans
Fat: meat fats, butter, oils, fish fats, cream, cream cheese
Carbohydrates: cereals, grains, vegetables, honey, syrup
Vitamin A: eggs, milk, greens, peas, beans, some vegetables, liver
Vitamin D: fish, fish liver oils, eggs, fortified milk
Thiamin: eggs, muscle and organ meats, vegetables, grains, milk, yeast
Riboflavin: liver, milk, green leaves, beef, yeast, egg yolk, wheat germ, chicken, cottonseed meal
Niacin: lean meats, liver, yeast, milk
Ascorbic acid: tomatoes, citrus fruits, raw cabbage (vitamin C, or ascorbic acid, is manufactured by your cat from glucose)
Iron, calcium, and phosphorus: blood, liver, milk and milk products, eggs, vegetables, bone and bone marrow, soybeans, oatmeal

Major, minor, and trace mineral elements necessary to the cat's well-being are found in the dietary essentials listed.
Proteins are composed of amino acids and form the basis of all life, for living cells are composed of protein molecules, and new body tissue is formed from amino acids, which differ in combination with the various proteins. The protein content of your cat's diet is best derived from a combination of both animal and vegetable proteins.
Fats produce heat that is translated into energy; fats are also a source of energy storage against emergency. Approximately 95 percent of most ingested fats are digested by the cat, give taste appeal, and produce over twice as much energy as an equal amount of proteins and carbohydrates. The value of fat as a nutritional essential cannot be denied.
Carbohydrates furnish cats with the fuel for both growth and energy. The fatty acid contents of most cereals are highly unsaturated, so some cereals and grains are a splendid source of fatty acids. The fibrous

material from carbohydrates stimulates intestinal action and aids in maintaining a healthy digestive tract. Carbohydrates can provide a much less expensive source of calories than other foods. In adult cats, when milk sugar passes into the large intestine it is prone to undergo fermentation, and results in diarrhea and gas. This effect has been particularly noticed in Siamese cats and breeds that owe their origin to the Siamese.

Vitamins are the necessary sparks and regulators of the life process. They fall into two broad categories—one group includes the water-soluble vitamins, and the other the fat-soluble vitamins A, D, E, and K. Cats do not need vitamin K.

How to Feed Your Cat

In feeding your cat it is most important that all the nutritional elements in its diet are balanced. Under normal conditions, 30 to 35 percent protein, 8 percent fat, and 40 percent carbohydrates in a cat's diet will meet its nutritional requirements. Pregnant and nursing queens and kittens need comparatively more food, calcium, phosphorus, and vitamins than the normal mature cat, particularly vitamin A and vitamin D, the "sunshine" vitamin. The pregnant queen's food intake should be increased gradually from the fourth week until parturition. If your cat has been ill, discuss a recuperative diet with your veterinarian. Indoor cats may need supplementary vitamin D, especially during the winter months. A nursing queen should be fed five times a day, weaned kittens four, and later three, times a day; mature healthy felines should be supplied with two meals a day. Active cats will consume more food relative to body weight than will lethargic felines.

A good commercial cat food manufactured by a reliable company and containing all the necessary nutrients for a balanced diet is the best way to keep puss healthy and happy. Never feed your cat more than it can eat at each meal, and try always to serve its meals at the same time and place every day. If the cat does not finish its food after about fifteen minutes, remove it and do not feed again until the next mealtime. Cats do not need variety in their diet. So when you find a good cat food that puss enjoys, stay with it and feed it fairly consistently at every meal.

If you wish to serve tidbits, delicacies cats particularly enjoy are raw beef heart, kidneys, lean fish, chicken giblets, and liver. These feline favorites can also be used to tempt an ill cat who refuses to eat its regular diet. Some owners add a bit of catnip to meals two or three times a week. Cats also enjoy chopped greens in their food, such as spinach leaves and dandelion greens. Orphaned kittens or those needing supplementary feeding can be given cow's milk or evaporated milk but with added protein and a bit of melted fat (sweet butter). The difference between cow's and cat's milk is important because it concerns the protein content: cow's milk offers only 3.8 percent protein compared to queen's milk's 7.0 percent protein. Feed five times daily using a small doll's milk bottle and nipple or a medicine dropper; approximately 8 cc. of milk should be offered at each feeding (see also Chapter 12).

The human animal has made a fetish of food intake. We no longer eat; we "dine"—and many of us dine so well that we become obese, suffer digestive and metabolic disorders, and slyly label ourselves "gourmands." As the old aphorism has it, we "dig our graves with our teeth." Let us not transfer our own frailties to our pets: felines must be offered only enough food to keep them in prime condition, and they must be fed portions at each meal that will not make them either overweight or emaciated. Some select table scraps may be given prudently, but never as the entire diet. To repeat: your cat's meals should be nutritionally balanced, a goal not easily achieved unless you base its diet on a complete manufactured cat food. Incidentally, a teaspoonful of mineral oil given once a week is an aid in ridding puss of stomach hair, which results from incessant personal grooming.

GENERAL CARE

Whatever pleasure we find in life must be paid for in some kind of coin, and we pay for the pleasure we derive from our cats in their constant care. They in turn repay us with their own unique brand of devotion and the enjoyment of the cat-human relationship. Cleanliness and sanitation, balanced nutrition, correct grooming, adequate bedding facilities and living quarters, and a periodic visit to your veterinarian to check for any incipient problems, plus a little love, are the keys to correct cat care. Whether you have one cat or a cattery filled with felines, good husbandry pays by manifesting itself in kitty's glowing coat, sparkling eyes, and dainty, dancing feet. It pays also in freedom from anxiety and in the prevention of sickness and perhaps death. Finally, it pays in dollars and cents—in the hard cash you can save in veterinary bills, the cost of expensive medication, nursing time, and the monetary value of an expensive show cat that can be lost through negligence.

Feeding Utensils

Cats are fastidious creatures and depend on their owners for clean food and water receptacles. Metal pans are best for these purposes since porcelain has a tendency to chip, and plastic pans have little weight and can be easily overturned unless molded with a special outer lip (most plastic pans made specifically for cat or dog feeding possess this lip). The food dish should be rather shallow, because a cat finds it unpleasant and difficult to lean over with arched neck and attempt to feed from a deep bowl. Use plain soap, water, and "elbow grease" for food and water utensil cleaning, and rinse thoroughly. Rubber mats placed under the pans will help eliminate mopping or cleaning the floor under and surrounding the pans.

Beds and Bedding

Your cat's bed should be raised off the floor a few inches and located in a place free from drafts, where it will not be too hot in summer or too cold in winter. A large choice of commercial beds can be purchased for puss, including a cat carrier with a detachable bottom that can be converted into a bed. We have not yet heard of a water bed for cats, but the possibility exists—perhaps for ship's cats. A cardboard box will suit a cat just as well as an expensive bed and can be replaced when necessary without financial loss. Many cats prefer an old chair, and often puss selects its own sleeping quarters on a shelf or mantle. A piece of old carpet, a padded seat with a removable and washable cover, loose bedding of cedar shavings or less expensive pine shavings, are all adequate, though loose bedding can be tracked out of the box and so present another small cleaning chore. Flea powder (formulated especially for felines) should be dusted on the bottom of the box, and the bed and bedding aired in the sun frequently.

Cats enjoy privacy and a feeling of security when sleeping, so be sure the bed is in a quiet place where puss can rest undisturbed. Damp cellars or basements were not designed as proper places for your cat's sleeping quarters, and if used for this purpose can lead to respiratory ailments. More than any other pet, your cat has a need, asleep or awake, for a light, happy environment.

The Sanitary Tray

Fertile imaginations have devised a multitudinous selection of sanitary trays, ranging from the simple, basic open tray to a completely enclosed, chemicalized cat toilet. One can purchase liners for the trays for easy disposal of the contents, tray deodorants, and a variety of litter materials—the last preferable to more prosaic substances such as sand, sawdust, wood shavings, shredded paper, peat moss, and so on. One part of common baking soda on the bottom of the litter pan topped by three parts litter material is recommended for absorption and sweetening.

The most obvious way of keeping the contents of the toilet tray from becoming odorous is to keep it clean. Cats do not enjoy using dirty toilets any more than humans do, and they may seek another place to use if their trays are not clean. Kittens can be supplied with more than one tray until completely housebroken. It is easier to teach the kitten to use the tray if you supply it with the same material in the litter box that it had become accustomed to in the maternity or queening box. Used litter can be put into a plastic bag, sealed, and relegated to the garbage pail for disposal.

Bathing Your Cat

The domestic cat who enjoys being bathed is decidedly rare. Most cats detest baths as a monumental indignity. A cat generally keeps itself clean by licking its coat—employing the tiny, clawlike hooks on its tongue as a grooming tool and saliva as a cleansing agent and emollient.

To remove a small area of dirt or grease on your cat's coat, an overall bath is not necessary. A dry shampoo can be purchased at a pet shop, sprinkled on the area, and allowed to remain a short time until it has absorbed the offending stain, then brushed out. If your outdoors cat walks in fresh road tar, it can be removed by dipping his paws in mineral oil and confining him to a small area with flooring that is easily cleaned, until the tar has loosened and dropped off or until it can be removed with a dry cloth. Oil paint can be removed with turpentine, which must be immediately washed out with warm water and soap, then rinsed thoroughly. Most paints used today have a water base and can be rinsed off with water. A quick cleansing of your cat's coat can be achieved with a damp cloth or a wet sponge gently applied to remove surface dust. Puss's coat should be dried well with a towel before grooming.

If your cat becomes filthy, muddy, flea-ridden, or if glamour-puss is entered in a cat show and you have no other cleansing recourse but a bath, then you must take your courage and your cat in both hands and prepare for the ordeal. Be sure the temperature in the room in which this horrendous event is to take place is about 75 degrees Fahrenheit. Use a shampoo manufactured for cat bathing or, if puss harbors fleas or lice, a shampoo guaranteed to rid the cat of its vampiric pests. Attire yourself in old work-around-the-house-and-yard clothes and set out the necessary cat-bathing paraphernalia, which should include two thick towels, a sponge, and the shampoo. Attempt to inveigle a friend into aiding you if this is your first experience in bathing a cat. After a time or two you should be able to handle the chore alone.

Nylon booties that tie across the shoulders can be bought or made, and are very useful in covering puss's paws to protect you from scratches. Many owners trim a cat's claws before bathing. It is best to use two tubs of water (warm but not hot), one for bathing, the other for rinsing. For long-hairs, add a bit of vinegar to the rinse water to prevent hair tangles. Be gentle during the bathing procedure, for puss is not likely to be amused by your antics. Care must be taken not to allow soapy water to get into your cat's eyes, nose, mouth, or ears. A drop of mineral oil in each eye and a plug of cotton in the ears will help.

Carefully, maintaining a firm hold on the cat, pour handfuls of water over its entire body until puss is completely soaked; then apply the shampoo, beginning with a collar of the cleansing lather around the neck and working backward toward the tail. When this has been accomplished, wash the head and face very carefully with a sponge or washcloth. Speak quietly and cheerfully during the whole process— a practice, it is said, calculated to ease your cat's fear of and exasperation with the proceedings (a dubious assumption).

Clean and swab the cat's ears carefully with a Q-Tip, then rinse away most of the shampoo with which puss has been lathered in the partially soapy water of the first tub, followed by a last, thorough rinse in the pristine water of the second tub. Be certain there is no vestige of soap left on the cat before you dry the coat briskly with the thick towels (even though puss is not an Angora or a Van cat, it is permissible to use a Turkish towel for drying). If you own a hair dryer and kitty is not agitated by it, by all means use it to dry and fluff the newly washed coat. Hair dryers are particularly effective in fluffing the pelage of long-haired breeds: brush the coat gently against the lay of the hair while the dryer does its job. Keep puss away from drafts until completely dry.

Grooming

Allocate five to ten minutes each day to comb and brush your cat. Not only will you keep the coat clean and shining and remove loose hairs that could develop into hairballs, but you will make this a period of complete and wonderfully close kinship with your cat, a silent dialogue that both of you will look forward to each day. Grooming is not only an absolute necessity for long-hairs, but also a time for examination for skin disorders or other physical irregularities that can immediately be treated before they become troublesome. For heavily coated Persians, quotidian grooming is a definite necessity. With all long-haired kittens an early introduction to brush and comb is desirable so that the cat will become accustomed to the ritual of grooming, and its coat trained to lie correctly. Brush first, then comb—and finish with careful long-stroke brushing and a silk or chamois light rub.

For the long-hairs, a bristle brush and long, wide-toothed comb is recommended. The comb should have about ten strong teeth to the inch; a finer-toothed flea comb is also useful. Unravel hair knots slowly and carefully, moistening around the knot to part it with greater ease. Be certain every area of kitty's coat has been thoroughly curried. Glandular secretions in the skin will keep the cat's coat shiny, but only if dust and dirt have been removed by grooming, for the feline's skin, unlike man's, has only a small number of sweat glands in restricted areas.

Short-haired cats do not require as much brush-and-comb care as the long-hairs, but they do need regular grooming. A fine comb and stiff brush can do wonders for kitty's coat. The uppermost layer of skin (in both hair lengths) is shed as the inner layers grow to replace it, and as the outer layer of skin loosens the hair is shed with it. This shed hair and dandruff-like skin is removed during the grooming process.

Best results are obtained if you first brush against the lie of the pelt, then brush briskly with short strokes with the lie of the hair. To put a finish to the coat, stroke strongly with your open hand and then with a piece of chamois.

Under normal conditions cats shed their coats according to the number of hours of light, or the length of the days, to which they are exposed. On the longest day of the year, which occurs in June, the coat is shortest; on the shortest day, in the month of December, the pelt is at its thickest—a natural phenomenon designed to keep the cat warm when the weather is frigid and cool when the sun is hottest. But the house or cattery cat, living in an artificial habitat with electric light, heat in winter, and air conditioning or fans to control its environment in summer, indulges in almost constant shedding, so the need for continual grooming is obvious.

Care of Your Cat's Nails

Cats enjoy exercising their toes and claws and, in the process, honing their nails by strongly scratching a tree trunk or any upright solid object. A cat's claws are retractable, as are the nails of all the *Felidae* (except the cheetah), and consist of a hard outer shell with a vein encased within. If you supply puss with a scratching post of wood that won't splinter, or a wooden post covered with carpet, it will please your pet and perhaps save your furniture from the ravages of kitty's claws. If your cat's claws are very sharp, you can trim them with an ordinary pair of nail clippers, or a small pair of dog's nail clippers of the guillotine type.

Indoor house cats should have their claws trimmed once a month even when supplied with a scratching post. By holding the cat's toes up to the light and examining the claws from the underside, you will be able to see the transparent section at the nail's end, which you clip off. This makes it easy to avoid nicking the vein. Do not trim the outdoor cat's nails.

Care of Teeth

Most grown felines will need the tartar removed from their teeth at some time in their lives, but, unlike trimming the nails, this is a job for your veterinarian. Examine your pet's mouth once a month, perhaps at the time you trim its claws, and check for tartar buildup, infected gums, and broken teeth. The few minutes this examination takes can save puss much mouth trouble, as can quick care by your veterinarian. When a cat's mouth is well cared for and the tartar removed, its breath is sweetened. Occasionally feeding your cat soft rib bones aids in the removal of tartar since its teeth pierce the bones and the tartar buildup is scraped off.

Ear Care

If puss shakes his head or holds it to the side, or if he scratches at his ears, immediately examine each ear carefully, for such behavior indicates one or more of the following conditions: dirty ears, ticks in the ears, ear mites, or ear canker.

Drop some alcohol or propylene glycol into each ear to dissolve dirt and wax, then clean out the ears thoroughly (but gently) with a Q-Tip. If ear mites or canker are present, there will be an accompanying distinctly odious smell. Your veterinarian will know how to cope with the problem.

See also Chapter 28.

Eye Care

Your cat's eyes seldom need particular care. Sometimes the eye fluid will overflow and stain the hair, but this is only a cosmetic problem and can be cleansed with the application of a little warm water on the stained area. Of course, medical eye problems can occur and we have covered them in Chapter 28.

RANDOM THOUGHTS ON CAT CARE

If you allow your cat to roam outdoors, it should be supplied with a collar with an attached identification tag, and a small bell to help both you and the neighborhood birds locate it. If puss is a house cat but trained to walk out with you on a collar, or harness, and lead, use a round collar for a long-hair and a flat one for a short-haired cat. It is a moot question whether to use a collar or a harness for this purpose; there are advocates of both. After you stroll is over and puss is once again at home, remove the collar or harness so that the coat is not worn by the rubbing of the leather.

Make your house a safe home for your cat. Be certain that all the myriad poisonous products that are present in every home—cleaning fluids, plumbers' liquid helpers, paints, varnishes, weedkillers, bug killers, rust eradicators, and so on—are locked up or placed safely beyond kitty's reach. Teach your cat that electric cords and sockets are not to be played with. Many houseplants are poisonous to puss, and all cats are inveterate plant, leaf, and flower nibblers. Dangerous common houseplants include philodendron, chrysanthemum, holly, calla lilies, rhododendron, poinsettia, mistletoe, and a host of others. Plant mold and mildew also pose a threat to cats.

Supply puss with toys made of rubber or polyethylene, but not soft, furry, or woolly playthings that he can chew, tear, and swallow. Find toys made for cats: a mouse that squeaks, a rattling ball-like toy, a catnip trinket; playthings that can keep a cat amused for hours at a time.

The scratching post you supply should be high enough to allow your cat to stretch full length with front legs extended upward before digging its claws in. Commercial posts can be bought that are well made and often supplied with a catnip toy at the top. Cats will instinctively scratch, so to save your furniture, a scratching post is a very worthwhile investment.

If you take your cat on a car trip with you, don't feed it for four hours before starting. If it is an extended trip, carry a supply of plain meat to feed puss to cut down on his elimination. Bring with you a comfortable cat carrier so puss can have privacy and a familiar place to snooze.

If you find it difficult to give your cat a liquid medication and the quantity to be given is not great, you can rub it on the tip of the nose and he will inevitably lick it off. This trick can also be used to introduce puss to a food that is good for him but which he has definitely indicated is not to his liking. After a few licks have made him accustomed to the taste, he will generally begin to consume it—then again, he may not, but it is worth a try.

If you are an ailurophile who has some connection with the medical profession, or are simply the kind of individual who likes to check a pet thoroughly to ascertain the state of its health and well-being, you might want to know that a normal adult cat has a temperature reading of 101 to 102 degrees Fahrenheit; respiration 25 per minute plus or minus 5; and pulse (femoral) should read 120, or up to 130 when excited.

FERAL CATS

All that you have read here in reference to the general care of domestic cats can also be applied—within reason—to feral felines. We would not advise you to attempt to bathe any of the larger wild felines. If accumulated dirt becomes a hygiene problem, a hose can be used to clean the soiled pelage. We remember well an incident that occurred some time ago when a lion and a tiger, supplied by International Films for a publisher's publicity stunt, were brought to a nightclub in New York City where they were to appear in the main room of the club. The tiger was brought in through the bar on a leash and collar, all 400 pounds of him sliding and protesting across the slick surface of the tile floor. Unfortunately, our King of Beasts had defecated in his cage during the journey and was a complete and utter mess. In an attempt to save the day the senior author (at the time, managing editor of the publishing company), inspired by a quick drink at the bar, drove the caged cat to a nearby carwash to be cleaned. Though years have passed since this event took place, the operator of the car-washing establishment has probably not yet quit running and screaming.

Of course the quantity of food ingested by a feral cat, unless the cat is one of the smaller species similar in size to a domestic puss, should be greater, in proportion to the feline's weight. But the same balance of nutritional essentials must be observed if the cat is to be kept healthy. One cannot find cans of manufactured foods large enough to feed a jaguar, but muscle meat should be given in huge chunks that have been injected with the necessary vitamins and minerals, and the inner organs of slaughtered cows and horses can be found with some diligent research, thus rounding out your feral pet's diet. A periodic health check by your veterinarian is a must.

Sadly, many owners of feral cats have the teeth and claws of their charges removed to keep the cats from injuring people. Usually such cats end up in zoos where they must lead solitary existences for the rest of their lives, unable to protect themselves, and thus unable to share a habitat with others of their kind.

CHAPTER 9

Training Kittens and Cats

Because of their independent spirit and intense desire to control their own destiny, cats are difficult animals to train, but the fact that lions, tigers, and leopards can be trained to perform is ample proof that they have the capacity to learn. The performing *Panthera* are trained, not tamed, and do not live with humans or share human family life. They are caged and given only minimum freedom in the performing cage. They are prodded and threatened into engaging in certain acts that they often execute reluctantly as the line of least resistance and that are followed by a food reward. In contrast, the domestic cat is a tame feline, which lives closely with humans, sharing their lifestyle and which, if we would keep its love and devotion, must be trained with the utmost kindness and understanding, and a bit of firmness.

THE CAT'S "MENTAL ABILITY"

We explore the brain and nervous system in the chapter on feline physiology, but a quick explanation here will aid you in understanding the physical elements that enable a cat to absorb training.

Mammalian nerves are long, thin fibers that form "bundles": the largest packet is the spinal cord, from which nerves branch out, not unlike a tree's limbs, with the end divisions forming tiny twigs. Other nerves emerge from the brain (cranial nerves) to service the head and the various organs of the body. These approximately forty-two pairs of nerves (cranial and spinal cord) control the total body of the cat: its glands, organs, all muscular movement, its mental and physical actions, voluntary and involuntary.

The feline brain consists of two main sections, the cerebrum and cerebellum (which includes the medulla), composed of gray (cellular) and white (fibrous) matter. Conscious, voluntary actions evolve in the cerebrum (the anterior and upper sections of the brain), which receives messages sent it by the sense organs. The lower section of the brain, the cerebellum, highly developed in the felids, is concerned with everyday, functional living, such as muscular coordination, body balance and movement, breathing, and all the involuntary pumping, expanding, and contracting in which the inner organs indulge. It is evident, therefore, that the cerebrum responds and evokes the proper responses to training. The more an animal learns, the more responsive the cerebrum becomes, and the easier it is to teach the animal new things.

The key to all animal training is *control,* and control is gained through *conditioned response,* or the shaping of the animal's reflexes to outside stimulus until the reaction becomes habit. *Consistency* is brother to control, and *patience* is a vital requirement for the trainer. *Firmness* is also essential, for without it control can slip away and be lost. When training your cat, firmness must be tempered with compassion.

Cats must be in the mood to be trained for you to attain any kind of success. They must be coaxed and cajoled into obeying commands, and never punished for not complying, except under certain circumstances which we will define later. Never, ever lose your cool during the training session, for if you do, you will have blown the whole training and will never again reach the rapport with your cat that is necessary for success.

RULES FOR TRAINING YOUR CAT

Here are some essentials for feline training that you must observe and that, in some instances, differ from training tips used for other animals:

1. Observe your feline pupil to determine what natural actions it indulges in when playing that can be fashioned into a training accomplishment. Example: If your cat sits up to use his front paws to reach for an object above his head, the command, "Sit up!"—prefaced by the cat's name spoken when he does it of his own volition—will eventually result in a conditioned response and the cat will ultimately perform the act upon command.

2. Always preface every training command with your cat's name. This immediately makes the training act pertinent and personal by attracting the cat's quick attention and interest, and making him receptive to the command.

3. You cannot pick a definite time to train a cat as you can with other animals. One cannot declare, "We will have a training session each afternoon at one o'clock sharp." Your cat may not be in the mood for training then and will not cooperate despite any proclamation you make.

4. Training should be undertaken at a quiet time of day, in an area where there are no other activities that will distract the pupil.

5. Short, distinctive words of command should be used, and the same command used consistently, the word or words always the same, and always spoken in the same tone of voice.

6. The training period must be approached as a time of quiet communication between you and your cat. Remember, you cannot push a cat into obeying commands if it chooses not to.

7. Training periods must be short and should terminate before the cat becomes bored. Attempt to end each session on a note of triumph, when the pupil has performed a training act perfectly and is given praise and reward.

8. Never scream at, slap, or in any way drastically punish your cat for not obeying. Control over your pupil begins with control of yourself. Praise and reward puss for accomplishment. Reward should be immediate, consisting of praise, petting, or a tidbit.

9. Be patient. Repeat the exercise over and over and reward any step in the desired direction. Be calm, be sweet, but be firm, no matter how long it takes to achieve the desired results.

10. Training time should never take place immediately after your cat has been fed. Puss will be sluggish and less likely to appreciate the tidbit you offer as a reward for accomplishment.

If all this sounds like a great deal of time-consuming work, you are correct—it is. Training any animal is a slow, patient process. Actually, if you housebreak your kitten or cat and teach it to comply with the few rules necessary to become a good citizen and house pet, you can rest on your laurels. But for those of you who wish to continue training further, there are some more hints that may be helpful.

In general, you will find that cats have certain characteristics that can be used to mold training response. They are, for instance, natural retrievers, and will chase and retrieve an object in play. You can cause a conditioned response by engaging in this pleasant activity with your cat, using the command, "Matilda [assuming your pet is named Matilda], fetch!"

Of course, the first instruction for the kitten is to teach it to come when called. We assume that should you acquire a mature cat, it will readily recognize its name and respond. The easiest way to train a kitten to come when called is to use its name at mealtime. When you set down the victuals you have prepared, call the cat to you, "Hannibal, come!" The kitten will quickly associate its name and the word "come" with a very pleasant experience and will soon become conditioned to come when called. Later, a whistle can substitute for the oral command. Once puss is trained to come when you whistle, you can call him to you even when he is outside.

Cats possess unusual powers of concentration. Your cat will sit for hours, unmoving, before a mousehole, its entire being concentrated on the prey it knows hides within the hole. If you could possibly channel this concentration into the training period, the results could be phenomenal. Unfortunately, a cat's attention to training sessions is like a child's—short and easily distracted.

The domestic cat is a mimic and often learns by imitating the actions of its peers. A kitten, through imitation, can learn many things from an older, well-trained cat, should you happen to have one in your home. Both feral and domestic felines, though instinctive predators, learn the fine points of hunting by imitating the actions of their dams. Cats are also inveterate teasers. They will tease their own kind, their human family, dogs, and any other nearby living creature.

Cats have an unusual aptitude for fathoming the manner in which simple mechanical objects function. They can become adept at opening latched doors, or doors that can be opened by manipulating a pull or loop. One great virtue our feline friends possess is a particular plus in training: cats never forget anything that they have once learned.

HOUSEBREAKING A CAT

Housebreaking is an easy chore because cats are innately clean animals. After the kitten or cat has eaten or drunk, bring it to the litter box. Gently restrain it from leaving the pan for a sufficient length of time and chances are it will eliminate. Praise puss extravagantly and allow him his freedom. Repeat this performance a few times and the kitten will get the message. When the inevitable occurs and kitty makes a mistake on the rug, try to catch him in the act, pick him up, and sternly tell him "No!" But do not otherwise chastise him. Then deposit him in the litter box gently, pet him, and hold him there for a few minutes. Do not clean the litter pan for the first couple of times, for felines (and most other animals) will return to use an area they have previously soiled. Once the habit of using the pan has been formed, and the catling has been conditioned to use the litter box, you may clean it frequently with hot soap and water but no disinfectant—a product cats abhor. Cats, when completely housebroken, dislike using soiled trays, which do nothing for the atmosphere in the house either. The country cat need only be allowed its freedom out of doors at regular intervals and it will quickly learn to be clean in the house.

Occasionally, a thoroughly housebroken cat will have a relapse, soil the floor, and act as though it had never been taught to use the litter box. The cause for this behavior is not always clear to us, but the cat undoubtedly has a valid reason, generally based on some act or event that has upset it. If, after you use the stern "No!" command and bring puss to the box several times, he still persists in his unmannerly behavior, he must be firmly scolded and incarcerated in a carrier or small enclosure, immediately following his misdemeanor, for several hours. This treatment should be repeated each time he soils the floor. Your cat is intelligent and knows that this is punishment for his misdeed. He will soon decide to use his sanitary tray again.

If you want to, you can also teach a cat to use the family toilet. We, personally, do not applaud this practice. We have even heard of cats trained to this way of elimination who have been taught to flush the bowl—and one or two who continued to flush it, over and over again! We think it best to train puss to use a litter box. It must be remembered that the male feline is a tom cat—not a john cat.

DISCIPLINING YOUR CAT

When you groom your cat, teach him to "Stand!" or, if you prefer to groom him while in your lap, use the command "Stay!" during the process. We have already mentioned the virtues of the scratching post. A bit of catnip (derived from a harmless plant related to the mint family) applied to the post will make it more attractive to your cat. When your pet attempts to climb the curtains, or chew and claw the furniture, you must discipline him sternly and convince him that such behavior is definitely forbidden. Pick him up and, while holding him close to the article he has damaged, tap his front paws briskly with your finger and admonish him, "Hannibal, NO!" Repeat sternly several times, then bring him to his scratching post and, holding his front legs, indicate to him how the post is to be used. The command "No!" spoken in a forbidding tone must become an important word in your cat's lexicon in the early stages of training. With luck you will not have much occasion to use it later.

Watch your cat at play and supply it with toys for its pleasure. A feline that has nothing to do—particularly a young one—becomes bored and, in attempting to find occupation, frequently finds trouble instead. Often the manner in which puss plays, by himself or with a toy, can suggest some kind of cute trick you can teach him to accomplish.

TAKING YOUR CAT OUTDOORS

Should you wish to train your kitten to walk outdoors using a collar and leash, attach a small, soft, light collar to his neck and to it tie a piece of light cord to hang loose. Puss will play with the hanging cord and in so doing, adjust to the pull of a leash. After a few days, remove the cord and replace it with a lightweight leash, pick puss up, and, when it is just beginning to turn to twilight, take him out. At first he will probably pull in all directions, but you must guide him by gentle tugs on the leash to move in the correct one. Never drag him, rather, direct him. Pulling or dragging with the leash will only make him dig his claws in and resist more firmly. Gentle, quick tugs in the right direction give him an incentive to move and not resist angrily. Alas, we must confess that some cats completely oppose the leash, so if after several earnest attempts you make no progress, it is best to forget the whole project and admit that yours is not a leash-cat.

If you should wish to try a harness instead of a collar, the same training method can be used, but control is much more easily gained through the use of a collar. A harness can wear the cat's coat in more body areas, and it can sometimes result in the cat's becoming "out" at the elbows. If you want kitty to be a complete indoors cat, never allow him to go out at all unless taken out on collar and leash. If he attempts to sneak out when you open the door, block the entrance with your foot and leg and push him back, uttering a stern "No!" and accenting the vocal command with an admonishing finger.

CATS AND FOOD

Cats are inveterate food thieves, and it is difficult to keep them from reaching up and deftly removing food from the table. The forbidding "No!" often proves inadequate in controlling the atavistic urge of the sneak thief in this instance. When such an impasse occurs, we must trick the cat into bringing retribution upon himself. Place a piece of food on the table close to the edge and within easy reach of puss's thieving paw. Tie a string to the bait food which has been attached to bells, small tin cans, and anything else you can think of that will make a resounding racket. When puss sneaks up on silent feet, stands on his hind legs, and deftly scoops up the bait and pulls it down, he brings with it much more than he had bargained for. A cacophony of sudden noise is anathema to any sneak thief, and he will rush away in consternation and alarm to some quiet place to think it over.

We once owned a cat who insisted on pulling the kitchen waste can over to seek for food tidbits when we left her alone in the house. It was probably a gesture of pure pique at being deserted. The obvious solution was to remove the object of her temptation and put it in the garage when we left the house. But sometimes (being only human and not feline) we forgot to do this and would return to find the can inevitably tipped over and garbage strewn all over the floor. Scolding was useless, so it was necessary to outsmart puss—a rather difficult accomplishment. We finally broke her of this habit by setting several mousetraps on top of the waste in the can, covering them lightly and carefully with a sheet of paper. When she tipped the can over, the traps snapped shut, startling her considerably. It was necessary to resort to this trap trickery twice before Mandy was cured of her propensity for garbage-can tipping.

CATS AND FURNITURE

If you wish to cure your cat from jumping on furniture, the same trap method can be used with good results. Remember always to spread paper over the set traps: you are not trying to catch the cat in the traps, but merely to startle her enough to keep her from repeating her indiscretion.

Many cat owners use a water pistol in their training. This is a method of reaching puss from a distance when he is scratching up a plant, or a piece of furniture that he has been told is out-of-bounds, and you know he will run if you approach close enough to chastise him. To some felines who enjoy water (such as the Turkish cat), the water jet would be a pleasure rather than a disciplinary action. You may try the water pistol method with a truly recalcitrant cat if you wish, but we were not born in the Wild West of the 1800s and refuse to spend precious time practicing a fast draw with a water pistol in a dripping house with a wet cat.

We would be less than honest if we did not warn you that there are some cats (happily very few) who view any attempt at training with Olympian detachment and complete lack of cooperation. It is generally a waste of time to attempt to train such individuals in anything but the most necessary basics. With dogs, and a few other pets, it is the instructor's fault if the pupil does not learn its training lessons within a reasonable time limit. It indicates faulty methods. A cat, on the other hand, can understand perfectly what it is you want it to do. But if it, at the moment, does not desire to perform, it will simply ignore you and your commands. Exasperating? Yes! But very typical of the cat's innate independence.

CHAPTER 10

Cat Genetics

The science of genetics advances so rapidly that this is an extremely important chapter if you are a cat breeder. Even if you are simply a cat lover, you may find this chapter as interesting to read as it was to write. Geneticists, biologists, and biochemists have now learned the secrets of DNA, the central gene control and the basic life molecule. Sociobiology, a new theory of behavior, is arousing worldwide interest. On these pages, we will explain as simply as possible how you can use the science of genetics to best control type, coat, and breeding value in your stock, and to upgrade that stock to breed fine domestic felines. Please do not be alarmed by the term "genetics." It is associated with the word "science," and science simply means knowledge. Certainly, we can all use a bit more of that scarce commodity.

A LOOK AT DARWIN AND MENDEL

The story of the study and discovery of the true mode of inheritance must begin with Charles Darwin's fabulous theory of evolution published in his monumental work *The Origin of Species,* in which he propounded the hypothesis that all living things struggle for existence, and that only those fit to survive endure and prosper. Through a process of natural selection there evolved all of the many contemporary living creatures, including cats, birds, and man. His theory caused a furor among scientists, laymen, and particularly the clergy. In the resulting pandemonium, the issue between science and religion was mortally joined and has not abated to this day. Darwin, a scholarly and gentle man, was disturbed by the subsequent savage attacks upon his character, morality, and scientific integrity. But, true scientist that he was, he held staunchly to his belief in the evolutionary theory he knew to be correct.

Darwin was aware that something was missing in his theories, that there had to be factors that caused variation in inherited material, giving their creature carriers the ability to survive. He indulged in years of plant experimentation, but failed to find the pattern of inheritance he knew had to exist. Meanwhile, in Europe, an obscure farmer's son, a Moravian monk, Gregor Johann Mendel, was studying at the University of Vienna. In 1856, Mendel, a brilliant man with an insatiable mind and an abundance of patience, began a long series of experiments that was to lead at last to the solving of the riddle of inheritance and to the beginning of a new and vital science—genetics.

After a period of testing, Mendel selected the common garden pea as the vehicle for his experiments in the variable characteristics of living matter. He found that in hybrid peas one character (round peas) prevailed and was visible, but that there was another character present (wrinkled peas) hidden in the germ of the pea seed. He called the visible character *dominant* (A), and the hidden character *recessive* (a). When two pure dominants (A × A) united, the result was the production of only the dominant (round) peas. When two recessives were paired (a × a), the result was a double recessive and the production of only wrinkled (a) peas. Mendel then took his experiment one step further and found that when the dominant (A) and the recessive (a) were combined, the result was a hybrid pea (Aa) with the dominant

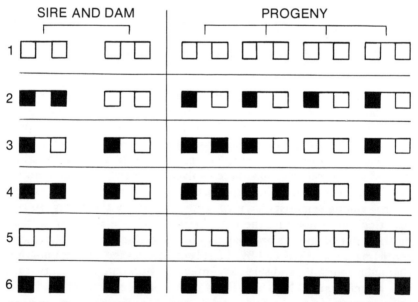

Mendelian Expectation Chart: the six possible combinations that can be formed by a pair of determiners. Ratios apply to expectancy over large numbers of progeny, except in the matings numbered 1, 2, and 6, where expectancy should be definitely realized. Exceptions can be caused by mutation or crossing-over. The black squares here are dominant determiners and the white squares are recessives.

round (A) of course visible. He then paired the hybrid peas (Aa × Aa) and found that three kinds of combinations could be formed: pure dominant (AA); visibly dominant but carrying the recessive in a hidden state (Aa); and double recessive (aa). Mendel noted that the dominant-recessive (Aa) occurred in approximately 50 percent of the hybrid cross; the double dominant (AA), and the double recessive (aa), each in 25 percent of the subsequent plants. This formula resulted in the famous 3 to 1 Mendelian ratio (three apparent dominants to one recessive).

As more factors were combined the probable combinations became more numerous, but Mendel proposed that there were six basic possible ways in which a pair of determiners or genes (Mendel called them "units") could unite, and this simple Mendelian law holds true in the breeding of all living things, including plants, whales, mice, birds, dogs, cats, and people.

In 1864 Mendel read a treatise he had prepared, comprising his eight years of experimentation and the results he had formulated, before the local Brünn Society for the Study of Natural Science. The small group was completely bewildered because Mendel's hypothesis was so totally contrary to the generally accepted theory that blood was the vehicle of heredity. His monograph, "Experiments in Plant Hybridization," appeared in the society's small, limited-distribution magazine in 1866 and was promptly buried in dusty archives and forgotten. Two years after the death of Darwin, Mendel also died, on January 6, 1884. It seemed that Mendel's great contribution to science would be buried with his body and his theory turn to dust with his human remains.

DE VRIES, SUTTON, AND MORGAN

At the time when Mendel made his experiments and quietly and precisely recorded his findings, there was little or no exchange of ideas within the scientific community, so Mendel had no way of knowing that other scientists were painstakingly working toward the same basic theory he had advanced. It is not surprising, therefore, that in 1900 a Dutch botanist, Hugo de Vries, amassed much data similar in direction to Mendel's, and that while hunting for any parallel research on plant hybridization, he found reference to Mendel's work and subsequently discovered the paper Mendel had published. De Vries immediately realized that the gentle Moravian monk was the first to find the answers to the riddle of inheritance, and he gave Mendel's work to the world.

In 1902, W. S. Sutton of Columbia University theorized that the chromosomes might be the physical carriers of Mendel's invisible "units." In 1933, after the experimental breeding of millions of fruit flies *(Drosophila melanogaster)*, Thomas Hunt Morgan, an American biologist, won the Nobel Prize for proving that Mendel's "units" were indeed encased within the chromosomes. Morgan renamed the "units," calling them genes, and became known as the father of modern genetics.

GENES AND CHROMOSOMES

With this very brief background of the puissant science of genetics, we will explain how you can actually utilize this knowledge to breed better cats. Remember, when using the tools genetics provides, that you must envision your breeding goals through a devised system of values so that short-term advances are weighed against the ultimate purpose.

Your cat as an entity is composed of a multitude of cells, and each of these cells contains a given number of chromosomes. In the female feline, there is a total of nineteen pairs of chromosomes in each cell; in the male, we find eighteen pairs, the sex cells not being paired. Packed within the chromosomes are the genes (Mendel's "units" of heredity). We, you and I, and all other living things, are programmed by our genes.

The paired chromosomes resemble twin strings of beads that mirror each other, except for the sex chromosomes, which in the female are alike and are labeled XX. But in the male they are not alike and so they are labeled XY (X representing one kind of chromosome, Y the other). Each gene has a "locus" or special location within the chromosome. The genes are paired like the chromosomes, linked and passed on to the next generation as units. When each gene of a pair is identical, we call the specific influence of that pair *homozygous* (pure for a given trait); but if each gene of the pair is different, then we label the influence it exerts *heterozygous* (not pure for a given trait). A homozygous pair of genes can be either dominant or recessive. A heterozygous pair consists of one dominant and one recessive gene. The dominant gene of such a pair, if it affected a surface area on the cat, would be visible, while the recessive allele (a gene that differs from its sister gene) would be hidden.

Cells constantly renew themselves, multiplying through a process called mitosis (or dividing), and when the cells divide, the chromosomes split lengthwise into exact halves (called chromatids) and form two separate nuclei. As the cell divides into two cells, each new cell possesses one of the chromatic nuclei in exact duplication and becomes complete and capable of dividing again. But in the sex cells (gametes), a different process takes place. There, when cell division occurs ("reduction" division), only half of the chromosomes and their genes are acquired by the gametes, male and female (sperm or ova). Selection of chromatic material is random, but when the split group of chromosomes in the male spermatozoon unites with the split group carried by the female ovum (egg), the two groups pair so that the embryo that develops from the breeding has its full complement of paired chromosomes, half from one parent and half from the other parent. Gametes also carry sex-linked factors, and there are more sex-linked characters coupled to the X chromosome than to the Y.

If the male Y of the pair of sex chromosomes carried by the tom unites with the X chromosome of the queen (remember the female carries a pair of X chromosomes), the resulting kitten will be a male (XY like his father). But if the male X chromosome is carried by the sperm that fertilizes the female egg, the resulting cat will be a female (XX like her mother). Since sperm are capricious and fertilization is random, the sex of the individual offspring of any mating is a matter of chance.

Now let us examine the genes that reside in their chromatic packets. Genes are securely insulated from exterior influence and can only be affected by some forms of radiation. Therefore, environmental modifications such as illness, stunted growth, and bone anomalies due to nutritional lack during the growth period, as well as other physical deficiencies of like origin, cannot affect the cat's genes. Its inheritable material will remain inviolate and the cat, when mature and bred, will pass to its offspring the genetic potential it was denied through improper environment.

Genes themselves are biochemical and contain chemical messages that control the metabolism and the growth and reproduction of the cells. Combined with cell enzymes, genes govern the sequence and speed of chemical changes in living cells, which are in a constant state of chemical modification. Genes are, therefore, regulators, and in this role they direct the development of the cell in which they dwell. Actually, the function of the genes in controlling and regulating the cells and chromosomes need not concern the cat breeder; it is mentioned here merely to lend completeness to this area of the genetic picture.

The chemical material of the gene is a wondrous molecule called DNA (deoxyribonucleic acid), which differs chemically from any other cellular tissue. A similar nucleic acid molecule, RNA (ribonucleic acid), created by DNA, aids DNA in its work, which is the directing of growth, body chemistry, cell specialization, and dictation of exactly what the aggregate living cells shall be and do. To put it more succinctly, the DNA helix encodes the sequence of the timetable of life.

MUTATION, MEIOSIS, AND "CROSSING-OVER"

When discussing genetics, you will frequently hear the word "mutation." Mutation is a sudden change in genetic material resulting in an unexpected and alien trait. The cause is probably due to accidents that affect atoms during DNA synthesis, which in turn affect the genes, which then fail to produce normal results. The loss of a gene, the gain of a gene, but more often a change in a gene, all result in mutation. Of great importance is the fact that most mutant genes are recessive and can lurk in the germ plasm for generations without being visible until suddenly, perhaps when drastic change in the environment makes physical change in a species necessary for survival, the mutant gene will link with another similar mutant gene when two animals mate, and the new pair of genes will create a dramatic change that allows the race to survive. Mutation keeps the gene pool of any species from becoming stagnant and can, for this reason, be called the fountainhead of evolution. Not all mutations are beneficial and some are even lethal, but gene recombination allied to sexual reproduction brings gene mutations into new unions. Then natural selection tests these combinations and either keeps or discards them, depending upon whether they help or impede the species.

A simple view of mutation at work can be found in the mutational color changes exhibited by the Australian parakeet or budgerigar. The normal body color of these birds in their natural habitat is green, and the color green is a mixture of yellow and blue. Suddenly, some budgies appeared that were solid yellow instead of green. Something had affected the gene that produced the mixture of yellow and blue to give the birds their normal color. The blue had been suppressed or lost completely and the result was a mutant yellow budgie. Not long after this occurred, another mutation appeared. In some few normal series birds the gene for color, due to injury or change, failed to produce yellow, and the result was the appearance of the beautiful blue parakeet. Both these mutations are typically recessive, so when either a yellow or blue mutant budgie is mated to a pure normal green, all the young in the nest are normal green, but carry the yellow or blue as a recessive. This is a very simple and easily understood example of how mutation works. Generally, though, mutant genes remain dormant and increase in variety in the germ plasm of a species until a drastic change makes their linkage necessary for species survival.

Change also results from normal sexual cell division in the reproductive organs of cats (or other animals), a process labeled "meiosis." This procedure results in egg and sperm cells each carrying 50 percent of the genes and DNA of the parent cats. When fertilization takes place, the sperm contributes half of the material of inheritance and the egg the other half. Thus the embryonic kittens are the recipients of a complete set of chromosomes, one half from the sire and the other half from the dam, that are different from the full set of either parent, making each kitten a unique individual.

One other way in which genetic change can occur happens just before the chromosomes divide in the sex cells, and is termed "crossing-over." It is caused by a twisting together of opposing members of the chromosome pairs, and it allows a gene or genes to relocate on another chromosome. This results in a change of genetic characters in the gene packet that is passed on to the progeny. A distinct variance in the expected genetic effect is caused by crossing-over since, not unlike mutation, it changes the Mendelian balance.

There are four known factors that cause change by interrupting genetic balance: selection, mutation, migration, and genetic drift. In the controlled breeding of pure-bred cats, only the first two factors apply. The last two can be replaced by a single pertinent factor—environment.

A triple chromosome phenomenon is caused by chromatic change, and the individual so influenced is called a triploid. An individual can possess too few chromosomes (anenploidy), or too many (polyploidy), and in some instances the effect could be lethal.

From what you have read so far you are aware that every cat you see—adult male, female, or kitten—is not just one feline, but from the breeder's point of view is actually three cats: shadow, substance, and a combination of both. The substance is the living, breathing cat that we see before us, the physical manifestation of genetic factors plus environment (the phenotype). The shadow cat is the total of the recessive genes that it carries unseen but ready to become apparent when a fortuitous linkage occurs. And the third cat, also amorphous, is the gene-complex cat, the total collection of its complete complement of genes, those seen and those not visible (the genotype).

DOMINANT AND RECESSIVE TRAITS

Here is where a complete pedigree of the ancestors of your cat, including color information, becomes important. If the breeder is not a neophyte, he or she will probably have owned or seen some of the specimens named in the pedigree, a circumstance that will also be a help in determining what type is behind the cat. Which are the dominant and which the recessive traits carried by the cat you wish to use for breeding? The following rules will aid you, for they are based on known patterns of genetic activity of dominant and recessive characters:

Dominant traits
1. Do not skip a generation;
2. Affect a relatively large number of kittens;
3. Are carried only by affected cats;
4. Minimize the danger of continuing undesirable characteristics;
5. Make the breeding formula of each individual cat very certain.

Recessive traits
1. May skip one or more generations;
2. Are carried by a relatively small percentage of individuals;
3. Are outwardly visible only in those cats that carry a pair of determiners for the trait;
4. Are hidden in a cat carrying only one determiner for the trait— only through the proper mating can the trait be ascertained;
5. Must be inherited from both sire and dam to be visible.

Knowing these rules for dominant and recessive traits, the genotype can be brought into sharper focus and the breeding potential of any cat made more specific. Be sure to remember that dominant traits *always* mask recessives, and that when two recessives link they become visible, though they still remain recessives; simply being visible does not give them dominant status. One cross to a male or female carrying a dominant genetic factor, and that factor will mask the corresponding double recessive, visible factor. Some dominants do not express themselves fully and completely but instead have varied penetration. Their effect is consequently unfixed and diverse.

BREEDING METHODS

Several breeding techniques can be utilized in the breeding of cats, and can aid in the application of the genetic material expressed in this chapter. If your aim is to establish a strain, or create a new variety, these methods can be used to advantage either singly or deftly merged. They can be employed as valued tools in the hands of the intelligent breeder, and when applied correctly, can help to clarify the potential of the breeding stock. These techniques are generally concerned with type and conformation, and coat quality, rather than with coat color.

To achieve the best results from any breeding program, it is essential that several characteristics never be less than normal in the stock used. These characteristics are fertility, vigor, and longevity. The choice of breeding partners that are as close to being faultless as possible—combined with rigid culling of the progeny, and a record of faults and virtues—is also a necessary adjunct to breeding success.

Inbreeding

To obtain the most intense purity of inherited material, one must inbreed. There are four avenues of inbreeding. They consist of the mating of father to daughter, mother to son, half brother to half sister, and brother to sister, the last breeding the closest of the four. Inbreeding consolidates both virtues and faults, strengthens dominants and makes recessives obvious so that both can be more easily evaluated. It lends the breeder control over prepotency and homozygosity. Close inbreeding is generally thought to produce degeneration and weakness. This is not necessarily true. It merely concentrates weaknesses, bringing them to our notice so that we can, through breeding acumen, eliminate them. Inbreeding, by its very nature, produces extremes from which the breeder can often select to better the basic stock. Purity in the strain is the end result of inbreeding, which has been used successfully with other genetic material including plants, mice, tropical fish, birds, and rodents.

Backcrossing

This method is allied to inbreeding, for it is based upon breeding back consistently to one specific animal, who must necessarily be a superb specimen of the variety. The process involves the use of a superior tom so magnificent in type that you wish to stamp your strain with his physical virtues. From the initial breeding, the best female is bred back to her sire. This first breeding can be son to mother if the super-male has acquired his genetic excellence from his dam. Then, in each subsequent breeding of father to daughter, the best female produced is bred back to her sire. The secret to success in backcrossing is to select, from each litter, the female that most resembles her sire, to perpetuate his type.

Linebreeding

Linebreeding is a broader, less intense form of inbreeding, that will help to preserve valuable genetic characteristics, and give the breeder enough control over genetic factors to develop a strain or "family" whose specific type is recognizable. Selection is made of breeding partners who possess one or more common ancestors. These ancestors must appear on both sides of the pedigree and should be excellent and prepotent felines. The method varies in intensity depending upon the closeness of the ancestors being linebred and the number of times they appear in both the upper and lower bracket of the pedigree.

Breeders who indulge in this course of breeding have a tendency eventually to select partners primarily from pedigree study. This practice can lead to failure, for choice of breeding partners must always be made through a knowledge of their genetic background *coupled* with their individual worth and appearance.

Outcross Breeding

The breeding together of two individual cats who have no common ancestry for several generations results in complete heterozygosity—this is outcross breeding. To exercise any control over the kittens from an outcross mating, one of the partners should be either line- or inbred. This is a breeding used essentially to correct faults and produce compensations. Through outcrossing, we introduce new and needed characteristics, add greater vigor (hybrid vigor), and generally find a lack of type uniformity in the resulting kittens. Outcrossing has a tendency to conceal recessives and support individual merit, and to disperse favorable genetic combinations, which lowers the breeding worth of the cat from an outcross mating.

(Heterosis, another breeding method that has been successfully used in agriculture and other areas, would not prove of importance in the breeding of cats, so is merely given mention here.)

Color Breeding

Now let us explore color in reference to its dominant and recessive traits as it concerns the animal to which we are dedicated, his majesty the cat. For percentage results in breeding, please check back to the Mendelian chart (page 106).

Basically, there are three color pigments that tint the coat of the cat: black, brown, and yellow. White is an absence of color, and a covering that can suppress color. The hue we designate as "yellow" is genetic nomenclature for red and orange. A list of the many color varieties and patterns that cats wear, and their dominant and recessive effects, follows:

White is dominant over all other colors. We refer here to normal white, not albino white, which is a recessive. Being dominant, white can mask other colors that are carried as a recessive.

The *tabby* and *black* are a genetic series. Tabby is dominant over black, and it is the basic wild color. Geneticists tag the pure tabby color design with the designation AA, perhaps because the tabby hair is banded or "agouti" hair. When a pair of genes is present for the loss of tabby banding (aa), the cat will be black. Tabby itself exhibits dominance as a pattern, in the following order: Abyssinian, wide-striped, narrow-striped (or mackerel), and blotched.

Black is dominant over all other colors but tabby, yellow (or red), and the dominant white with colored eyes.

Normal color intensity is dominant over all dilutes, and *silver* shows dominance over Burmese and Siamese, while Siamese is recessive to Burmese.

Self-color is dominant to the Siamese pattern.

Red cats (designated as yellow and with the symbol O for orange) are color–sex-linked. The red cat is actually a black cat with the black color suppressed by genes producing the red (yellow-orange) hue.

When a tabby or black kitten inherits a pair of genes for the dilution factor from its parents, it and its litter mates will be *dilutes*. The *self-blue* (Maltese) is a dilute black, and so is recessive to black. Self-blue × black is generally considered a good breeding to establish type because there seems to be correlation between these colors and good conformation.

In *Siamese-patterned cats,* there is a factor for color restriction with full color confined to "points." Genetically, Siamese are imperfect albinos, exhibiting the effect of weakened color-producing genes rather than a full absence of color. In breeding Siamese, it must be remembered that the color pattern is recessive to all other feline hues.

Seal-point is actually black (in the point pattern), and *chocolate-point* is modified seal-point. *Blue-point* is dilute black (seal), and *lilac-point* is chocolate modified by a doubling of the dilute blue-point factor. *Frost-point* is a double-dilute blue-point. When a Siamese is bred to a black cat, the progeny will be black with a gray undercoat. The Burmese is genetically allied to the Siamese but exhibits a greater penetration of color.

The *smoke* is a silver that lacks the gene for tabby markings. *Shaded silver* can be detected in the nest for, at that early age, the kittens display evidence of the dark, classic tabby pattern. *Chinchilla* kittens will show lighter, mackerel tabby markings. *Blue smokes* are a dilute phase of normal or "black" smokes. Do not use a tabby-marked cat in the breeding of smokes. *Silver* indicates a reduction of yellow and black pigment; the silver effect varies due to the production of several varieties of hairs.

The genetic picture of the *tortoiseshell* is quite interesting because it is a sex-linked color variety. We mentioned that the yellow (red, orange) cat is also sex-linked: it is an incomplete dominant carried on the X chromosome. A male carrying a gene for yellow carries in a masked state the gene to produce black, and when a female has two genes for yellow the color black is again masked, and the female will be homozygous for yellow. But if the queen carries only one gene for yellow, the black is not completely masked and we have a tortoiseshell. Torties are called an all-female variety since practically all torties are of the female sex. Tortoiseshell males are occasionally reported, but they generally prove to be sterile. As there are exceptions to every rule, we hear of a tortie male now and then who is said to be fertile. A favored breeding for the production of tortoiseshells is a black male to a yellow queen. The result will be yellow males and tortie queens. A yellow male bred to a black female produces black males and tortie females.

The handsome *blue-creams* are dilute tortoiseshells. Since blue is dilute black, and cream is dilute yellow (red or orange), it follows that to produce blue-creams one must mate a blue to a cream. The same breeding procedure as delineated for the production of normal torties is followed, using the dilutes of black and yellow. The blue-cream possesses the same sex-linked genetic formula as the normal tortoiseshell, so blue-creams are generally females and the occasional male is usually sterile.

To produce the pretty *calicos* (tortoiseshell and white), it is best to use a black and white bicolor stud × a tortie queen. Again, one can produce a dilute calico or blue-cream calico by using the same formula that produces the blue-cream but with the addition of white markings in one or both of the mated pair. The male calico is genetically XXY, a form of sex linkage related to certain kinds of Mongolism in human children.

In the lovely *cameos* (reds with silver undercoats), a popular breeding is the mating of a cameo stud to a shaded blue-cream or tortoiseshell queen; recommended because these color-variety females carry genes for red and silver. Smokes are also recommended in cameo production. With smokes there is no eye color conflict.

If it is at all plausible, it is best, in most breedings for color, to breed like to like. This will keep both coat color and pedigree pure and eliminate surprises in litters. But if you feel that the introduction of a cat of another color is desirable to bring an advance in type, coat quality, or for any other plausible reason, then your thinking is valid. Incidentally, the introduction of whites into a line to reduce color is not logical. They will not reduce color hue, but can introduce recessive colors (which they can carry invisibly) that can wreck a color-breeding program.

CHARACTERISTICS BEYOND COAT COLOR

Other important dominant and recessive characteristics that are not allied to coat color inheritance but are necessary adjuncts to the complete picture of controlled breeding should also be mentioned here.

Coat Length

Short hair is always dominant over long hair. Short-haired cats can carry a recessive for long hair, and can produce some long-hairs in a litter if their mate also carries the long-hair recessive. But long-hairs (carrying this genetic inheritance as a double recessive consistently) cannot produce short-hair kittens when bred together. Normal coat (short-hair or long-hair) is dominant to the rex coat and the wire coat. The Devon rex is a rexoid mutation on a different gene locus than that which influences the German and Cornish rex coats. In all three the rexoid genic factors are, of course, recessive.

Hairlessness can be due to mutation, or the result of a hidden recessive carried in a normal-coated strain, frequently for many generations. The Balinese, which initially appeared in normal Siamese litters in the early 1950s, is a prime example of a masked recessive lying dormant in the germ plasm and then suddenly manifesting itself to fashion a new breed.

Tail Length

Short tails or complete taillessness are examples of imperfect dominance and display various degrees of penetration. The complete absence of a tail in the Manx breed is considered by some geneticists to be a deformity and a semilethal dominant, but in its breeding results follows the pattern of uneven penetration. The Manx can produce taillessness as well as appendages of assorted lengths, including normal tails, in the same litter. Cats of pure Manx breeding that flaunt fully normal tails can produce tailless young.

Polydactylism (extra digits)

This is a characteristic determined by a dominant gene. If a polydactyl cat possesses a pair of genes for the trait, all its progeny will exhibit extra digits. A pair of visual polydactyls, each carrying one gene for the trait instead of a pair, when bred together will, in the usual Mendelian ratio, produce approximately 25 percent progeny with the normal number of toes.

Orchidism

When one testicle in the tom is retained (unilateral chryptorchidism) in the body and does not descend, the cat is popularly labeled a monorchid. When both testicles fail to descend into the scrotum, he is a cryptorchid (bilateral) and will not prove fertile since the sperm does not remain viable in body heat. Since this trait is recessive it must be carried by both sire and dam, which means that females can carry the characteristic in a hidden form and it will become visible only in affected male cats. Breeders must shun any cat as a producer that carries the taint of orchidism, for it is an insidious fault that can bring ruin to an earnest breeding program, despite CFA ruling that a male must have at least one descended testicle. Testicles that are retained in the body can also become cancerous and result in hormonal disturbances, androgynous behavior, and unstable temperament.

EFFICACIOUS CROSSES, ETC.

To bring this chapter to a close, a few quick notes on some of the efficacious crosses that have been used in color breeding, and a few other matters that you might find useful in your endeavors, would seem to be in order.

Blue and brown tabby should be bred pure; blue tabby × blue tabby, and brown tabby × brown tabby, if the specimens you have are worthy of such breeding. Solid blues (selfs) are often used to improve type and bone in brown tabby breeding. Blue tabbies, when produced from this breeding, mated back to a brown tabby will generally produce better type and excellently patterned brown tabbies. Silver tabbies are black when born, but indicate on their feet and the sides of their bodies the color of maturity. The beautiful chinchilla or silver is, in the Persian variety, a lighter-boned and daintier cat than the standard calls for. The shaded silver is a darker-hued feline than the normal chinchilla or silver.

Experiments seem to indicate that the gene responsible for silver and smoke is an allele of the identical gene that causes the Siamese coat pattern, and it is suspected that the Burmese coat color may be an intermediate between Siamese and silver. The silver coloring reduces the yellow drastically, turning it practically white. The red tabby represents an opposite variation extreme from that produced by the silver effect. When breeding smokes we must realize that, despite variation of color intensity, the smoke is actually a self-colored cat and crosses to other colors must be indulged in with caution. Silver × tabby crosses bring with them the unwanted tabby pattern.

Many Abyssinians bear a dominant white-spotting factor, manifested on the chest and chin. Selection for decreasing the size of the white areas is just about the only avenue of control. Incidentally, in pure white cats that are odd-eyed, faulty hearing is frequently found, confined to the side of the head that exhibits the blue eye.

The peke-faced Persian is best bred from an excellent red tabby × a fine peke-face. In all peke-faced Persians check for a bad bite (malocclusion), a fault in which the teeth in the upper and lower jaws fail to meet properly. This again is a persistent genetic fault that cannot be easily controlled and can wreak havoc with a breeding program.

The red-point Siamese was originally developed from a cross between a self-red and a seal-point Siamese. This breeding produced tortie females and black males. A tortie queen from this mating bred to a seal-point Siamese tom can result in seal-points, reds, blacks, tortie-point, and red-point kittens. Of course, the easiest way to get a full yield of all red-point young is by breeding red-point to red-point, because the red-point is homozygous. Red-self queens are rather scarce due to the genetic basis of the red self, but good females can be bred by putting a quality red male to a "typey" (excellent show type) black female.

A word of caution in breeding for type and conformation: one must not breed to extremes to reach a happy medium. Such practice generally results in catlings that exhibit both the extremes rather than the intermediate effect you hope to achieve. In all your breeding efforts plan each mating well, comparing the pedigree with the vital, animated characteristics of the living feline clay you wish to mold to a specific pattern. Tally your lists of dominants and recessives against the absolutes of the Mendelian chart to arrive at a fairly accurate prediction of what you can expect in the coming litter.

We wish you luck, for regardless of how much we may learn of genetics and allied sciences, the production of fine, show-worthy felines will remain a mixture of science and art, with a bit of creative innovation and luck to keep our interest and expectations high.

At the time of writing, geneticists have found the secrets of the prodigous DNA (the essence of life) and how to create new combinations of the master molecule in the bacterium *E. coli (Escherichia coli K-12)*. Biologists can now manipulate the sticky loops of DNA to accept splicing and combine animal genes with bacterial genes. The resultant recombinant DNA will revolutionize genetics and allied sciences. Genes that produce certain body regulators (such as insulin) will, in the future, be isolated and cloned. Injured or sick cells can be rejuvenated, and once techniques are developed for this new molecular biology, vast and wondrous advances in this area of research will occur, to progress so far beyond our most extravagant flights of intellectual fancy that the predictions of science fiction will no longer be fiction but fact. There is no doubt that science is on the verge of a dramatic breakthrough that will eventually result in the ability, through DNA control, to create new life forms in the laboratory.

Meanwhile, on a less lofty scale of achievement, cat fanciers have in their hands the power to fashion heredity and, in so doing, to mold life in a more limited field—that of feline breeding. Five million years or so in the past, when *Homo habilis*, man's earliest known ancestor, strode the still forming surface of an early earth toward his destiny of dominance over all creatures, unexcelled world·predator and unchallenged ruler of the planet, it was written in the galaxy stars that man would wield the wand of evolution and control its destiny.

Now it has happened!

You, the breeder, control and weave the intricate evolutionary pattern of the domestic feline species through the manipulation of its genetic characteristics; your tools are the units of inheritance, and your art, their infinite combinations.

Handle the assignment well and with dignity, for you are the most blessed of all people: in an era of machines and computers, you are a creator, an innovator, sculpting the cells and chromosomes of the flesh and form of the feline species into patterns of your own desire. You have the opportunity to play God. We hope that you will perform your role well.

CHAPTER II

The Queen and the Stud Cat

All living creatures on this planet are born with an ageless and necessary involvement with sex. The need to reproduce is a natural, inborn instinct, as strong as the defense of territory and the need to survive. Actually, it is even more powerful than the latter two inherited impulses, for without this compelling urge a species dies and journeys into oblivion. The process of replication for the feline is based upon an elementary urge to sow its genetic seed in a fertile field and create more of its genus to protect and project the species. You, the cat breeder, direct this fundamental impulse into a given channel, to create new life in an envisioned form and produce, as an end result, new and individually unique living creatures.

THE QUEEN

The queen is necessarily the hub of the breeder's endeavor. She represents the mother creature within whose womb the seed will be sown and nourished. She is the hope for the future and the fecund, phyletic symbol of a bountiful mother nature. Through the queen you can bring needed improvement to your feline stock, for she is the foundation upon which you will build your future generations. If the foundation is weak the structure will fall, so the queen must be a strong, healthy, and vital cat, and as near to breed perfection as possible, for she will bequeath 50 percent of her own genetic worth to her progeny.

If you do not possess a queen of such sterling worth, you must purchase a female of the very best quality you can afford. She should be young, six to ten months of age, and should indicate the virtues you want in a queen by this age. If you have been a breeder for an appreciable length of time, you will probably have a selection of queens from your own stock to choose from. Whether you buy one or have one, be certain she is a healthy and sturdy girl, and a "good keeper," meaning a female of good appetite who has grown well, without illness, and who always seems to stay in fine condition.

Temperament and character are also important. The ideal queen should have a sweet disposition and be easy to handle. Before she begins to "call," take her to your veterinarian for a general checkup, and bring with you a sample of her stool (about the size of a cherry pit). From the stool sample your veterinarian will be able to ascertain whether or not she has worms and, if she has, what kind. Proper medication will rid her of these toxic and debilitating internal vampires, a necessary precaution before she is bred because she can pass worms and their eggs to her young both before and after they are born. She should be clean of parasites and in top condition before breeding.

Queens will begin calling as early as six months of age, and some Siamese will call at the premature age of four months, but they should not be mated until about a year of age, when they are mature, fully developed, and ready for parenthood. It is not advisable to allow the queen to become much older than a year before she is mated for the first time, for some females, if allowed to go too long, become poor and unreliable breeders. Many queens are temperamental and when brought to the stud tom go out of season immediately, before a breeding can be consummated. One can imagine what this does to the stud cat's ego.

To achieve the correct genetic breeding often is not easy because sometimes it is difficult to get your temperamental female bred. Some queens come into heat only a few times a year, while others are only out of heat a few days when they begin calling again. Often queens nursing a litter of kittens come in season but must not, of course, be bred at this time. One or, at most, two litters a year are enough for the queen to care for; more and she will become debilitated from her matronly duties.

The onslaught of the heat period brings with it very definite physical signs, indicating that the magic of nature has begun. Puss is transformed from an individual to an important vessel of racial extension and a symbol of fecundity. She begins her vocal calling, rolls on the floor with ecstatic abandon, becomes restless, constantly cleans herself, and crawls with her front feet low and her hindquarters as high as they can be arched. She will crouch and "pad" with her front paws, her tail held to the side and, in general, indulge in highly amorous behavior. This period of heat will average from five to seven days in length. Her appetite will increase, she will show greater affection toward you, and there will be a slight swelling of the vulva.

Changes are also taking place inside the queen. Her ovaries display enlarging follicles, and the uterus is becoming larger in both length and diameter. The acceptance period follows as the follicles and the uterus become even larger, blood vessels and uterus swelling greatly. Theoretically the queen, at this point, is ready to be bred; nature's legerdemain has brought her to the peak of the mating cycle. It should be remembered that in the female cat the follicles, with their attendant eggs, do not spontaneously rupture as in most other mammals. Only the act of copulation causes ovulation. Because of this peculiarity, any small rodlike instrument (a cocktail mixer, for example) inserted into the queen's vagina will cause the heat period to come to a quick halt.

If you are not the fortunate owner of a top stud tom, about thirty days before your queen is due to begin her heat cycle, contact the owner of the stud you have decided to use and advise him or her of your choice. Discuss the stud fee, ask if you are entitled to a return service should the first breeding fail to take, and make all arrangements for the coming nuptials. Clip your queen's nails before bringing or sending her to the stud, which should be when she flags the signs indicating that she is approaching full heat. Generally, you will leave her at the cattery where the stud stands, and make arrangements for her to be kept until the stud owner is certain that a true breeding has taken place, when a telephone call will bring you back to pick her up. Pay the stud fee after the tom has serviced your queen. If she is to be shipped to the stud, be certain of your timing, and supply her with a strong, safe, warm carrier for the trip.

If she is a young queen, it is best that she be mated to an older tom experienced in the ways of love. But if she is a matron who has been bred before and has had several litters, she can be bred to a less experienced male; her own expertise in the art of amour will compensate for her mate's lesser knowledge. Once she has been bred to the stud, make very certain that she does not escape from you and breed to another cat (or possibly cats) of unknown ancestry and low social standing. The queen in heat is completely amoral, and the prowling tom instinctively a *macho* rakehell, willing and able at any time to seduce any female who crosses his path. (Although domestic cats are completely polygamous, some wild felines seem to be monogamous.) During the breeding process, as soon as the mating has been completed, the queen should be returned to the quarters assigned to her. These should be within sight and sound of the stud cat so that he can court her during the periods when physical contact is not taking place.

The producing queen must be fed a well-balanced diet containing all the necessary food essentials (see Chapter 8). But do not overfeed her. If she does become obese, put her on a lower-intake diet and turn a deaf ear to her plaintive protests, for obesity in the pregnant queen can result in problems in delivery, even though cats generally find littering an easy chore.

Sometimes the bred queen fails to conceive but goes through a pseudopregnancy, mimicking all the outward signs of impregnation but in the end producing nothing but exasperation for the breeder.

THE STUD CAT

The male feline, as in almost all species, is the swaggerer, the boaster of sexual prowess, of countless conquests in the field of fecundity. Ah, but in the case of the tom cat such braggadocio is not just idle bombast. The male cat is an amazing sexual machine. He is capable of copulating seven to eight times within a thirty-minute period, and at each breeding discharges millions of spermatozoa. Of course, the owner of a valuable, pure-bred tom would never allow such profligacy.

The sperm itself is an uncomplicated cell, fashioned to serve as an efficient transport system, and possessing a small head and a long tail. In the head is packed a nucleus of genetic material and a small amount of cytoplasm. The tail (flagellum) directs the movement of the head, which is capped by the acrosome containing enzymes capable of dissolving the cell and mucous layers surrounding the egg so the sperm can pierce it and deliver its payload of genes. Capacitation occurs and the egg is fertilized.

If there is more than one stud cat in a cattery they must be kept as far apart as possible, for they will engage in battle with all the feral ferocity of tigers should they make contact. Of course, the stud cat cannot share the home with his owners because he will "spray" and permeate the house, furniture, and drapes with a strong, disagreeable, and pungent odor that bears no relationship to Chanel #5. The spray is an atavistic attempt by the tom to define territory and to attract the female of the species. To humans the odor is a sickening stench that even the most ardent ailurophile must abhor. Tom will, of course, spray his own quarters, so everything in this area must be built of easily washed and de-scented materials. The stud's quarters will need frequent sterilization, particularly during and after the visitation of a queen.

Accommodations for visiting queens should be provided in the stud cat's area. Tom's quarters should be spacious and comfortable, with a large, enclosed outside run, complete with posts to climb and scratch, and hanging articles for him to paw. Exercise is essential to keep him fit and to alleviate the boredom of his necessary isolation. He must be supplied with a nutritious breakfast and a high-protein dinner, and his feeding 'and watering utensils and surroundings kept scrupulously clean. He must be considered an athlete, though his game is love, the lucky fellow.

A young male should not be used for breeding until he has reached early maturity—approximately a year of age (this can vary with the breed)—and should be used sparingly for the first four or five months after reaching breeding age. His first few breedings should be to experienced queens who will give him no trouble. If you intend to advertise his services and commercialize his breeding potential, it would be wise to exhibit him at shows and, if possible, make him a champion. The title does much to make him desirable as a stud in the eyes of the owners of queens.

To be successful commercially, the stud cat must be healthy and vigorous, a good breeder, from excellent stock, and closely mirroring the breed's standard of perfection. He should also be good-natured and gentle with the queens sent to visit him. Do not use him too frequently or he may become sterile for short intervals. Generally, breeders will allow their stud to copulate three or possibly four times within a period of two days. The stud's owner should not leave the tom and queen alone together until he has witnessed the initial mating. The visiting female should be kept two or three days and serviced by the stud on two successive days to be certain the breeding has been successful. A shelf should be built in the breeding pen to which the tom can leap to avoid the queen. After the mating she is likely to attack him, and if the stud is scarred it is at the risk of his owner.

Spend some time each day with your stud cat so that he will not be difficult to handle. In some countries, owners of studs allow them the constant companionship of an old queen who has been spayed after leaving her productive years behind her. This arrangement helps to alleviate the loneliness of the stud's imposed lifestyle.

The stud cat must enjoy excellent health, and a periodic checkup by your veterinarian can ensure this condition. A poor diet, worm infestation, and illness of any kind can affect his fertility and make him less able to meet the demands of his role. You will generally find that your stud's breeding commitments will be heaviest during the months of February and September.

As we have said, if you own a fine queen you bring or send her to a stud of your choice. Because of this latitude in stud selection, some breeders consider it unnecessary to keep a stud cat of their own with the attendant extra care it entails. But a quality stud tom, bred correctly, can be an asset to any cattery, particularly if you intend judiciously to line- or inbreed your stock in order to attain specific results.

The importance and precise definition of the male and female cat has, we hope, emerged here clearly. They are the containers of a precious heritage that will fashion the feline family of the future. If they are endowed with the many virtues of their variety, their genetic worth can mold excellence for generations to come.

CHAPTER 12

The Breeding of Cats

How far from the simple and basic reasons for our sexual heritage we have wandered since the first creatures breathed the warm air of a virgin earth. Sexual pairing is necessary to create life and to ensure the continuance of the species. It is as simple as that. But in the three thousand years since human civilization began, man has added an intricate design of social conduct to an artless act that is as elementary as eating, and more important than individual survival. Though it may not be recognized as such, we share with all animals, including our cats, an unnamed, all-powerful need to project our genetic heritage into the generations of the future, to make certain that the race continues through the ancient, compulsive sex act, the one and only means by which we can perpetuate ourselves.

Cat breeders have very few references available that offer them physiological and practical knowledge of the feline reproductive process. It is without doubt true that while pregnancy is the goal of this knowledge, it is also the greatest disease of the cat population. Due to unwanted pregnancies, overpopulation is a bigger problem in the cat than in other pet animal species. More suffering of both the pregnant queen and the unwanted kittens occurs in our domestic felines than is tolerable. Any person who accepts a cat into the household accepts the responsibility for the health and well-being of that cat. Among these responsibilities is keeping the female pet cat from becoming pregnant and so presenting the owner with unwanted offspring that may have to be destroyed or, even worse, eventually abandoned. Ovariohysterectomy (spaying) is the only practical solution to the problem. Spaying not only prevents pregnancy but totally prevents heat cycles during which the queen becomes quite noisy and demonstrative. It also has the advantage of keeping your cat at home, for spayed cats tend not to roam.

Since it takes two to tango, we must not forget the very *macho* male cat who roves the streets and alleys, seeking and finding young female felines to assuage his beastly appetites. Castration is simple and inexpensive, and the neutered male is a far superior household pet to the intact male. He will not roam, he seldom fights, and he is more loving and amenable. The pungent odor of the whole male cat's urine is greatly diminished, and if castrated he will not spray upward onto objects both inside and outside the house in an effort to mark his territory.

Both spaying and castrating can be performed after puberty, or better yet, shortly before puberty occurs—just so the cat is fully developed. This is at about six to seven months in the female; therefore, most veterinarians recommend spaying at five and a half to six months of age. Actually, spaying can be done at any age and after any number of litters, but both price and surgical difficulty increase with age.

In the male, puberty is usually reached at about six months of age, but depending upon physiological and mental development may range from four to eight months. Usually six months is an excellent age for spaying or castrating surgery, which is best accomplished before male habits are set but after the urinary tract is fully developed. Once roaming and fighting begin, and the longer they continue, the less likely surgery will be to reverse these instincts.

With the foregoing in mind, this section is therefore written for the fancier who is producing kittens that are anxiously awaited and who is attempting to improve type in the variety she or he is breeding. A proper understanding of reproduction in the cat may help breeders to avoid mistakes and give them information that will help them to appreciate more fully their own endeavors.

THE BREEDING CYCLE

To reiterate, puberty in the female usually occurs at six or seven months. Although the queen can conceive at this time, she is not yet physically mature and is comparable to a human female of about sixteen years of age. It is best to wait until the queen is at least one year old before she is bred. The time of puberty may vary with individuals and breeds. Siamese have a tendency to reach puberty at as early as four to five months of age and, if bred, can conceive at this time. But Persians may not begin estrus cycles until they are over a year old. The beginning of the estrus cycle is also seasonal, so that a queen reaching maturity in the fall may not begin to have estrus cycles until early spring. Most cats cycle from midwinter until fall. Anestrus, the true quiescent period, usually occurs from the autumn months through early winter. There are, of course, always exceptions.

The queen has two or three breeding seasons per year, during which she will have several estrus cycles, the most active cycles occurring during the spring season. Physiologically, the cycle is divided into proestrus, estrus, and metestrus. Proestrus is the beginning of the period of heat. The queen's habits and activities begin to alter. She may become more affectionate and exhibit increased urination. As estrus approaches, the intensity of these characteristics increases. Proestrus lasts about three days.

As estrus begins, the queen becomes very vocal. This is especially noticeable in the Siamese cat. Many owners, viewing the strange activity in which the queen indulges (see Chapter 11), will consult a veterinarian, believing their cat is ill or in pain. Vaginal swelling and discharge occur but are so minimal that they may not be noticeable. The estrus period lasts about three days, though it may occasionally continue for seven to fourteen days if no breeding occurs. The queen ovulates only from the physical act of coitus. After being bred, she will generally then go out of heat within twenty-four hours. If no breeding occurs, metestrus follows, during which time the female acts with complete normality. She will begin another proestrus period in about fourteen to twenty-one days. Some cats (again especially Siamese) may come back into proestrus even earlier. After several cycles, anestrus will follow metestrus, thus ending the season.

Natural breeding is the usual method of impregnating the queen. Artificial insemination has been accomplished with both fresh and frozen sperm, but it is not as yet really a practical method of impregnation in the cat. To effect a breeding, during the queen's estrus period the male and female are best placed in a large breeding cage or pen. If both queen and tom are experienced, you may have a cup of coffee, a spot of tea, or perhaps something a wee bit stronger, while nature takes its course. If one or both partners are inexperienced, adjustment time may be necessary.

The queen will usually first rub against the cage and then against the male. She will roll and present her genital area to him, signaling her acceptance of the mating rite. The tom will then approach the queen, sniff, and usually indulge in a mating call asserting his maleness. The foreplay is short: the male quickly mounts the queen, and grasping her by the skin of her neck, he will begin a series of thrusts. After a few thrusts, erection and, very quickly, ejaculation occur. The total time for the mating is often only ten seconds. After an intermission of about ten minutes, the mating may be repeated. The tom cat's ejaculation is quite limited, less than 0.2 milliliters, but can contain 100 million sperm or more. After mating, the female will emit a loud cry as the male withdraws, then roll and begin to lick the area surrounding her vulva. The male stalks away a short distance to contemplate this procedure superciliously.

Mating problems that prevent coitus are not numerous and several can be corrected. Some females exhibit so few signs of estrus that the important period is not identified by the breeder in time to effect a breeding. It may be necessary to keep such females near other queens

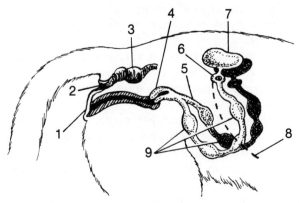

Female cat's reproductive system: (1) vulva, (2) anus, (3) rectum, (4) cervix, (5) uterine horns (uterus), (6) ovary, (7) kidney, (8) rib line, (9) embryos developing in uterus.

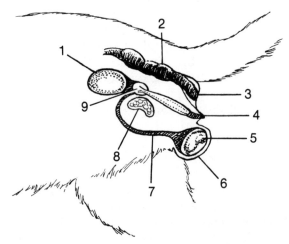

Male cat's reproductive system: (1) bladder, (2) rectum, (3) anus, (4) penis, (5) testicle, (6) scrotum, (7) vas deferens, (8) cross section of part of pelvic bone, (9) prostate.

in order to stimulate more expressive estrus. Occasionally a teaser male is used, and the queen left with him until estrus occurs. But this could prove to be impractical should the tom be in demand as a stud. Vaginal smears can be examined by your veterinarian to identify the time of estrus, and the female put with the tom at the proper time.

Some females will fight all toms, not desiring coitus, and must be manually held by the breeder. Holding may also be necessary if there is a size difference between queen and tom great enough to prevent proper mounting by the stud cat. Some females indulge in no vocalization during the foreplay, leaving the stud male uninterested. Other queens exhibit a very poor after-reaction, with a complete lack of rolling and licking. These deficiencies of physical reaction apparently cause reduced conception.

Male cats have their problems also. Some are overly aggressive, causing the queen to become defensive. Others are underactive and need tutoring, a chore that experienced queens delight in accomplishing. The presence of penile hairs can turn the queen off and cause her to refuse the tom. Of course, overuse of the stud cat can cause a decrease in viable sperm.

OVULATION

The female genital tract consists of a vulva, the entrance; a vagina, into which the tom deposits the sperm; a two-horned uterus, in which implantation of the fertilized egg occurs and fetal development progresses; an oviduct at the end of each horn of the uterus, in which the sperm fertilizes the egg; and an ovary at the termination of each oviduct, in which egg development takes place.

Ovulation occurs eighteen to forty-eight hours after coitus. The egg moves to the oviduct, where it meets the sperm and fertilization is realized. The fertilized egg then travels to the uterus and, after about fourteen days, a firm implantation is completed. The queen possesses an endothelial chorial placenta (zonary), and with this type of placentation a wide band of fetal tissue surrounds the fetus. The attachment is very strong, with close opposition of the blood vessels, allowing nutrients to move freely from mother to fetus.

GESTATION

Gestation averages about sixty-three days, and by the twenty-fifth day the fetus is fully formed and recognizable as a kitten. There are several periods during which the fetus undergoes accelerated growth and development. These periods occur on the twenty-eighth to the thirty-second day, the fortieth to the forty-fifth day, and the fifty-second to the fifty-sixth day. Queens should not be shipped or overly disturbed during these times, for stress may cause underdevelopment of the fetuses or even abortion. Hair develops on the unborn kitten on the fifty-eighth day.

Pregnancy diagnosis is accomplished through palpation and is not a difficult procedure except with the most resistant, or obese, queens. By the fourth week of pregnancy, the fetus is usually ¾ to 1 inch in diameter. The secondary signs of pregnancy are typical of all mammals: mammary development and an enlarged abdomen.

Abortion can be a problem. Early before implantation, stress may cause the reabsorption or expulsion of the fetus. Lack of the hormone progesterone, produced by a small body in the ovary called the corpus luteum, will cause the queen to abort at about thirty days. The corpus luteum develops in the area that contained the egg. Weekly injections of a reposital progesterone, starting at the fourth week and ending with the eighth week, can prevent abortion from this cause. Some viral infections such as distemper, upper respiratory disease, and leukemia cause abortion, fetal deformity, or early death of the kittens after birth.

Queens sometimes come into heat during pregnancy and will mate again at this time. This will not end the first pregnancy but can result in a second pregnancy, thus causing the queen to carry fetuses of different ages. Usually a combination of live and disintegrated fetuses is delivered, but rarely are there reports of two births several weeks apart. There can also be several sires for one litter of kits. If several different toms breed to a female within a single estrus cycle, they form a pool of sperm, any one of which can fertilize any egg. One sperm fertilizes one egg regardless of which tom cat it comes from.

Pseudopregnancy (false pregnancy) is rare in cats but does occasionally occur. No kittens develop, but the queen does not come back into heat; mammary swelling takes place and the abdomen may indicate some enlargement. Pseudopregnancy usually lasts thirty-eight to forty-five days. There is a pattern of hormones that follow estrus and pregnancy. Estrogen comes from the ovary and causes the physical appearance and expression of estrus. During this time a follicle stimulating hormone (FSH) is released from the brain and causes the development of eggs in the ovary. When bred, a luteinizing hormone (LH) from the brain causes the release of the eggs, and where the egg is released from the ovary, the corpus luteum develops and produces progesterone, a hormone necessary to maintain pregnancy.

When a queen exhibits no heats, or erratic heats, patterns of these hormones can be injected in order to start the cycling. FSH is often given to queens producing small litters to increase their egg production. These procedures should be accomplished only under veterinary supervision or more harm than good can result. If mismating occurs, the use of estrogens may prevent pregnancy, but the queen will remain in estrus for a prolonged period. Overuse of this hormone (estrogen) may injure the bone marrow and cause blood-cell deficiencies.

PARTURITION (BIRTH)

The cat's gestation period can vary normally from fifty-eight to seventy days. Abyssinians and Siamese cats often have prolonged normal gestations, and certain family lines in any breed may constantly exhibit long gestations. Stress may shorten gestation; poor health, overbreeding, excessive activity, and fright can all result in a shortened gestation. Litter size is also a factor, large litters resulting in a shortened period of gestation.

During the last week of pregnancy the queen may become less active and begin to seek a quiet, dark area in which to give birth. Her breasts will swell and the nipples become prominent; she will be listless but restless. She should, at this time, be introduced to her queening box and area, though many cats (particularly pet cats) will birth where they choose and not allow the owner to select the area for them. In the closet and under the bed are favorite areas for the pet cat to have her kittens.

The onset of labor is the first stage of the birthing. Queens are very restless, often going to and from a litter pan but producing little or no urine. This procedure is in response to early contractions. Many queens show a temperature drop to between 99 and 100 degrees Fahrenheit from twenty-four to a few hours before queening (birthing) begins.

Stage two is the delivery of the kittens. The queen usually lies on her sternum with her legs to one side during labor. She may vocalize periodically until the first kitten is born, then usually quits. As labor becomes stronger she may assume a squatting position to force the kitten out. As a kitten is presented (born), the outer sac (amniotic sac) ruptures, lubricating the canal and making passage easier. A kitten may be born with head or tail first; both positions are normal. If the amniotic sac is still intact, it will look like a darkish bubble protruding from the vulva. As the contractions become more vigorous, the kitten is forced out (delivered). The queen will now either clean the kitten after freeing it from the sac, and chew off the umbilical cord (often still trailing from inside the female's vulva, the rest of the afterbirth to follow), or she may begin to clean herself. Since licking the fetus helps to stimulate breathing, should the queen pay more attention to her own toilet than to the newborn kitten, the breeder must intervene and vigorously rub the kitten with a towel until it is breathing strongly and emitting some resisting cries. This action is similar to "spanking the baby's bottom" in human birth.

The final stage is the delivery of the rest of the afterbirth (placental membrane). Each kitten has its own placenta. The queen may attempt to eat the afterbirths. It is not at all necessary for her to consume them as many old wives' tales demand. The afterbirth, if ingested, is laxative and will usually cause unwanted diarrhea for several days after parturition, so it should be removed each time by the breeder and disposed of.

Once stage two begins, the first kitten may be born in a few minutes to an hour later. Kittens arrive with irregular timing, from ten minutes to one and a half hours apart. Most parturitions are completed in four to six hours. Occasionally, after the birth of the first kitten the queen will go into a rest period that can last from twelve to thirty-six hours. Afterward she will return to labor and deliver healthy, normal kittens.

Problems result from oversize kits and lack of labor. You will have to seek veterinary help if these conditions exist. Sometimes, during the process of giving birth, a queen will present a head, or two hind legs, and then stop laboring. It may then be necessary for the breeder to intervene to save the life of the kitten. If the head is through the canal, the rest of the kitten should fit. Having scrubbed your hands thoroughly, gently insert your little finger and attempt to hook the forelegs with it and extend them out of the vulva. Grasp the kitten's head, or the head and forelegs, and wriggle it from side to side with gentle traction as you would pull a cork from a bottle of fine old wine. The kitten will pop out and you will hold a vintage kitten in your hands. It is best to have someone to help control the queen while all this is going on, so she will not inadvertently bite you. If lubrication is necessary, dip your little finger in mineral oil, insert it into the vagina, and circle it around as far as possible. With a breech birth (hind leg presentation), seek the tail with your little finger to be sure it is not bent backward, then grasp the hind legs and proceed as above.

Your veterinarian should be called if strong contractions do not produce a kitten in three to four hours, or if contractions that were strong begin to weaken before a youngster is birthed. The queen's inability to remove a partially delivered kitten signals that professional assistance is needed. Finally, if no labor occurs but a bloody or reddish-green discharge becomes visible, your veterinarian should be consulted at once. This latter occurrence usually means that there is an inability of the uterus to contract (known as primary uterine inertia) and there may be a need for hormonal injections or Caesarian section to save the queen and kittens, as the placentas through which the unborn kittens are fed are breaking down and the babies will soon die.

Uterine contractions are initiated by a hormone known as oxytocin, which is produced by the posterior pituitary gland. Oxytocin can be injected to stimulate birth, but must be handled by an expert. If the kittens are too large for the cervix, or if the cervix is closed, an injection of oxytocin may rupture the uterus and result in the death of both queen and kittens.

If a delivery has been difficult, if human interference was necessary, or if the number of afterbirths is less than the number of kittens, a postpartum examination by your veterinarian is necessary. The veterinarian will provide drugs against infection and give injections to cause expulsion of retained afterbirths. Estrus may resume as early as a week after the birth of a litter, although the normal time is three to four weeks after parturition, and if bred the queen can conceive again.

Cannibalism is not uncommon in female cats. It is generally triggered by something or someone in the cat's environment that causes her to think her kittens are in danger. In her frenzy to protect and defend her young, she kills and eats them as an ultimate protection.

LACTATION

Most kittens will begin to nurse one to two hours after birth. If the queen does not have enough milk to support the kittens, milk letdown and quantity can be increased by a nasal spray called Syntocinin. This is a product for humans that has been most successfully used by the junior author. The Syntocinin is sprayed (not tilted so that drops run out) into the queen's nose three times daily. There may be some mild objection by the queen, but her milk flow will definitely be increased.

During lactation the queen will consume two or three times as much food as normal, depending upon how many kittens she has to support. Small catlings in large litters should be especially watched. If the breeder sees that they are not getting enough to eat, he or she should give them separate and controlled nursing periods. The first milk, the colostrum, contains antibodies against various diseases. This protection may last up to three months. Queens usually nurse for six to eight weeks, gradually and naturally weaning the kittens during the last few weeks. Breeders must be aware of this weaning process and begin to provide food when the kittens are four to five weeks of age (see Chapter 16, "Kitten Care").

NURSING PROBLEMS

At times a breast will cake. This most commonly occurs in the thoracic breasts because the youngsters do not nurse at these breasts as often as they do at the others. Hot moist packs, using toweling applied for fifteen to twenty minutes several times a day, will return the breasts to normal function. If the problem becomes intense despite this nursing procedure, your veterinarian may have to administer diuretics.

Mastitis is an infection of the mammary glands and is most common as an acute disease in the nursing queen. The milk may become infected and transfer infection to the kittens. The breast becomes hot and sore and the character of the milk changes, often becoming odiferous, thick, or displaying a change in color. The gland may even rupture, opening at the side of the nipple. This is a case for veterinary care, for the queen will need antibiotic therapy to cure the infection. The breeder can supply hot compresses to help drainage. If kittens are nursing at the time, it is best to tape over the breast involved during the periods of nursing until the infection is cured.

Acute mastitis, if improperly attended to, can become chronic, especially in older queens. After lactation is over, the infection causes small, round nodules of inspissated (thickened) milk and infection in the breast. Though antibiotic therapy and hot packs are the major treatment, sometimes it is necessary to drain a particularly resistant area surgically.

Eclampsia (milk fever) is the result of a low blood calcium. The disease occurs in queens nursing large litters, or nursing several fairly large litters too close together. The clinical signs begin two to four weeks after parturition when the demands on milk production are at their peak. Calcium is diverted to the milk and the blood level drops; the queen goes into a dramatic picture of muscle tremors and spasms, and soon is unable to stand. As the condition progresses, the muscle spasms are so intense that the respiratory muscles no longer function, and the animal dies. The clinical picture is similar to that of tetanus, the condition often being called calcium tetany because of the similarity. The whole course of the disease takes only a few hours, so it is a definite emergency for which treatment is necessary immediately. Calcium replacement is accomplished through intravenous injection, and the results are quite dramatic. The symptoms regress and the cat is returned to normal in approximately thirty minutes. After treatment, the breeder must control nursing and supplement it with bottle feeding.

Unrelated to pregnancy and lactation is breast cancer, which is the final problem concerned with the cat mammary gland. The most common tumor in cats is the adenocarcinoma, a highly malignant growth. Any nodule in a breast should be brought to the attention of your veterinarian. These tumors occur most frequently in unspayed and middle-aged queens. They will seed to the next breast or spread to the local lymph nodes, and thence to the lungs, liver, or other organs. Swift surgical intervention is the only solution. If the breast is removed before the growth spreads, the cat can be saved.

GENITAL TRACT DISEASES

We have comparatively few ovarian problems in cats, but almost any such problem will prevent conception. Follicular cysts, coming from the developing egg, can be quite large, sometimes three to four times the size of a normal ovary, and several cysts can be present on one ovary. The probable cause is an excessive amount of FSH (follicle stimulating hormone). Follicular cysts usually cause a prolonged and excessive heat and, because the cyst is persistent, no conception. Treatment can be attempted with LH (luteinizing hormone), by surgical rupture, or ovary removal. The queen can function fully with only one ovary. For the pet cat with follicular cysts, spaying is the proper choice.

Luteal cysts, occurring in the ruptured follicle, are the result of too much luteinizing hormone. When these are large and pathogenic, they cause the queen to stay out of heat. Treatment is by FSH, or surgical removal of the damaging cysts. Again, the pet cat with luteal cysts should be spayed because they are prime candidates for pyometra (see below).

Tumors are rare in felines, and usually involve hormone changes similar to cysts. Some females become masculinized by specific tumors. In such cases, ovary removal or spaying is the corrective procedure.

The uterus, the "house of life," is the organ that causes most of the medical problems. It is Y-shaped, displaying two horns and an elongated body. Congenital anomalies are rare, but occasionally there may be a horn that is different in size or not fully developed. Sometimes the horns do not develop at all and only a ligament-like structure is present that is a remnant of the embryonic mullerian duct.

Several diseases of the uterus are caused by an excessive amount of progesterone. These conditions may be simple and present not much of a clinical problem except infertility, or they may progress to a final and dangerous disease—pyometra. They are:

Cystic endometritis. The lining of the uterus proliferates and contains small to large multiple cysts, sometimes occupying only a local area.

Usually the cat is asymptomatic except for sterility. Cysts can rupture causing hemorrhage that, while slight, will continue for several days.

Mucometra. Here the uterus is slightly enlarged and contains small amounts of mucoid material. Cats so affected are sterile and often retain this problem all their lives. Some may become infected with bacteria.

Hydrometra. With hydrometra, the uterus is grossly enlarged similar to in late pregnancy, but with a watery solution. This fluid is not infectious, and again the cat may exhibit only infertility plus an enlarged abdomen.

Pyometra. In this case the uterus is very much enlarged and filled with pus. Numerous bacteria can infect the excellent culture media fashioned by endometritis, mucometritis, and hydrometritis, and the result is a highly virulent and deadly disease. The cervix may be closed, allowing no drainage of pus. When this happens, toxic products of the infection are retained, and the queen not only has a highly dangerous bacteremia but also a toxemia. Affected females can succumb very quickly. In other cases the cervix is open, allowing drainage of the infected material, which usually results in much quicker diagnosis. In either case you have an emergency on your hands that needs immediate attention or death will ensue. Pyometra and its lesser disorders can only be treated surgically. Total ovariohysterectomy is necessary, followed by antibiotics and fluid therapy.

Metritis. This is an infection of the uterus. Unlike pyometra, there is no great bag of pus. Bacteria are the commonest cause, but fungus, viruses, and possibly yeasts can cause metritis. Bacteria are the most common agents, causing over 99 percent of the infections. If we are to preserve the uterus, proper identification of the bacteria by laboratory analysis is the initial step, followed by specific drugs to kill the bacteria involved. Many cats stricken with metritis, if treated correctly, can be returned to full fertility.

UTERINE PROBLEMS IN PREGNANCY

Other than the problems already discussed, such as abortions and birthing complications, the queen can exhibit a few other rather rare conditions during pregnancy.

Torsion of the uterus can occur during fetal growth. The uterus will twist, and the cat will be unable to give birth. Caesarian section is the only reasonable solution.

Prolapse of the uterus can occur following the completion of parturition—generally within forty-eight hours. The uterus should be replaced and the cat treated with antibiotics. If the organ protrudes, place cold compresses on the uterus and, through gentle manipulation, attempt to mold it back into place. If you are unsuccessful, call your veterinarian at once. If by any chance you cannot reach your veterinarian, make a cold solution of water saturated with sugar and pack the uterus with it. This will help shrink the tissue and make replacement less difficult. Even if you succeed in replacing the uterus, bring the cat to your veterinarian as soon as possible to prevent recurrence and infection.

The uterus may rupture during parturition due to excessive straining. Should this occur, the fetuses can migrate into the abdominal cavity. Surgery is indicated if a rupture is suspected.

Hemorrhage after parturition is not particularly common. There is a normal bloody discharge for three to five days following parturition. The presentation of large amounts of bright red blood and blood clots indicate hemorrhage in which there may be tears in the uterus or general uterine hemorrhage where the placentas were attached. Treatment involves the use of ergotine or oxytocin. Intravenous liquids or whole blood may be needed. Obviously, professional help is necessary.

The vagina may become infected from discharges issuing from the uterus, or from the surrounding external environment. Infections of this type are generally treated with local flushes and antibiotics. The area will also become irritated during cystitis. The signs of vaginitis are a discharge, clear to thick and white in color. The odor may attract male cats, but the queen will not permit copulation.

THE MALE CAT

Tom cats are relatively free of genital problems. Perhaps the fact that most males are castrated lowers the incidence of such problems. The penis can develop a hematoma (blood-filled swelling) at the tip. This can be caused by small bladder stones attempting to pass from the bladder, or from external trauma. If crushing occurs with the trauma, the cat can lose the tip of the penis due to gangrene.

Cryptorchidism is the retention of one or both testicles in the abdomen or inguinal canal. It is the result of a recessive gene and therefore most common in purebreds where inbreeding in the face of the offending gene is practiced (see Chapter II, "The Queen and The Stud Cat").

Orchitis is an inflammation of the testicles. This affliction is commonly caused by bite wounds. Treatment is by antibiotics. Sometimes orchitis is caused by systemic disease (infectious feline peritonitis). In such cases the basic disease must be identified and treated.

Glandular disease is almost unreported because the prostate and the bulbourethral glands (secondary sex glands) atrophy with castration. Prostatic old age enlargement does occur and may cause urinary problems. Prostatic cancer is also rare, but when it occurs it is most often terminal.

Infertility may be physical or psychological. Novice stud cats, or cats that have undergone a change of environment, may display temporary infertility. Viral infection of the newborn, especially if due to distemper, may leave a male infertile. Malnutrition may cause a secondary infertility, as may also obesity. High liver diets often result in testicular degeneration. Finally, a poorly functioning thyroid gland can cause reversible infertility.

Despite the list of breeding problems that can affect the cat, if you contemplate increasing the feline population for a good and valid reason, such as the production of superior specimens of your breed, do not be unduly alarmed. A healthy, well-cared-for queen generally gives birth easily and raises her family with little or no trouble. Breeding and birthing are natural processes of species perpetuation, and if accompanied by constant difficulties the feline race would long ago have succumbed to the basic law of survival of the fittest.

CHAPTER 13

What Is a Cattery?

A cattery is a house or enclosure in which cats are kept. It can be very elaborate or quite simple in structure and appointments, and in either case serve its primary purpose quite well. It can be large, medium, or small, depending upon the number of cats in residence, and the ambitions and desires of the cattery proprietor.

The above description of a cattery is completely valid, but it is only the bare bones of what a cattery actually is. In reality, a cattery is not so much a material structure as an abstract concept, a dream that begins with the first planned litter of purebred kittens produced by the ardent ailurophile. Or the dream may begin during the first cat show the neophyte attends, when he or she is exposed to the insidious malady known as "show fever." It is while in the virulent throes of this chronic disease that the miasmic, fever-induced dream invades the consciousness and slyly subjugates the feline fancier's momentarily weakened mentality.

Flushed with great expectations, the embryonic fancier takes the first confused and catatonic steps toward a distant, chimerical goal, and enters the best kitten from the initial litter in the next cat show within driving distance. Poor puss, against highly professional competition, wins no ribbons and the dream becomes a wee bit tarnished. But eventually newly absorbed knowledge and revived determination help to restore the original fantasy to its former luster. A better queen is purchased and bred to a top stud, another cage is necessary—and another when the best of this important litter is kept for future shows and breeding.

A ribbon or two are won, vivifying the dream, embracing a vision of breeding a rosette winner, and then—who knows? In an illusion the sky is the limit, and the stars are reflected as a gleam in the ailurophile's eyes. Like Topsy, the feline population "just grows." You consider the cost of stud fees and shipping expenses, and conclude that to continue successfully in the hobby, you must have a fine stud cat to use on your own females and whose fees, bred to queens other than those on the premises, could help defray expenses; and another queen of specific bloodlines must be found. . . . The cat population has now expanded to a point where there is (you tell yourself) but one sane solution—a cattery must be built. And so, to

[141]

the mental hallelujah sound of a trumpet fanfare, the dream is realized and a cattery is born.

THE IDEAL CATTERY

In building a cattery certain basics must be understood and utilized —a necessity in the erection of any edifice designed for a specific purpose. One can convert a garage or some other available space into a cattery; but the ideal is a building set a short distance from your home or living quarters that is attached by an enclosed areaway for easy access during inclement weather. The building should be deeper than it is wide to allow for quarters for stud toms and their outdoor runs to the rear of the building. Use materials indigenous to your area to cut the building costs. The cattery should be well insulated against both heat and cold, and should have ample tightly screened window space for light and air.

Of vital importance are the surfaces of the walls, ceilings, and floors. Sanitation will be one of your biggest problems, so all surfaces must be covered with easily cleaned and disinfected materials. Walls, floor, and ceiling should be faced with smooth, hard-surfaced substances such as linoleum or vinyl (sheets or tiles). The floor can be tiled, covered with linoleum or, if of smooth cement, finished with a coat or two of a good grade deck paint. Drains should be situated judiciously toward the center of compartment floors to accelerate cleaning and drying.

If you are starting from scratch (an appropriate word when referring to a cattery), consider the use of cement or cinder blocks for the building's structural material. They are easy to use and go up quickly, and are usually less expensive than other materials. Be sure you have a well-realized and complete plan, clearly drawn and blueprinted, with separate plans to indicate electric wiring, plumbing and water pipes, air conditioning and heating elements. You may find that some of your friends or acquaintances will offer help in these areas of planning. Complete architectural drawings are necessary for the contractor who will build your cattery, or for you should you—with help, of course—assume the job yourself.

It is important to install a unit for both heating and cooling that can maintain a constant and comfortable temperature during any season of the year. It should be automatically controlled by an accurate thermostat.

CAGES

Cages can be bought or made. If purchased, they should be made of metal. If hand-built, all solid sides (floors, tops, and enclosed sides) should be covered in vinyl, plastic tiles, or any material that can be washed and disinfected quickly with minimal labor. Where two surfaces butt (sides and floor for example), it is advisable to use concave metal strips to cover the seam, for no matter how tightly joined the fit may be, the space will eventually harbor a buildup of unsanitary dirt and its accompanying odor.

All cages should be large enough for a cat to walk comfortably around within their confines, and they should be stack cages; that is, cages that can be stacked or fitted one atop the other from the floor to eye height. Tall enclosures can be built that can, through the use of sliding partitions, be converted into several enclosures similar to stack cages. All larger enclosures, suitable for accommodating several cats together, should be uniform in size and placed flush with the walls (as should the cages also) so that the free space is in the middle of the room. Open wall space in the pens and any part of the room not enclosed should be furnished with shelves at different levels for cats to jump up to and lie or sit upon.

One corner of the main room can be used for felines brought to the cattery for boarding. In the areaway leading from the house to the cattery an area can be sectioned off, fitted with a stack of cages, and utilized as an isolation area for sick cats needing special care. Visiting cats can be kept in this area while they are being examined for fleas, skin disease, or any other anomaly that could be transmitted to your own healthy felines. Once given a clean bill of health, they can be transferred to the boarding area of the cattery.

BOARDING CATS

In a cattery where boarders are accepted, cards should be printed that list all the particulars about the feline guest: name, breed, sex, age, description, vaccination data, name of owner, address, telephone. Each card should be numbered and a corresponding number appended to the cage allocated to the boarder. The comprehensive cards should be filed in numerical order in the office section of the cattery. An indemnity form should also be made available for the boarding cat's owner to sign, which simply states that, though everything possible will be done for the comfort and well-being of the guest feline during its stay, the cattery cannot be held lawfully responsible should an accident or act of God occur that results in injury or death to the boarder. Have your attorney draw up this little contract: it will not be as simple or as clear as we have put it but it will be legal, and it will, we hope, save you from liability and a lawsuit should anything happen to a visiting cat.

COMMUNITY CAGES AND RUNS

Within the cattery there should be one or more rather large and roomy walk-in areas that can be utilized by several females at the same time, or by litters of kittens that have been weaned and are on their own. These areas (or smaller caged areas not high enough to walk in) can also be used to accommodate cats or kittens whose cages you are cleaning during your daily chores. Another group of cages, larger than those used for individual cats and kept in a section of their own, can be used for the queens who are littering.

There should be at least one outdoor run connecting with the large indoor enclosed areas in which the groups of females or kittens are kept. This outdoor run should be high enough to afford easy entry for the cattery owner, and it should have shelves at various levels for cats to climb on for resting or catnapping. Such outside runs should be about 6 feet high (or 1 foot less), 4 feet wide, and about 6 feet long. These dimensions are adequate for a group of cats to share. Cement flooring for the outdoors run is easily cleaned and can be slightly sloped toward the far end for run-off drainage. When cleaning up stools from the run, shovel up each one separately into a container, dump the contents into a previously prepared pit, and cover with a layer of earth. Hose out the container and apply disinfectant, and the job is done with a minimum of bother.

You might consider a soil-cement run, a type of subsurface employed on small light-traffic airfields and some suburban roads. To use this method, remove the top sod, then with a spade loosen and pulverize the soil to a depth of about 4 inches. Scatter two-thirds of a sack of cement to a square yard of soil and mix thoroughly. Hose with a mist spray until the soil-cement mixture will mold in your hands, then rake to full depth and level the surface. Quickly tamp down the run to compact the surface, then roll with a garden roller until smooth. Mist-spray again and cover with damp sawdust for about a week. Sweep off the sawdust, and the run will be hard and ready for use.

Plain dirt or sand flooring for the run can also be used, but the run wire must then be sunk at least 1 foot below ground level to discourage the cats from attempting to dig out. Dirt runs must be raked, sweetened with applications of powdered lime, and the surface burned off two or three times a year, for the run will harbor worm eggs and unsanitary material that the most diligent raking and cleaning will not remove.

THE STUD SECTION

The rear section of the cattery should be partitioned off from the rest of the building. This is the realm of the swaggering toms and the visiting amorous queens. Inside, each stud should enjoy one large cage with another cage adjacent but divided with a partition between the two. The second cage is for the visiting queen, so the lovers can become acquainted before being put together to consummate their tryst. In the rear wall of the tom's pen there should be a guillotine-type door that opens to his outside run. If there is more than one run for the stud toms, and they are side by side, the walls between them must be solid to prevent fighting or biting. Plastic with wire mesh, fiberglass, or polyethylene sheets (heavy duty) are all excellent for this purpose. These materials are transparent and will allow light to enter the runs.

RUN MATERIALS

Welded mesh wire, not chicken wire, should be used for all outdoor runs, for a cat can chew through chicken wire. The corner posts can be made of metal or piping, or of wood (2" × 2"). Side framing can be of the same material. If wood is used for the framing it should be treated and water-proofed, and the bottoms of the corner uprights creosoted: all corner posts, timber or metal, should be set in cement. Inside the runs, set a log upright for a scratching post and build shelves along the sides for the cats to use. Doors should be hung at the far end for easy access, and a small safety entrance built out to trap any cat that manages to get through the door as the owner enters. Adequate locks or bolts should be used on all doors.

Each living box or cage should be furnished with a bed, nontippable bowls for food and water, and a toilet tray; all of this equipment should be made of easily washed and cleaned fiberglass, heavy plastic, or metal (stainless steel is recommended). Fresh water should be supplied every day, and all occupied cages should be cleaned and sterilized daily. A daily and weekly sanitation routine should be established and adhered to. Once the procedure becomes a fixed habit, it will cease to be a chore and be instead a segment of your feline-oriented lifestyle.

THE WORK AREA

Incorporated into the scheme of the ideal cattery should be a walled-off area or room with a sink, a tub for washing cats, a dryer or drying cage (with controlled heat), a medicine cabinet above the sink containing necessary feline medical supplies, as well as a thermometer, bandages, cotton, ointments, and the telephone number of your veterinarian. He will give you a list of necessary medications and medical supplies for your first aid box.

A closet can be built in this area for mops, pails, and other necessary cleaning paraphernalia. Built-in cabinets in this area are also useful for the storage of food, bedding material, extra feeding and watering pans, and many other items. In the work area a small table, upon which cats can be perched for examination or any other purpose, will be handy.

A small office, containing a desk and a sofa or a couple of chairs, is an ideal place to greet visitors and a haven to which the cattery owner can escape at intervals and relax. The walls can be nicely decorated with ribbons and rosettes, and possibly a few trophies won by cattery residents. Tastefully exhibited, they and the lovely framed photos of fine show cats that are progenitors of the cattery's stock cannot fail to impress visitors. Here all the paperwork can be done and the files kept, along with the pedigrees and registration certificates of the cattery's population. Litter registrations should be filed and kept with breeding records. A fire extinguisher should be readily accessible. Some catteries use extractor fans to keep the air inside the structure constantly flowing and changing.

NAME REGISTRATION AND TAXES

You can register your cattery with the Cat Fanciers' Association, Inc., and once it has cleared and accepted the name you have chosen, you will have no difficulty registering it with any of the other associations. Write to the organization secretary and request that all pertinent information on registering a cattery name including fees and forms be sent to you.

If your cattery is registered, you can set it up as a taxable property. You must keep records of all monetary transactions and, if you show a profit, must pay taxes on that profit. If you show a loss, it can be deducted from your taxes. You can take a depreciation on your cattery building, and the purchase price of any cat or kitten you may have bought. You will, we are certain, show a loss each year, and this could result in a very nice deduction from your tax total. Should you consider exploring this financial avenue, discuss it first with a qualified tax consultant. Tax laws seem to change every year.

Last, but by no means least, do introduce music to your cattery: a radio or, if you wish to be more sophisticated, a stereo set, to fill the cattery with music. It will make your cleaning chores more bearable, and a bit of tuneful humming, a few lilting bars of song, and perhaps a terpsichorean step or two can brighten up your whole day. Your feline friends will like it, too, for most all creatures love the sound of music. Remember, it has been said (ad nauseam), that "music hath charms to soothe the savage breast."

FERAL FELINE HOUSING

One does not generally keep more than a single (neutered) specimen of the larger feral cats, otherwise one is an immediate prospect for the psychiatrist's couch, unless the keeping of more than one large cat is a professional or commercial endeavor. The strongest wire to be found is usually not heavy enough for the cages and runs of the large predacious cats. We have seen jaguars in a South American military zoo that had chewed through the thickest chain-link fence available. It follows that the safest material for the caging of large feral cats is steel or iron bars.

Any housing enclosure must be stoutly built since the strength of the large *Panthera* is enormous. A house and a reasonable-sized run is necessary for the physical well-being of the feral feline. The animal will pace back and forth for needed exercise. A platform from 4 to 6 feet off the ground to which the big cat can jump to sun and snooze is practical and can, in fact, be the top of its house or cage. A cement-surfaced run is necessary for easy cleaning. Or one can furnish the run with actual trees, rocks, water, and vegetation similar to the environment of the animal's wild habitat.

The smaller feral cats, such as the ocelot and margay, can be kept in much the same fashion as the domestic cat but should definitely be given the opportunity to spend several hours a day in an outside enclosure.

To reiterate, build your housing and runs for the wild brethren of our domestic felines as strongly as possible, for should one escape and do harm to any person or other pet, the liability will be yours and the consequences will make you wish that you had never heard the word "cat."

We do not feel that any schematic descriptions are necessary to end this chapter. If you have given a good deal of intelligent thought to the cattery concept and decide definitely that it is what you want, then build your cattery well; we are sure that the original dream will become a wonderful reality. We cannot win unless we take the gamble. But are the spoils worth the risk? It is for you to answer.

CHAPTER 14

Cat Shows and Showing

If you have established a cattery or are in the process of building one, you are probably eager to become a part of the cat show fraternity. Perhaps you have already dipped a tentative toe into the warm waters of this enchanting world, and are keen to know as much as possible about this exhilarating area of cat culture. We will attempt, therefore, to give you a broad report of the most important aspects of the cat show and the show cat.

The first cat show in the United States was held in New York City in 1895, and the beginning of what one could refer to as an organized fancy occurred in Chicago in 1899. The cat show, in general terms, has many facets though it is basically a feline beauty contest. Through elimination it elevates deserving cats to prominence in the various breeds and categories, so that the cat fancy is made aware of the excellence of individual cats and the breeding that is producing the top contenders for show honors. The show also enables the exhibitors and the cat-conscious spectators to select and possibly arrange to purchase a specimen of the variety that has captured their interest, a fine kitten from show-winning parents; or to arrange a breeding to a particularly handsome, winning stud cat.

The prospective exhibitor should pick a show within easy driving distance of home for his first venture in exhibiting. Write to the secretary of the show-giving club for an entry form (see pages oo–ooo for a typical form). This must be filled out and the entry fee paid. At the show, a catalog may be purchased in which you can find the competition in the class in which you have entered your feline pride and joy. Make friends with other exhibitors and be alert to answer the call for your class!

CAT SHOW CATEGORIES

Cat shows fall into two main categories: those where competition is available in all the numerous recognized breeds of felines; and the specialty show, which is generally dedicated to a single major feline group such as short-haired cats or long-haired cats. Classes and subdivisions for the different breeds and colors are featured at the all-breed shows. Since there are several cat associations, or organizations, in North America, the procedures, classes, and standards (of breeds) at the various shows sponsored by the different associations can vary, but not to any great degree.

PREPARING FOR THE SHOW

Because queens are likely to be littering in the spring and summer, resulting in some difficulties at the shows in handling toms when females are in season, and because long-hairs lack full coat at this same time, the most prestigious shows are usually held between the months of September and February.

Your cat or cats, when being prepared for a show, should be made accustomed to the show-type cage and brought into top condition and coat just prior to the show. The cat's claws should be clipped, its ears and eyes cleaned, its body solid and flealess and, if female, not obviously pregnant. No cat should be shown if there is a communicable disease at its cattery. Ignoring this rule can put any number of felines in jeopardy. For this reason, we advise all exhibitors to isolate their show cats from others for a week or two after they return from a show, to make certain they have not been exposed to a contagious disease (possibly in a hidden viral form) in the show hall.

Do not feed puss for several hours before the show, and convey him or her to the show hall in a comfortable and familiar carrier. Once he has settled in the show cage, a light snack of a well-liked food can be offered to your hopeful.

As you enter the hall where the show is to be held, you will be presented with a card on which is typed your name, your cat's name, and the number of its cage. You will also receive a schedule of classes and the names of the judges (usually four in number) who will be handling the various classes, with their location in the hall. You will want to purchase a show catalogue to learn who will be exhibiting at the show and who your competitors will be. Along with other ailurophiles and their cat carriers, you will have to approach the show veterinarian presiding behind his examination table.

If given a clean bill-of-health by the busy veterinarian, you will carry your entries to the assigned cage, and tastefully arrange the decorations you may have brought with you. Use colors that complement the color of your cat's coat for the cage-floor blanket or rug, the cushion or pillow, and the cage decor. When puss has been made

THE CAT FANCIERS' ASSOCIATION, INC.

OFFICIAL

ENTRY BLANK

It is the responsibility of the Exhibitor to enter his cat under its correct registered name, registered ownership, and in the correct class. Consult the CFA Registration Certificate for the **EXACT** registered name, registered ownership, and other data required for entry.

The Show Management is expressly **PROHIBITED** from accepting a Championship, Premiership, Provisional Breed or AOV entry unless the Entry Blank contains the registration number as shown on the registration certificate.

AVOID ERRORS — TYPE OR PRINT

NAME OF CAT

MO / DAY / YR

CFA REG NO.   BIRTH DATE   SEX   EYE COLOR

BREED   COLOR   COLOR CLASS

SIRE

DAM

BREEDER   AGENT

OWNER   PHONE: AREA CODE   NUMBER

STREET ADDRESS   CITY   STATE/PROVINCE   ZIP/POSTAL CODE

CIRCLE NUMBER OF REGION OF RESIDENCE (IF KNOWN)	1 NORTH ATLANTIC	2 NORTH WEST	3 GULF SHORE	4 GREAT LAKES	5 SOUTH WEST	6 MID WEST	7 SOUTHERN

I hereby enter the above named cat, at my own risk, subject to the provisions of the Show Rules of the Cat Fanciers' Association, Inc. in effect for this show, and I state that I am familiar with the provisions of these rules. (A copy of the current Show Rules may be obtained from the CFA Central Office, PO Box 430, Red Bank, NJ 07701. Price is $1.00.)

I hereby state that the information provided on this Entry Blank is true and correct to the best of my knowledge.

SIGNATURE OF OWNER: _____
(If owner is under 18 yrs. of age, this blank must be signed by owner's parent or guardian.)

CAT TO BE ENTERED IN: (Check Proper Class and List Names of Shows)

NON-CHAMPIONSHIP	CHAMPIONSHIP	PREMIERSHIP	NAMES OF SHOWS
☐ KITTEN	☐ OPEN	☐ OPEN	
☐ HOUSEHOLD PET	☐ CHAMPION	☐ PREMIER	
☐ PROVISIONAL BREED	☐ GRAND CHAMPION	☐ GRAND PREMIER	
☐ _____ OTHER		☐ *for Sale*	

FORM 501

comfortable, locate the "ring" where your entry or entries will be judged.

The "ring" consists of a large table with a central, small platform, behind which a very knowledgeable judge will examine his or her quota of cats during the show, classify them as to merit and, sometimes after a few quiet but pertinent and pithy remarks, award them the ribbons they have earned. Surrounding this absolute authority is a U-shaped complement of approximately ten roomy cages, situated behind the judge and reaching in two arms on either side. At one side of the table sits the clerk who keeps all the records, checks numbers against the catalogue, and calls the entries to the ring on a loudspeaker. Each ring is also graced by a steward, a hardworking individual who retrieves the cats from their cages (always gently and with their hind ends emerging first), who is responsible for the cats in his/her particular "ring," returns the cats to their proper ring pens after they have been judged, and who has a myriad of other chores that aid in keeping the show running smoothly.

The judge is provided with a looseleaf notebook in which are recorded the identification numbers of all the entries to be examined in the allotted classes, but no other information that could possibly identify the cat or its owner. As each class is called, the numbers assigned to the cats in that class are attached or hung on the cages that form the "ring" around the judge, and the owners or agents (show handlers acting for owners) bring the animals called for (generally draped over a shoulder not unlike half of an expensive furpiece) to the "ring" and put them in the cages bearing their respective numbers.

One by one the judge or steward removes the cats from their "ring" cages and puts them on the small platform. Then the judge, with deft and knowing touches, begins the examination. With a hand and forearm under them, he or she holds each cat up with virtuoso efficiency, inspecting head and eye shape, eye color, ears, coat quality and color, feet, legs, body and tail, structure, weight for size, and muscle tone. Between each individual examination, he disinfects both hands and table with a spray bottle, using clean absorbent toweling to dry the surface.

When the judge has reached a final decision (working by comparison and point evaluation against the breed standard), the ribbons are awarded; from first to fifth prize in each class, the brilliantly colored ribbons or rosettes are hung from the cages of the cats who have won them. Owners and agents retrieve their cats, the cages are quickly disinfected, and the next class is called. The decision of the judge is always and inevitably final.

CAT SHOW CLASSES

The classes we shall discuss here are those in effect now in shows sponsored by the Cat Fanciers' Association, Inc. (CFA), the most prestigious feline association in North America. The other associations use much the same formula in both show classes and registration of cats, but with some variations.

All domesticated felines of both sexes, whole, neutered, or spayed, eight months of age or older, are called cats. To qualify as a "kitten," a youngster must therefore be under eight months of age. Spayed or neutered kittens are not eligible for cat show entry. A castrated male is named a "neuter," and an altered female a "spay." A "ring" is an area of competition assigned to a single judge. The "show" is a concurrent series of "rings" (usually numbering four).

There are three major competitive categories: Non-Championship; Championship; and Premiership ("alter"), the last for neutered cats. A "class" refers to a competitive division within the structure of the three categories. Non-Championship classes include: Kitten; Any-Other-Variety (AOV, registered cats who do not conform to their breed standard and cannot earn a championship); Provisional Breed (eligible for award only in this class); Miscellaneous (noncompetitive); and Household Pet (only eligible for award in this class).

Championship classes include: Novice, a cat who has never won a winner's ribbon; Open, for felines who have not yet achieved the title of Champion; Champion, obviously the class for Champion cat competition; and Grand Champion, for cats who have garnered enough wins to have reached this exalted status. Premiership Classes list registered spayed or neutered cats of recognized breeds. These special Alter Classes include Novice, Open, Premier, and Grand Premier, in each color and coat class. There are three diverse systems of award: the CFA asks that Best and Second Best be chosen in each category, but most of the other associations want Best and Best Opposite Sex cats selected in all colors and divisions.

To acquire the title of Champion, a cat must have won six or more winner's ribbons as the best cat of its sex in its specific color division in combined Novice and Open competitions under a minimum of four different judges. To reach the pinnacle of Grand'Champion, or Grand Premiership, a cat must amass 150 points under at least three different judges. These points are awarded 1 point for every Champion it defeats in breed or division.

The Cat Fanciers' Association will, for a very nominal fee, send you a comprehensive booklet, *Show Rules,* which contains twenty-eight articles concerning all aspects of the cat show. They also print a worthwhile booklet, *Show Standards,* and other rewarding literature from which the feline enthusiast can glean much information. Other cat organizations also can supply you with interesting literature.

Besides the major all-breed cat associations, there are individual clubs representing the many breeds that find favor with cat fanciers in North America, and that are affiliated with one or more of the all-breed national organizations. These specialty clubs publish literature featuring news of their particular breeds.

BRITISH CAT SHOWS

Our British cousins, fantastic animal fanciers that they are, were the initial ailurophiles to sanction and stage the world's first cat show. This important event occurred in 1871 at the Crystal Palace and enjoyed an entry of 170 cats. Today, the National Cat Club's annual exhibition in London has an entry of over two thousand cats. The National Cat Club, guiding organization for the feline fancy in Britain, was founded in 1887, and eleven years later the Cat Club, a rival organization, came into being. Both clubs maintained their own cat registrations and stud books. Then in 1910 the two clubs, with typical British foresight, merged into one under the banner of the Governing Council of the Cat Fancy (GCCF).

Specialty clubs were quickly born, became affiliated with the national club, and came under its rigid jurisdiction. The Council has complete and autocratic power over the entire cat fancy in Britain, and is certainly a stabilizing influence. As a single governing entity, it eliminates some of the confusion found in North America where the several separate associations project some slight differences in standards, show procedures, and general rules, resulting in duplication, added expense, and a bit of chaos.

A cat in Britain cannot be shown more than once during a fourteen-day period, which makes it necessary for show-giving clubs to stage their exhibitions beyond the two-week limit if they are to be assured of a large entry. The hall in which the competition takes place is not open to the public until about noontime, and the exhibitors are requested to vacate the show hall from ten o'clock, when judging begins, until noon. This ruling enables the judges to have two quiet and undisturbed hours in which to judge the very significant open classes. In the United States, spectators are allowed access to the show at any time and the exhibitors are always present.

British shows are one-day affairs, all judging being accomplished and ribbons and awards given in that single day. In North America, some of the larger shows are two-day affairs. Considering the comparatively greater number of entries at British shows, their efficiency in completing the task in one day is rather amazing. The proficiency of British judges is recognized throughout the feline show world, and the excellence of cats bred in the British Isles cannot be disputed. In fact, the British have long been recognized for their ability to breed and produce outstanding livestock in any number of animal categories.

THE CAT SHOW JUDGE

Judges are unique individuals who put their expertise on the line each time they accept an assignment. Since only a comparatively few cats of the many entered at a show will be granted the winners' awards, the judge will be beloved by a few of the exhibitors and castigated by many. But these attitudes the judges learn to ignore, for they are content in the knowledge that their special skill in the art of judging cats, based upon experience and integrity, cannot be questioned.

The American CFA requires that a cat show arbiter must prepare for this elevated position through a vigorous training program as a trainee and an apprentice judge. Add to this the experience accumulated previously in the roles of breeder, exhibitor, steward, clerk, and cattery owner, and there can be little doubt that the adjudicator is qualified. The various parent clubs and associations in North America, as well as clubs in other countries, have slightly different methods of selecting judges, from committee appointment and special examinations to the apprenticeships previously mentioned. In Britain, the specialty breed clubs generally recommend judges to the GCCF for approval, with details of the chosen individual's years of experience in stewarding, breeding, and exhibiting. The name of the future judge is then considered at a meeting of the GCCF. Generally, the aspiring candidate must serve a probationary term during which he or she is assigned to judge classes at three shows.

The CFA has ruled that judges cannot accept work at two shows at different locales during one weekend, even though it is estimated that they should be capable of handling approximately eighty cats a day at a North American show. Judges evaluate show cats in two ways: by comparison to an envisioned standard (informal evaluation), and by the point system allocated to each breed. Though standards are essentially "abstract aesthetic ideals," each judge must completely assimilate the standards of the breeds he or she wishes to adjudicate. Each competing cat must be a completely balanced entity within the physical scope of its individual breed or variety. Any cat that behaves in a vicious, threatening, or recalcitrant manner during the judging will be disqualified. Judges are not present to prove their courage, and a nasty bite or scratch can incapacitate them. It follows, therefore, that exhibitors must train their show cats to behave in an exemplary manner.

Since the standards depict an abstract ideal, judges can vary slightly in their interpretation of a written standard, which can result in different placements for the same cats from show to show. Though no cat shown can possess all the perfection necessary to embrace the standard's ultimate, judges bear a great responsibility because their interpretation of the standard can set type in a variety for generations to come. There can be no doubt that judging is a satisfying and highly stimulating experience.

CAT ASSOCIATIONS

The cat organizations and registries of North America include the American Cat Association, the oldest show-giving organization, incorporated in 1904, which maintains the feline registry begun by the Beresford Cat Club of Chicago in 1897; the American Cat Fanciers' Association, Inc., organized in 1955; the Canadian Cat Association, organized in 1960 and offering International Championships; the Cat Fanciers' Association, Inc., organized in 1906, which at present holds more than two hundred shows each year in all areas of the United States, Canada, Hawaii, and Japan; the Cat Fanciers' Federation, established in 1919 based upon the principle of equal representation; the Crown Cat Fanciers, incorporated in Texas in 1965; the Independent Cat Federation, youngest of the cat associations and particularly interested in the household pet cat; the National Cat Fanciers' Association, favoring the concept of several organizations with different approaches for an area as large as North America; and the United Cat Federation, of Los Angeles, California.

For exhibitors, the cat show can be a wonderfully exhilarating experience, an opportunity to indulge in a highly competitive endeavor and to contend for top awards with living entities acquired through their own knowledge or fashioned by their breeding acumen. The cat show world is unparalleled in the heady excitement and sense of achieve-ment it can engender. Competition adds spice to life, and the cat show is a competitive arena that embraces all people regardless of sex, age, physical condition, race, creed, or color. Yes, there are disappoint-ments too, as there are in all contests, but they are inevitably erased by the finally achieved triumphs.

CHAPTER 15

Feline Physiology

Before entering the rather technical pediatric and medical sections of this book, you should know about the physiology of the feline.

Cats, whales, mice, and men all have much in common because they, along with a whole host of other creatures, are mammals. They share the presence of body hair, milk-secreting glands, a diaphragm, and, with the exception of the monotremes (the lowest order of mammals, restricted to the Australian region), they bear living young; for this last reason they are termed "viviparous." All mammals feed or give sustenance to their young by means of milk from the mammary glands—from which, indeed, the name of this most important class of living creatures is derived.

Mammals are warm-blooded, four-limbed vertebrates (with certain exceptions, such as whales), who breathe air and possess numerous glands for varied purposes. They have a complete diaphragm, lungs with air cells (alveoli), and teeth that generally display full roots. Each mammalian creature is, beyond doubt, a fantastic multiplicity of specialized cells. The precious heart of a mammal is sectioned into four areas, and the brain is well developed, which, more than any other factor, has made mammals the dominant life form on our planet.

Considering the present energy crisis and our growing awareness that we must learn to reuse our waste products, it is perhaps ironic to remember that during the long process of mammalian evolution many body organs became obsolete. Frequently, however, such organs adapted themselves to new functions in a kind of physiological recycling.

In cats, mutation and selection for desired attributes have resulted in many different breeds. But unlike the dog, cats are essentially similar in size and basic type, a phenomenon that attests to the strength and aptness of their inherited form and their eminent fitness for survival. Most domestic breeds have short hair, but there are also long-haired breeds of great beauty. Most cats have long tails, but there are a few breeds, particularly in Southeast Asia, that have short tails. Manx cats are, in show specimens, completely tailless, with large, strong hindquarters to give them the balance that tails provide for other cats.

THE EYES

The cat's eye is a remarkable and complex organ that is a particularly important part of the animal's receptor system. In daylight, muscles attached to the suspensory ligaments contract and change the pupils to narrow slits, controlling the amount of light that enters. At night, in dim light, the muscles of the iris relax to admit all available light into the wide-open pupils. Cats actually have much better vision in dim light than in bright. Being basically nocturnal creatures, they have excellent night vision if there is a modicum of light to cast some luminescence. No one knows for sure if the cat can distinguish color, but we think that it cannot since cats are nocturnal and don't need color to recognize an object in dim light. The 280 degrees of visual field possessed by felines is extraordinary. Like all nocturnal creatures, the cat has comparatively large eyes with a light-reflective layer called the tapetum (membranous layers in choroid or retina) associated with the retina. At night when rays of light are reflected back from the tapetum, the cat's eyes exhibit the familiar glow in the dark.

THE SKIN

The external covering or integument of the mammalian body is the skin: it is also the single largest organ of the body. The cat is not a thin-skinned creature, mammals never are; but the feline skin is not as thick as that of many other mammals, and it is also more flexible and loose. The outer skin, the epidermis, is composed of thin layers that are constantly being renewed. Immediately below, or underneath, the outer integument is the dermis. Thicker than the outer skin layer, it supports nerves, blood, and lymph vessels, as well as sweat and sebaceous glands that lubricate the outer hair and ensure the normal growth of the hair coat and claws of the cat. Beneath both these layers is subcutaneous connective tissue that stores fat and acts as an energy reserve and protection against chill for cold-country cats. The skin is also the initial barrier against disease entering the body.

The pelage or coat of the cat, feral or domestic, varies greatly. It can be patterned, short- or long-haired, self-colored, and can differ with age, as witness the lion, whose young are born spotted. All

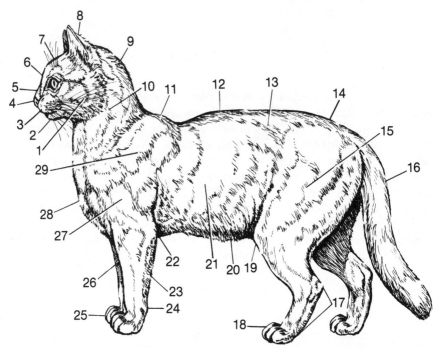

External anatomy: (1) cheek, (2) chin, (3) muzzle, (4) nose leather, (5) nose, (6) stop, (7) skull, (8) ears, (9) neck crest, (10) neck, (11) withers, (12) back, (13) loin, (14) croup, (15) thigh, (16) tail, (17) hock, (18) foot, (19) knee, (20) belly, (21) ribs, (22) elbow, (23) foreleg (ulna), (24) heel, (25) forepaws, (26) foreleg (radius), (27) upper arm, (28) forechest, (29) shoulder blade (the upper arm and the shoulder blade together form the shoulder assembly).

wild cats exhibit coat colors that are adapted to blend with their environment. A tawny coat indicates that the cat who wears it lives generally in dry country where the land, earth, and vegetation are dry and sere. Through such country, lions—African, Indian, and American—can move unseen, silently hunting their unsuspecting prey. The tiger's striped coat mimics the shadows of long blades of coarse grass in moonlight, and the feral cats who sport spotted pelts are climbers who search for their kills from the boughs of huge jungle trees, their coats aping the dappling of light and shadow filtering through the leaves. The exception to this rule (as it is to other cat-cult canons) is the cheetah, who wears a spotted coat but hunts in open country by running down its quarry. Man, who at a cursory glance appears to be a rather hairless mammal (with some exceptions), actually is not. A microscopic view of the human skin reveals as many hair follicles as those of our much-removed relative the chimpanzee.

THE MUSCULAR SYSTEM

A muscle is a separate bundle of contractile fibers whose function is the production of movement in the animal body. The muscles lie under the cat's skin and there are two basic kinds, voluntary and involuntary. The voluntary muscles are the skeletal or striated muscles that aid in holding the bony structure together and move, flexing and relaxing, when the skeleton is in motion. These muscles, under voluntary control, respond to messages from the cat's brain. Cats possess

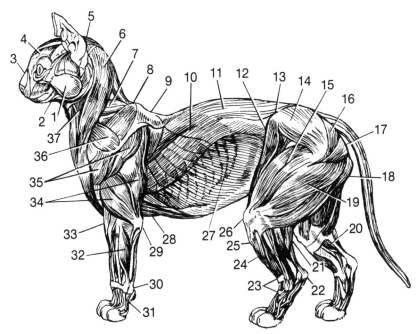

Musculature: (1) cheek muscle (masseter), (2) lower jawbone muscle, (3) nasal cartilage, (4) skull muscles (temporalis), (5) levator of auricle, (6) neck muscles (cleidomastoideus), (7) cervical serratus anterior, (8) supraspinatus, (9) spina scapulae, (10) latissimus dorsi, (11) lumbo-dorsal fascia, (12) anterior sartorius, (13) tuber coxae, (14) glutaeus medius, (15) quadriceps femoris, (16) glutaeus maximus, (17) abductor cruris anterior, (18) semitendinosis, (19) biceps femoris, (20) flexor hallucis longus, (21) end of semitendinosis, (22) superficial flexor tendon, (23) annular ligaments, (24) tibialis anterior, (25) tibia (swelling of), (26) patella, (27) aponeurosis, (28) pectoralis minor (posterior section), (29) olecranon, (30) os pisiforme, (31) Mm. interossei, (32) extensor carpi ulnaris, (33) extensor muscles, (34) triceps brachii, (35) deltoideus, (36) shoulder-tranverse-process muscle, (37) sternomandibularis.

more than five hundred of these controlled muscles, and it is through the use of such muscles that they are able to walk, run, jump, stalk, raise the hair on their backs, and perform divers other movements. Felines also have a leverage mechanism that permits them to twist their limbs and body in the air and land upon their feet.

The second group of muscles, the smooth or involuntary muscles, are in general those that the organs utilize in their all-important tasks. These are the muscles that control the functions of the liver, bladder, blood vessels, digestive tract, and all the other organs and glands that keep the cat alive and healthy. These involuntary muscles must respond automatically and spontaneously to the demands of the animal's inner body and not wait for a command from the brain.

The musculature of mammals is a remarkable interwoven skeletal covering of tough, pliable armor. It gives the family *Felidae* enormous strength, quick agile power, and the controlled stealth and exquisite balance necessary to their roles as successful predators.

THE SKELETON

This is the bony or cartilaginous framework of a vertebrate animal. The bony structure that lies under the skin and muscles of the cat is of a type classified as endoskeleton, which simply means that it is internal—in contrast to an external type, named exoskeleton. The latter skeletal structure is worn as an outer body armor or shell, such as the lobster displays. The difference between the two kinds of bony structures can be recalled if you will remember that some exoskeleton creatures are best when dipped in warm butter, but an endoskeletal cat certainly isn't.

The human skeleton and the skeletal structure of your cat are quite similar, yet they differ in some few important aspects. The vertebrae are biplanar and separated by discs (epiphyses), which lend pliability to the vertebral or spinal column. All mammals, including the cat, giraffe, pig, whale, and man, have seven cervical (neck) vertebrae. Moving from the neck toward the rear along the spinal column, we find the thoracic, the lumbar, the sacral, and the caudal (or tail) vertebrae in that order—all part of the long spine. The sacral vertebrae are fused (not pliable) and the pelvic girdle is attached to them. The ribs are joined to, and spring out from, the thoracic vertebrae.

In man, the caudal vertebrae are reduced to a very few rudimentary bones, but the cat, with the exception of the few tailless and bobtailed varieties, sports a full number of vertebrae in its caudal appendage, or tail. Another difference between the skeletal structure of man and

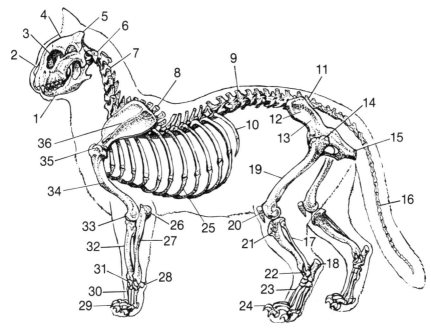

Skeletal structure: (1) lower jawbone, (2) os nasale, (3) eye socket (orbita), (4) cranium (os parietale), (5) occiput, (6) first cervical (neck) vertebrae, (7) neck vertebrae (seven in all), (8) thoracic vertebrae (dorsal with spinal process), (9) lumbar vertebrae, (10) thirteenth rib, (11) sacrum, (12) ilium (pelvis), (13) ischium (pelvis), (14) trochanter major (head of femur), (15) pubis (pelvis), (16) tail vertebrae, (17) fibula, (18) tuba calcanei (point of hock), (19) femur, (20) patella (knee cap), (21) tibia, (22) tarsus, (23) metatarsus, (24) phalanges pedis (toes), (25) ribs, (26) olecranon (elbow), (27) ulna, (28) os pisiforme, (29) phalanges manus (front toes), (30) metacarpus, (31) carpus, (32) radius, (33) external epicondyle, (34) humerus, (35) external tuberosity, (36) scapula (shoulder blade).

feline occurs in the clavicle or collarbone. Man's is fully developed, whereas the cat's clavicle is vestigial. The shoulder bones (scapula and humerus, or shoulder blade and upper arm) are separate entities with no skeletal connections to the body.

The cat is, of course, quadrupedal or four-legged, with a leg at each corner of its body, a design highly recommended for balance. The feline walks on its toes (digitigrade), and is therefore considered a running animal. In this respect also the cat differs from man, who uses the plantigrade method of locomotion with the foot, from heel to toe, touching the ground (considered a more primitive way of moving than that enjoyed by the cat). Digitigrade motion produces a greater degree of elastic mobility and silence—a definite advantage for a predatory

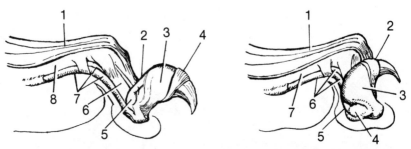

Retractable claws: (1) tendons on phalanx of toe, (2) strong elastic ligament, (3) phalanx tertia, (4) ring-shaped skin fold, (5) ligament connecting phalanx secunda with phalanx tertia, (6) phalanx secunda, (7) flexor carpi ulnaris muscle, (8) olecranon.

cat. Your cat (unless of a short-tailed variety) can boast of 230 bones in its skeletel structure, while you have only 206.

The leg to which the cat's foot is necessarily attached is called a pentadactyl limb (bearing five digits). The front feet of all *Felidae* (except the cheetah) possess sharp, powerful retractile claws, and beneath each toe of both front and hind feet is a thick pad and a larger, rather triangular-shaped pad, placed in the foot's center. The front feet also bear two small pads for the dewclaw (fifth toe), and the carpal bones. Cats perspire through their footpads. Your cat should have five toes on its front feet and four on the hind feet, but some cats carry more than this number of toes and so are designated as being polydactyl, meaning that they possess a greater number of digits than is normal.

The bones of the skeleton vary in shape and composition according to their purpose. Some are round, some oblong, others flat. Some are dense and hard, others pliable and honeycombed with inner tunnel structures that carry nerves and nourishment in the form of blood. Generally speaking, the skeletal structure provides a protective armor for vital organs, a connective arrangement for the muscles, and a solid framework for the body as a whole.

THE SKULL

The skull is a part of the skeletal structure, but treated separately here because of the great importance of the dentition and eyes of the cat to its lifestyle. The skull consists of the foreface or muzzle, with the essential movable lower jaw or mandible, and the cranium, the bony box that holds and protects the wily feline brain.

Since they are carnivorous, the *Felidae* have dentition typical of their predacious way of life. The large powerful canine teeth are designed for stabbing, seizing prey, and fighting; the sharp incisors are for biting and ripping; and the molars for grinding. Felines can also boast of modified molars that form knifelike carnassial teeth to slice through sinew. Each separate tooth of the thirty they possess (sixteen upper and fourteen lower) consists of a root set into a pit in the jawbone (alveolus), and a crown. Like most mammals, the cat has two sets of teeth; the milk or baby teeth, and the permanent set that must last the rest of its lifetime.

The skull provides a pair of sockets to accommodate the complicated eyes of the cat. Each eye is a hollow sphere embedded in these sockets and is formed by three layers: the sclera or outer coat, which forms the cornea; the choroid, composed of blood vessels and pigment, which shapes the iris; and the retina, which encompasses nerve cells, fibers, and light-sensitive cells, and ends behind the ligaments from which the lens is suspended. Feline eyes are unique in that they possess a slit pupil, not a round one such as those shared by man and most other mammals. Cats also have a third eyelid, called the nictitating membrane, that is situated under the lower lid and closes horizontally.

Sphincter muscles surround the pupil of the cat's eye, some of which cross and have a side attachment. These muscles display a scissors action when they contract, shaping the pupil to a vertical slit. The tapetum, a part of the retina, has special light-absorbing cells necessary for night sight.

THE ALIMENTARY TRACT
AND DIGESTIVE SYSTEM

The lips of the feline's mouth are fleshy and the tongue is quite muscular, with a smooth underside and covered with minuscule fleshy hooks on the upper side. This arrangement is an aid to swallowing food, and to the incessant grooming indulged in by cats. The old query "Cat got your tongue?" could be given more credence if it were changed to "Cat hooked your tongue?" The hooks on the tongues of the larger feral cats have enough of a rasp to draw blood if allowed to lick human flesh, so if you own one of the larger wild cats, do not encourage it to lick you.

Continuing down the alimentary canal, we come to the palate and the epiglottis, which might sound like Italian pasta to you but is actually a thin, valvelike cartilaginous structure that covers the glottis

involuntarily during swallowing, preventing food and drink from entering the larynx. The cheeks are exceedingly muscular in all felines,
and the salivary glands are enough to make the mouth water, which
is their primary function. Next we reach the elastic-walled stomach
where some digestion of food takes place. Liquid acid supplied by the
glands breaks down proteins and fats. From the stomach we move to
the gut, which is divided into the ileum, or small intestine, and the
colon, or large intestine. Here bile from the liver and pancreatic
starch-digesting substances become active, breaking down food substances to their component parts, which in turn are absorbed and
distributed by the blood. Carnivores have only a rudimentary caecum,
and the intestines of carnivorous creatures such as the cat are much
shorter than those of omnivores (eaters of both plant and animal foods)
and herbivores (plant eaters). A sheep, therefore, can possess 90 feet of
intestines, and a tiger 20 feet or less, though it is difficult to believe that
a sheep has more guts than a tiger or lion.

The liver and pancreas are next in line, both fairly large and necessarily highly functional. The liver is actually the cat's largest internal
organ.

RESPIRATION AND CIRCULATION

The larynx and the several cartilages that form the Adam's apple
in the throat of the cat and are accompanied by the vocal cords, the
glottis, and epiglottis, must all be considered as segments of the respiratory system. Air is carried by the trachea (windpipe) to the bronchi (tubes that enter the lungs), passed on to the bronchioles, and
then to the pulmonary alveoli (air cells of the lungs). There is also a
membrane in mammals that separates the lungs from the rest of the
chest area and that varies in strength with different species. In the
cat it is very thin.

The feline's heart is divided into four chambers (as it is in man) and
a single aorta (the main artery) branches from the left ventricle. The
aorta is an animal's lifeline, delivering blood from the heart to the
arteries and other blood vessels throughout the body. The blood
nourishes the body, brings needed substances to the cells, and delivers
waste products to the organs of excretion. Though fluid, the blood is
itself an organ composed of specialized cells and important chemicals.
The corpuscles circulating in the blood, and the act of breathing,
combine to keep the cat's temperature normal (approximately 101.5
degrees F.). The cat's purr, which we accept without thought, is specific to the cat alone in the animal kingdom. It originates through the

vibration of a large blood vessel in the chest which, transmitted to the air passages of the throat, causes the purring sound.

THE NERVOUS SYSTEM

All mammals have a highly developed nervous system composed of fibers that control the entire body's activities. The spinal cord is the seat of the largest group of nerves. The expression "I'm a bundle of nerves" is actually precise, because the nerve fibers are formed into bundles. The nervous system is animated by the cerebral hemospheres and the cerebellum sections of the brain, a very complex operation. In the *Felidae,* hearing, seeing, and smelling are all highly developed senses and all part of the animal's receptor system, which provides the central nervous system with definitive information about conditions existing in the immediate environment every split second. Cats react quickly to nerve stimuli, so the old expression "nervous as a cat" is quite appropriate.

Tactile corpuscles throughout the skin result in high sensitivity to touch, and the cat's muzzle is well supplied with vibrasse, or whiskers, which are acutely perceptive sensory organs that supplement the scenting ability and nocturnal vision, allowing the cat to move with sureness in the dark. The surface of the nasal passages is increased by the complexity of the turbinal bones, which intensify the properties of scent, and the taste buds of the tongue (coupled with scent) aid felines to select and appreciate their food.

Only mammals can boast of an external ear and three tympanic ossicles, if one considers this something to boast about. A cat's ear is a complicated and interesting organ. It is pricked and cupped externally to catch the slightest sound. Audible waves move downward through the auditory opening to the eardrum, and beyond the drum is a delicate instrument that registers vibrations and sends them, via the semicircular canal, to the nerves. In turn, the auditory nerve communicates all sound stimuli to the brain. Beyond the visual ear the auditory system is well protected by the skull case.

The eustachian tube (auditory canal) passes from the middle ear to the feline's throat, as it does in man. As a matter of fact, the entire auditory mechanism of the cat is very similar to our own, but with an extremely pertinent difference that is characteristic of most of the comparable senses: man's sensory faculties have become dulled through disuse, for we no longer must depend upon them to survive; but the animal's senses must remain functional, quick, and keen, for in its world, perception can mean the difference between life and death.

THE UROGENITAL SYSTEM

The urinary and reproductive systems are considered parts of the same system by embryologists, so we will incorporate both under this heading and explain that the pelvis kidney is a metanephros (developing from the lowest portion of the nephric blastema cords, according to the *American College Dictionary*). This illustrates how clarification can result in complete bewilderment unless the reader is a practitioner in one of the fields pertinent to the study of the reproductive system.

The urine flows through independent ureters that empty into a reservoir known as the bladder. Developing initially in the lumbar region, the male's testes (or testicles) descend into the scrotum. Sperm is produced in the testes and is stored in the epididymis (in which the spermatozoa ripen), located on the outside of the testes, and in the vas deferens, a duct that conveys the sperm to the urethra, the passage through which both sperm and urine are discharged. Felines do not possess a seminal vesicle as does man.

The cat's penis becomes erect when infused with blood, and it is provided with spines which cause difficulty in the process of withdrawal after copulation, but which are necessary to trigger ovulation in the female.

The female organs of reproduction comprise the uterus, cervix, vagina, clitoris, and vulva (the mammary glands can also be added to this list). Female domestic cats have two or three breeding cycles a year, but the wild *Felidae* have only one cycle per year, and therefore can produce only one litter annually. There is some speculation that the tigress produces a litter only every other year. Unlike the testes of the male, the ovaries are situated within the female's body and are protected by the lumbar muscles. The ovaries do not connect with the fallopian tubes, which end near them in a fringed funnel. The ova (eggs) are discharged from the ovary into the abdomen and thence go through the oviducts to the uterus. (More about the processes of mating and conception can be found in Chapter 12.) Of exceeding interest are the many stages of the evolutionary process evidenced in the reproductive systems of animals. The *Monotremata*, most primitive of all living mammals, with only two modern surviving members, the platypus and the echidna, and the marsupials (infraclass *Methatheria*, or pouched mammals), more advanced than the *Monotremata* but archaic in comparison with the placental mammals in the evolutionary scale, both possess two genital tracts that end in two vaginas and two uteri. In placental mammals during the evolutionary process the two vaginas merged into one organ, and the uteri, which have remained distinct as two in rodents, became incompletely fused in insectivores, carnivores (which includes the *Felidae*), and the ungulates. Only in the primates (monkeys, apes, and man, the ultimate mammals) has the complete fusion of the uteri been accomplished.

THE GLANDULAR SYSTEM

The glands are the regulators of the body; without them, the body would not function. There are ductless and ordinary glands, and each gland has its own functioning area, though it can also influence the accomplishments of other glands. Some of the glands have awesome capabilities, with a performance range that seems almost incredible. The pituitary is a sterling example of such a grand gland. It is found at the base of the brain and is the most important body regulator of all the glands. It has the capability of stunting growth or causing gigantism; it brings on the estrus cycle and affects sexual development; it helps regulate the metabolism of carbohydrates; it causes hair shedding and obesity; it raises blood pressure; and it does other chores as well. The pituitary is a busy little gland.

The pancreas manufactures digestive ferments (enzymes), and consequently is important to digestion. It also, in conjunction with the liver, regulates the amount of sugar in the blood and urine. The adrenal glands produce adrenalin, a chemical that affects the heart and the blood vessels and is vital in the regulation of blood pressure. The adrenals, located near the kidneys, also affect urinary salt, and fat and sugar metabolism.

On either side of the neck, and connected below the larynx by a thin isthmus of tissue, we find the thyroid, a bilobate ductless gland. It secretes a chemical regulator, thyroxin, that is rich in iodine. When functioning properly, it prevents goiter, which is a swelling of the gland itself. Basically, the thyroid organizes the life rhythm of the cat. The parathyroids are small glands that are located beside the double sections of the thyroid. Their function is to regulate calcium metabolism so that the bones of the skeleton grow normally and maintain continued pliability and renewal during maturity.

The ovaries are also concerned, to a degree, with growth. Their removal before the cat is sexually mature will increase the final growth and allow the formation of excess fat, the latter effect probably due in part to the fact that a spayed female is less active than one that is normal. Combined with the pituitary gland the ovaries bring on estrus, and when this occurs a hormone, estrone, is produced in the blood, causing the female feline to go through all the physical manifestations of the mating cycle. In the testes of the tom cat there is secreted a hormone (testosterone) that needs the help of the pituitary gland to function properly. The combined efforts of the pituitary and the hormone help tom to become the sexy, swashbuckling character he is.

Each part of this masterly work of art and mechanics, the feline physiology, fits into its adjoining section with awesome precision to produce a flawless, animated creature, pulsing with vital life forces. Shakespeare called man "the paragon of animals," but were it not for the sapient human brain it is possible the accolade would have better fitted our friend the cat.

CHAPTER 16

Kitten Care

Fortunately for most cat owners and neophyte breeders, "mama cat" has an inherited instinct to care well for her kittens; but sometimes a nervous queen with her first litter will need help. It is usually best with the uneasy queen for only one member of the breeder's family to assume the necessary nursing duties. Keep the mother in a quiet and relatively darkened area in order to soothe her, and when you approach her and handle her kittens, do so quietly and calmly. The human "nurse" should make certain the kittens are suckling by examining them for full bellies several times a day. If they are not nursing, you may have to put the kittens on the queen's breasts five to six times during a twenty-four-hour period and monitor the feeding. If this does not prove to be successful, bottle or tube feeding (see "Orphan Kittens" below) will have to be resorted to. As the queen becomes more experienced, she will probably instinctively take over more and more of the duties of motherhood. Keep the temperature of the "nursery" at about 75 degrees Fahrenheit; the queen will provide body heat to increase the nest temperature.

Weaning time usually begins when the kittens are about five or six weeks of age. You will now have to provide milk and food for the babies. A sudden switch to cow's milk often causes diarrhea. We have found that evaporated milk diluted with 50 percent water makes a good early supplement and causes little or no diarrhea. A tablespoon of Karo syrup added to a pint of this mixture will augment the diet with some ready energy for the kittens.

During the first week, gradually flake some hamburger or meaty cat food into the mixture until the kittens are ready to accept solids. As the kittens become self-sufficient, slowly change the diet to fresh milk and separate solids. This procedure is best begun at four weeks of age. Use a flat, shallow pan filled with milk, and introduce the kittens to it by dipping your finger in the milk and then rubbing it on their mouths. As the kits become excited by the flavor, gently grasp them by the head and individually dip their chins and mouths into the milk in the pan. Soon they will be wading in the pan and lapping up the milk as though they were starving. As the kittens grow, their table manners will improve, we promise you.

ORPHAN KITTENS

If the queen dies or is unable to care for her kittens for any reason, you will find it necessary to hand-feed the babies. There are two accepted methods of hand-feeding: by bottle or by feeding tube.

The task of raising orphan kittens is challenging, though not quite as difficult as it may seem. Kittens have been raised on as few as four feedings a day, but it is best to feed as often as every three hours the first week to ten days, then six times daily until they are three weeks old. From three to six weeks, four to five meals a day are sufficient until the catlings reach the age of six weeks, when three feedings daily will supply them with enough nutrients for their needs.

Small nursing bottles are available in most pet stores, or you can generally find one at your veterinarian's. To tube-feed, use a number 8 French catheter or a "feeding tube." Catheters can be purchased at drugstores and pet stores, or veterinarians may have feeding tubes, which are specially adapted catheters. The catheter is passed over the tongue and down the esophagus into the stomach. The number 8 catheter is too large to go into the trachea and lungs, a safety factor that will keep the kitten from being drowned when the milk mixture is introduced. Another precaution you can take is to lay the catheter alongside the kitten and measure the length from the mouth to just beyond the last rib, where the stomach is located, and mark the tube where it will enter the mouth. Now pass the catheter gently down through the kitten's mouth until it reaches the mark. If the catheter is in the lung, it will stop 1 or 2 inches before the mark. Attach a 10 cc. syringe containing the milk supplement to the catheter and inject the milk slowly into the stomach. The entire amount can be injected in five to ten seconds.

If too much milk has been given, the kitten may regurgitate the excess from its mouth or nose. If this occurs, hold the kitten upside down so the milk does not run into its lungs, and gently shake it to clear its mouth. Never use an eye dropper for feeding except in a dire emergency, as the catling cannot control the introduction of supplement into its mouth and, if it is inhaling at the time of introduction, it may get milk in its lungs, which can lead to pneumonia. If you must use a dropper because it is all you have at hand to feed the kittens with, there is a blizzard raging outside, the bridge has been washed away, and the world is coming to an end, then feed the milk mix drop by careful drop gently into the kitten's mouth or onto its tongue.

There are two kinds of supplements available and both are reliable:

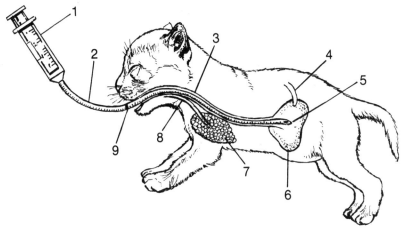

Tube-feeding a kitten: (1) hypodermic syringe, (2) French catheter, (3) esophagus, (4) last rib, (5) end of tube just behind or parallel to last rib, (6) stomach, (7) lungs, (8) trachea, (9) mark on tube.

the home formula or the prepared formula. The latter can be acquired at a pet store or from your veterinarian. These formulas are made mainly for puppies but are also the closest available formulas to queen's milk. The most common products to look for are Esbilac or Vetalac. Use as recommended on the label.

Home formulas are just about as good as prepared formulas, and the ingredients are closer to hand in an emergency. Goat's milk is the easiest to use—if you just happen to keep a milking goat around the house. But if someone has gotten your goat, use the following home-made formula:

> 8 oz. evaporated milk
> 8 oz. water
> 1 Tsp. Karo syrup

Mix the ingredients well and feed. We also like to add a little liquid vitamin supplement to the formula, especially one high in the B vitamins. Your veterinarian can supply you with such a supplement.

Kittens require 60 calories per pound of weight a day when in an incubated environment (80 to 90 degrees F.), and 100 calories if they are not. Formulas are about 1 calorie per cc. Therefore, a ¼-pound kitten should receive 15 cc. to 25 cc. of formula per day. Use this as a guide, but check for full tummies and adjust accordingly. Once again, if it is an emergency, do not be afraid to use cow's milk, or even diluted coffee cream, until you can acquire the correct formula ingredients.

After nursing, you must "burp" the kittens just as you would a human baby. To produce urination and defecation, use a piece of cotton moistened with warm water or baby oil and gently rub the kitty's tummy. Orphan kittens should be kept in a warm environment since there is no mother to supply body heat. Eighty to 90 degrees Fahrenheit is the proper temperature. Keep the orphaned kittens in a small bed so they can cuddle and not wander away from each other's warmth. As they become more independent reduce the heat to 75 degrees, and then 70 degrees. If their skin becomes dry from the heat, rub in a bit of baby oil to relieve the condition.

KITTEN DISEASES AND DISORDERS

Kittens and Disease

Colostrum, the milk produced by the queen during the first twenty-four hours of nursing, contains antibodies against the many diseases that can afflict kittens, and it protects them during the first few months of life. If the babies are orphaned and this initial milk has been denied them, they are unprotected, though they can accept early vaccines against distemper and respiratory diseases.

Kittens that become ill succumb rapidly to disease since their ability to fight infections is less than an adult cat's. Every breeder should be aware of the normal body values of the kitten, which differ slightly from those of an adult cat. Normal kittens have:

Heart rates of 150 to 200 beats per minute.
Respiratory rates of 20 to 30 breaths per minute.
Temperatures of 100° Fahrenheit.
Mucus membranes that are pink.
Skin that is elastic and springy.
Their eyes open at ten days of age.

You can feel the heart rate by placing your hand on the chest (count for fifteen seconds and multiply by four). Observe the respiratory rate, and examine the mucous membranes by looking at the gums or inside the eyelids. The temperature can be taken with any human rectal thermometer. Lubricate the thermometer with Vaseline or other gel before inserting in the rectum.

Sick kittens are cold, wrinkled, and cry almost constantly, and a cold, calmmy kitten is in danger of expiring. A whole litter of kittens can waste away and die. This "fading kitten" syndrome is not uncommon and can be caused by a number of different factors, both infectious and noninfectious. Queens are very careful mothers and seldom smother a kitten, so if a dead baby is found in the nest check immediately for the cause. Chilling, starvation, and neglect are common causes for fading kittens. If the queen will not stay with her litter, and you have not provided a warm enough environment, the catlings will chill—a condition that leads to pneumonia. If you suspect this to be the cause of "unthriftiness" (the signs that indicate a kitten is becoming ill), immediately warm and feed the kittens and seek veterinary help as fast as possible, as the youngsters may need antibiotics or other treatment.

Starvation can occur if the owner is not alert. Examine to see if the queen has milk. She may spend many hours with her kittens trying desperately to provide them with milk but, if the well is dry, the kittens will starve. We once had a queen who, when she found she had no milk with which to nurse her kittens, came to us meowing and lamenting, then ran to the stairs leading up to the nursery, drawing us to the litter, where we found five empty kitty bellies. She performed this rite several times. All five kits survived, thanks to mama's intelligence and the immediate aid of their "godfathers."

The largest number of fading kitten deaths occurs because of bacterial infections. These infections can enter the kittens before birth via their mother, after birth through the raw umbilical cord, or by ingestion. The symptoms are the same: basically sick and dying kits. Only your veterinarian can save them.

Virus also plays a role in the fading kitten syndrome. Colostrum usually protects the kittens from distemper and respiratory viruses, but at times the protection can be low or altogether absent. Even your veterinarian will find it difficult to save a virus-infected kitten. Professional care and good nursing will provide the only chance these little creatures have. When "nursing" fading kittens, raise the temperature in their environment (to 90°–95° F.), and feed every two hours. Feeding should be done by the human nurse to make certain that the babies are receiving enough of the milk mix, as the kitten may have lost its ability to suckle. Vitamins are an important supplement. Your veterinarian will provide medications and vitamins.

Congenital Malformations

Every kitten should be checked for malformations at birth. Some malformations may not be discernible for many weeks, but others are immediately noticeable. Cleft palates are seen at birth; the cleft may extend to the lips, forming a facial disfigurement. Such kittens are difficult to raise as they cannot suckle, and the deformity will require surgical repair. The condition may be inherited, so they cannot be used in a breeding program.

Hernias are sometimes obvious, but can also be so small that they are not identifiable until the catlings are six to eight weeks of age. Umbilical hernias are the most common and are not dangerous if small, for they can easily be repaired surgically. If the veterinarian feels that the hernia is small enough, surgery can be delayed until the cat is taken to be neutered. The umbilical hernia can be traumatic or inherited, so cats exhibiting this anomaly should not be used for breeding. Inguinal hernias are not common in cats, but do occur occasionally. They can be so small that they are not seen, in female cats, until the queen becomes pregnant. Then the pressure of the full uterus opens the hernia and the uterus enters the inguinal canal. Repair is surgical, but if an organ is trapped at the time of discovery the condition may be classified as a surgical emergency.

Cryptorchidism—the retention of one or both testicles—has been discussed previously. It may be difficult to determine early, since the testicles are so tiny at birth, but it becomes obvious at about eight weeks of age.

Hydrocephalus

A hydrocephalous kitten has excessive amounts of cerebrospinal fluid, and exhibits an enlarged head. Often the breeder can feel fluid under the skin, and usually there is an open fontanelle (soft spot) on the top of the head. Open fontanelles can occur on newborn kittens that are unrelated to hydrocephalitis. If you find a kitten with a soft skull spot but a normal-sized head, you can be sure the bone will usually close in a few weeks and the kitten will be normal. Hydrocephalitis is inherited as a recessive genetic fault and is most often found in Persians and Himalayans. Such kittens can possess a head so large that normal birth is prevented and Caesarian section is necessary.

Hypoglycemia

This is a condition of low blood sugar that affects young kittens who are under great stress. The very young catling has poor storage of glycogen, which converts to sugar. As the kitten grows, his liver becomes a better warehouse of glycogen. But young kits that are ill or under stress may use up their blood sugar and deplete their liver storage more rapidly than the body can cope with. Stricken kittens will go into convulsions, followed by coma and death. This condition is one reason why we stress the addition of Karo syrup in the early weaning formula. Treatment is via injectable sugars, which your veterinarian can provide.

Rickets

Rickets is a nutritional disease of growing cats. The disease is caused by a lack of calcium in the growing bones, leading to malformation and fractures. Calcium is provided in milk and cat foods that contain supplements. Vitamins and mineral supplements also provide calcium. Cat foods usually contain whole fish or chickens ground into the preparation, and therefore provide ground bone as a source of natural calcium. But kittens must also have vitamin D to utilize the calcium. Vitamin D is provided by sunlight and vitamin supplements in the diet (fish liver oils are rich in vitamin D). The treatment for rickets is simply to supply these elements to kitty. But you must be careful, for too much vitamin D in the diet can be harmful because it interferes with calcium absorption. The worst diets to feed kittens are all-red-meat diets. Consult your veterinarian for the proper supplements to combat rickets.

CHAPTER 17

Immunity
and Vaccinations

The cat's most important weapon against infection is immunity or a resistance to disease. There are two factors involved in building immunity: the antigen and the antibody. The antigen is usually a foreign protein that, when introduced into the body, causes the body to react to eliminate the invasion. Microorganisms and their toxic products (poisons) are common antigens involved in disease. Other proteins are related to allergy, cancer, and many more physical antigen invasions that can also produce antibodies.

Antibodies are anti-disease units that have been built by the body to protect itself against antigens. Antibodies are constructed in the reticulo-endothelial system (netlike tissue) and are released to circulate in the body fluids. High amounts of antibodies are found in the bloodstream in association with serum globulin.

The antibodies destroy antigens in the following ways:

Antitoxins (antibodies) chemically neutralize toxins (antigens).
Agglutins cause bacterial cells (antigens) to clump and influence an inability for invasion.
Lysins dissolve antigen cells.
Precipitins precipitate and alter the antigen protein.
Opsonins stimulate the white blood cells to destroy antigens.

Immunity also occurs on the cellular level. The immune cell becomes able to block the antigen from entering and destroying the cell. Premunity is an immunity where a balance exists between the antigen and the antibody, halting disease while the antibody and antigen continue to co-exist. There are other immune reactions in the body that are yet to be discovered and classified.

The measurement of antibodies in the blood has been accomplished for many diseases, but it only indicates circulating immunity and does not include immunity in other body fluids or intercellular immunity. Circulating immunity is important to the pregnant queen, as these antibodies can cross the placenta, or be acquired by the kittens from suckling the first twenty-four-hour milk, the colostrum, and they build immunity for the newborn kitten during its first few months of life.

The amount of immunity a cat can build from antigen invasion depends upon the cat's hereditary ability, the blocking of antigen by antibodies already present, and the ability of the antigen to fight immunity. Each cat has an individual ability to produce immunity. Some felines can build only a limited immunity regardless of the antigen introduced. If it is a very low immunity, such cats often succumb to disease early in life. Some antigens are introduced in the presence of already existing antibodies and these antibodies attack and destroy the antigens. This reaction is fine if the antigen is a disease antigen, but sometimes a vaccine antigen is given (by injection) to a kitten who has antibodies received from his mother's colostrum. The introduced vaccine is destroyed, and shortly thereafter the maternal antibodies die out, leaving the kitten unprotected. This is why your veterinarian may recommend more than one visit during vaccination procedures. Finally, some antigens are very poor stimulators of immunity reaction, and may only cause a weak immunity or a very short-lived one.

No immunity is for a lifetime. All immunity begins to fade after the peak of antibody production is reached. Depending upon the amount of antibody production, the immunity may last for months or for years. If it is an immunity produced by vaccine, your veterinarian will recommend vaccine boosters to fit the situation.

With some vaccines the immunity is built up with two injections. This double vaccine procedure causes a multiple response known as anamnestic reaction. The second injection is administered a few weeks after the first vaccine, when antibody production is at its peak, and causes a higher and faster rise in antibodies that far exceeds the single value of either vaccination.

PRODUCTION OF IMMUNITY

The first line of defense the cat has against disease is its physical ability to destroy the antigen. These physical defenses basically include the unbroken skin, tears, and gastric juices, which either block or kill the antigen.

The second line of defense is immunity. There are several categories of immunity based upon how the immunity was produced.

Inherent Immunity

This is that immunity with which the feline was born. It is usually considered on the species level, although breed levels are also thought to exist. Very little investigation has been done on the breed level, but the clinical experience of veterinarians indicates that certain breeds of cats are more susceptible and clinically more debilitated by certain diseases. On a species level we can see, for instance, that cats have an inherent immunity to human measles, and therefore are unaffected by the presence of this virus, while humans are species-immune to cat distemper.

Acquired Immunity

More important in the immune picture is acquired immunity, which is divided into two categories: passive and active immunity.

Passive immunity is only temporary. It is produced by transferring the antibodies of one cat to another cat, with the purpose of protecting the second cat, who received the antibodies. *Natural passive immunity* is that which the newborn kitten receives from the queen's colostrum, which contains high amounts of antibodies. Transferred to the kitten, these antibodies protect him for the duration of the antibodies' life, which may be several weeks to several months. *Artificial passive immunity* is produced by extracting serum containing antibodies from an immune cat and concentrating the solution. This serum is then injected into the cat, causing a protection that will last for several weeks. Passive protection is only of a temporary nature, but it is a method that may be used in the contaminated or diseased feline as a protection against the disease. It is frequently utilized in distemper cases.

Active immunity is produced when an antigen enters the unprotected cat and it responds with antibody production. Active immunity is usually long-acting.

Natural infection will cause *natural active immunity*. If a cat can build enough immunity to survive the infection, the immunity is usually quite strong. Unfortunately, many animals die because they cannot build immunity rapidly enough to protect the body. This is in the pattern of nature's (and Darwin's) survival of the fittest.

The production of *active immunity by artificial means* is the method with which most people are familiar—the method called vaccination. There are six basic types of vaccination procedures, but not all are used for cats:

1. Extracts of organisms are accomplished through the use of ground, dried cells to obtain the extract. It is not used for cats.

2. Aggressins are utilized in some sheep and cattle diseases (anthrax, for instance).

3. Metabolic products, though not used in cats, are familiar to most people. For instance, toxins and toxoids are used to vaccinate human beings against tetanus (lockjaw).

4. The combination of virulent virus and immune serum was once used for protecting dogs against distemper, but this method has now become completely outmoded. The vaccination procedure was to introduce a full "hot" disease virus simultaneously with an injection of high-immune serum. The serum would theoretically protect the dog, and the body would be stimulated to produce antibodies by the presence of the antigen. In fact, the method was dangerous and often produced active disease.

5. Killed organisms is a method commonly used to protect cats against feline distemper and rabies. The virus is killed by heat or chemical treatment, and a standardized dose is injected into the cat. The disadvantage of this vaccine is that immune production is usually slow, taking two weeks to reach a protective level. Also, regardless of the age of the cat, two doses of distemper vaccine are often necessary. All rabies vaccinations consist of one dose (as long as the cat is over three months of age).

6. Vaccines containing live organisms are the vaccines of choice of most medical authorities. Some live vaccines are used in a sublethal dosage, administered in an abnormal area. Laryngotracheitis (a throat infection of poultry) is protected against by depositing the live vaccine in the cloaca of the chicken. This method is not used for felines. Attenuated live vaccines are commonly used in cats. The organism is grown on successive recipient tissues (that are abnormal for the organism) until it has lost its power to produce disease but retains its ability to create immunity. This method is commonly used to produce feline distemper, respiratory, and rabies vaccines. They produce an immunity in the animal more quickly than killed vaccines. Protection often begins in as little as seventy-two hours after introduction to the cat. Most live vaccines need only one dose if administered after the cat is nine to twelve weeks of age.

VACCINATIONS

The following is the vaccination program utilized by most veterinarians.

Panleukopenia (distemper)

Antiserum. Antiserum is used for passive protection only. Its sole true clinical usage in a vaccine program may be in young kittens in a cattery when confronted with a sudden and virulent outbreak of disease. This product given subcutaneously gives protection in hours, and when furnished intravenously offers almost immediate protection. It may also be used as a treatment for felines with suspected panleukopenia when the disease is diagnosed in its early stages. Because antiserum may interfere with vaccines, it is recommended that active immunity be delayed two to three weeks after antiserum is administered but, since the half-life of the product may be much shorter, there is doubt whether it will protect for the necessary length of time. Therefore antiserum, used in a program of normal vaccination, can result in a period of unknown protection longer and more dangerous than simple, active vaccination.

Inactivated vaccines. Killed (inactive) vaccines take at least six days before protection begins. The best inactive vaccines are of the tissue culture type. They should be started at about nine weeks of age, and a second vaccination is recommended after the kitten is twelve weeks old. Some inactive vaccines claim protection with one vaccine, but at less than twelve weeks of age maternal antibodies can cause vaccine interference. Since most immunologists recognize that live virus vaccines produce stronger immunities, it is best to booster the first killed vaccine in a month no matter at what age the vaccine was administered.

Modified live virus vaccine. Live virus vaccines contain a live virus treated so that it will act as an antigen but will not cause disease. These vaccines produce immunity in approximately seventy-two hours. If there has been a known disease contact, and if the feline has a live virus vaccination within a reasonable time limit, the vaccine can provide protection before the incubation period is over, thus preventing the disease. The speed of active immunity produced by live vaccines is their greatest advantage. Again, the kitten is given its initial vaccination when it is about nine weeks old, and a second vaccine injection is recommended between the ages of twelve and sixteen weeks. Kittens over twelve weeks of age need have only one vaccine shot. This vaccine cannot be furnished to pregnant queens as it can produce birth defects in their young. It can also be harmful to kittens that are under four weeks of age.

An annual booster should be given for all distemper vaccinations. Nobody really knows how long a feline's immunity lasts. For many years the prevalence of the "street virus"—the virus of the natural disease—gave most cats a continuing immunity. Since the disease itself is the best antigen, contact with it was akin to receiving a booster shot. But the house cat, who has no street contact, will always need boosters —much more so than will the wandering tom.

Today, however, the picture is changing. More cats have been vaccinated, and the amount of street virus has decreased so that veterinarians no longer see daily cases of distemper. Instead, the disease seems to appear in outbreaks depending on the area and the protective level of the local feline population. Without the natural protection from street virus, booster programs for all cats are even more important, and booster schedules should be followed. Your veterinarian will advise you on when to return for boosters.

Pneumonitis

A modified live virus vaccine is available for pneumonitis. It is not generally recommended by veterinarians unless their area has a particularly high incidence of disease because the antigen does *not* supply a truly effective antibody response.

Upper Respiratory Disease Complex

A combined vaccine is available against rhinotracheitis and calici virus, two of the most virulent and dangerous disease entities in the respiratory disease complex. The other viruses in this disease complex are much milder and, as yet, no vaccine has been developed against them (see Chapter 22, "Diseases of the Respiratory Tract").

Two types of vaccine are available. One is an intramuscular vaccine dispensed in one injection or in two injections approximately one month apart. Vaccination is started at about nine weeks of age. This vaccine has been available for several years and is acknowledged to be effective in blocking these diseases.

Another vaccine has reached the market. It is an oculonasal live virus vaccine. Drops of the vaccine are deposited in the eyes, nose, and mouth of the cat. It is claimed that while circulating antibodies are produced, local protection through exposure of the respiratory tract enhances the protection. Sneezing or coughing is caused in some animals treated by this method, but the symptoms pass after several days. Kittens can start vaccinations at eight to ten weeks of age, and should be given a second vaccine after they reach the age of twelve weeks. Cats that are vaccinated after twelve weeks need only one vaccine treatment.

Rabies

Modified live virus vaccines. Live vaccines furnish immunity in about thirty days. The immunity thus bestowed is strong and probably lasts two to three years. At present, federal laws and world health recommendations limit the advertised immunity to one year; therefore, annual boosters are necessary. Vaccination can be administered as early as three months, but in a nonrabies area it is often delayed until panleukopenia vaccination is completed at five to six months of age.

Inactive tissue culture vaccines. There are two types of inactive vaccines that can be utilized. One requires two injections given thirty days apart; the other is a single injection. Both are administered when the cat is from three to six months old.

Vaccine Failures

At times laymen attempt to vaccinate their own cats, usually sooner or later with a tragic result. Granted it is no great chore to lift the cat's skin and inject subcutaneously under it. But only a veterinarian is constantly aware of the newest procedures and scientific findings concerning vaccination programs. The veterinarian's inspection of a cat may determine the presence of disease that can make vaccination contra-indicated at the time. Laymen may also purchase their vaccines from unethical sources and acquire defective vaccines.

The major causes of vaccine failure are listed below:

1. Vaccine spoilage: Improper storage, heat, premixing, out-of-date vaccine, or even exposure to light can completely destroy the antigen.
2. A cat is already infected with the disease before immunization and before the vaccine has a chance to build antibodies.
3. A queen mother has bestowed enough antibodies to block or destroy vaccines given too early in life.
4. Chemical sterilizing of the syringe used or, at times, of the cat's skin, can kill a live vaccine. Only disposable syringes should be used.
5. A cat may have an inherent inability to build antibodies.

Your veterinarian can protect you against failure from the first four causes. Kittens that are embraced by the fifth category are rare and usually succumb to the disease early in life. When purchasing a kitten, be sure to inquire what diseases it has been vaccinated against, what products were used, and the name and address of the veterinarian who administered the vaccine. The last is most important, for your veterinarian can confirm by phone the first two questions of vaccination history.

Most important of all is to remember that the key to feline health is prevention, not attempting to salvage the health of a cat that is already sick.

CHAPTER 18

Infectious Viral Diseases

A virus is any of a large group of submicroscopic infective agents, smaller than common microorganisms, that require living cells for multiplication and growth, and frequently attack the nerve tissue, which is then easily invaded by many types of bacteria. Secondary infections can be treated by the newest "wonder" drugs, but there is no known medication that is effective against the virulent viruses themselves.

Feline Panleukopenia (distemper, infectious enteritis)

Panleukopenia is a contagious disease of felines caused by a DNA-type virus. The disease not only affects domestic and exotic cats but also raccoons, coati mundis, ring-tailed cats (cacomistles), minks, and ferrets. The virus may persist in the environment, or a host cat, for many months (a host cat is a nonsymptomatic carrier to healthy felines).

The diseased puss is usually dehydrated and depressed. Fever ranges from 103 to 105 degrees Fahrenheit, and vomiting and diarrhea are common symptoms. Usually the cat will refuse all offered food.

The most commonly affected cats are the younger ones under two years of age. The young kitten of under eight weeks of age has only approximately a 25 percent recovery rate. As the age of an infected cat increases the prognosis brightens, so that cats over four months of age show a 50 percent or better chance of survival. The disease is not limited to the young, though; any susceptible cat can get distemper. Vaccination or natural immunity will *not* last for life, and as immunity fades the older cat becomes vulnerable to the disease.

Pathologically the virus affects the bone marrow, the mucosal cells of the intestines, and the lymphatic system. The virus is present in everything the animal discharges: the feces, vomit, urine, and saliva. The route of infection is by ingestion. Blood counts usually show a depletion in white blood cells involving both the lymphocytes and the neutrophils (white blood cells produced in the infected lymphatic system and bone marrow). Because of the effect upon the marrow, anemia (red blood cell loss) usually occurs after about five to seven days.

The incubation period is two to nine days following contamination. If it is known that a cat has had contact with the virus, rapidly taken preventative and treatment methods may abort or lessen the disease. Diagnosis is arrived at from the clinical picture and laboratory findings. There is no specific test for panleukopenia. Postmortem is the only positive way of definitely diagnosing the disease, and is important only where multiple cats are involved, as it is information acquired after the fact of death.

Distemper is often complicated by secondary infection. With its resistance weakened, the sick cat is very susceptible to generalized bacterial infection, or concurrent viral infection of a different disease, especially the upper respiratory viruses.

Treatment involves both direct and supportive measures. Direct treatment includes immediate vaccination of contaminated but clinically well felines. Cats whose condition indicates that they have just become stricken with the disease derive the most help from whole blood transfusions. If there is no whole blood available, serum derived from immune cats is most helpful. As supportive treatment, intravenous fluids combat dehydration and restore physiological balance. Antibiotics are administered to halt secondary infections, and a broad spectrum of vitamins is recommended. Vitamin B complex with iron is particularly helpful in the blood-rebuilding processes. The cat with panleukopenia will often relinquish its will to live, so affection, hand-feeding, and using heating pads are extremely important nursing procedures.

Vaccination is the key to the prevention of this lethal disease. Vaccines should begin to be administered at about eight weeks of age. Both killed and modified vaccines are available, and boosters are available on a yearly basis.

Feline Respiratory Disease Complex

Perhaps the most common illnesses seen in felines are the upper respiratory diseases. The complex presents clinical diseases that vary from a simple "head cold" type to a very deadly illness. Many owners, seeing the symptoms, think their pet has a common cold and watch it diligently for several days before seeking help. By this time dehydration and secondary infection have turned a controllable situation into a sad and deadly ending. Cats are not susceptible to the human "cold," and veterinary advice should be sought immediately when upper respiratory disease symptoms appear in order to assure a happy outcome.

Many cats are carriers of the causative agents without having any clinical symptoms. Of course, all really sick cats will readily spread the disease, and some recovered felines shed disease for many weeks.

The signs of the disease vary from a mild conjunctivitis (redness of the eyes with discharge) to ocular nasal discharge accompanied by nasal and oral ulcers. Pneumonia can follow several of the complex infections. Occasionally, one of the viruses (FVR—herpes virus) can produce encephalitis.

For clarity it is best to classify the feline respiratory diseases in the table form that can be found on the following page. The chart is a simple method of characterizing the pure diseases, but often a cat may acquire more than one URD (upper respiratory disease) infection at a time. Furthermore, the bacterial secondary infections in the final column often attack cats with other URD, making the clinical case more virulent and the mortality rate higher.

Diagnosis on clinical examination is difficult, especially early in the disease. Often, as it progresses, the character and course of the illness in the face of difficult diagnosis will inspire some veterinarians to allocate a label, right or wrong, to the disease. Even the most expert practitioner can be deluded when confronted with this confusing complex. More often we can diagnose by hindsight, after the disease is over. Bacteria can be grown for identification, and special tissue culture methods are available for virus identity; but the latter procedures are expensive and time-consuming, and only of definite value in a cattery where a chronic problem exists.

Basically, all the diseases of this complex are treated in a like manner. Good supportive treatment is necessary, and warmth, good food, and fluids are essential to prevent dehydration and general debility. Wide-range antibiotics are administered continually: they will not kill viruses but will help control and eliminate secondary infections. Antibiotics will also eliminate chlamydia, the agent of pneumonitis. Without the antibiotics, many FVR- and FCV-stricken cats will contract secondary infections leading to a long and debilitating disease or a deadly pneumonia. At times hyperimmune serums are used to attempt to slay the virus or to limit its range.

Today, the control of the most serious of these diseases is through vaccination. FVR and FCV can be vaccinated against simply and inexpensively. The vaccines, although new, produce a high rate of immunity. Pneumonitis, a milder disease, can be vaccinated against, but the vaccine provides a lower protection rate and is not very long-lasting so it is seldom recommended by veterinarians except for known group problems. Cattery owners who constantly attend cat shows where disease contact may be high often take advantage of pneumonitis vaccine.

Feline Respiratory Disease Complex Chart

	Rhinotracheitis (FVR)	Caliciviral Disease (FCV)	Reovirus (FRI)	Pneumonitis (FPN)	Bacterial
Cause	Herpes virus	Calicivirus	Reovirus	Chlamydia psittou	Mycoplasma, staph pyogens, strep pyogens, *Pasturella multicida*
Incubation	2–10 days	1–9 days	4–19 days	6–15 days	Basically secondary to other URD
Severity	Severe	Moderate	Mild	Mild	Mild
Signs:					
Tearing	Yes	Yes	Yes	—	—
Sneezing	Yes	Yes	—	—	—
Mouth ulcer	Yes	Yes	—	—	—
Conjunctivitis	Yes	Yes	—	Yes	Yes
Coughing	Yes	—	—	Sometimes	Sometimes
Nasal discharge	Yes, serous to purulent	Yes, serous	—	Often	Rare to purulent
Convulsions	Yes	—	—	—	—
Course	2–4 weeks	1–2 weeks	1–3 weeks	1 week to chronic	1 week to chronic
Morbidity	High	High	50%	Variable	Variable
Mortality	High in young and old	Variable	Low	Low	Low

Finally, scientists have identified other viruses that attack the upper respiratory area of other species of animals and birds. It is reasonable to assume that they might yet identify some of these viruses as affecting our felines, to further confound our confused URD scene.

Feline Leukemia

An infectious, cancerous disease of the lymphatic system, feline leukemia is caused by an oncornavirus (a division of viruses). This virus was initially discovered in 1964, and represented an important breakthrough in cancer research as only a very few cancers have been found to have a specific causative infectious organism. Feline leukemia closely mimics the disease in humans, providing an excellent subject for the study of viral cancers in man.

Clinically, several syndromes (a combination of symptoms resulting from a single cause) of cancer may be present. The thoracic form produces cancer of the chest. The thymus (a gland in the chest, present only in young animals) and the lymph nodes may be infected. The gland can grow to occupy much of the chest cavity, limiting expansion of the lungs and causing breathing to become labored. Lymph nodes also enlarge, but do not usually occupy as much room so the breathing is unaffected, but the cat gradually becomes emaciated. Finally, fluids are produced that can eventually fill the chest cavity and compress the lungs, causing labored breathing, followed shortly by the cat's demise.

The abdominal form will involve the liver, kidneys, spleen, lymph nodes, and mesentery (the fold of the peritoneum attaching the intestine to the posterior abdominal wall). The feline becomes a "poor doer," inappetant (lacking appetite), with a dry coat and weight loss. It may fade and die, or may die as a result of organ damage, such as kidney failure due to cancer replacement of normal kidney tissue.

The alimentary form of feline leukemia (FeLV) involves the lymph nodes and the intestinal tract. Finally, there are some unusual forms such as brain, spinal cord, and skin leukemia. This last group affects cats only rarely.

Diagnosis of FeLV is made by two basic methods: (1) Coupling the clinical findings with positive cancer cells, either in blood smears or smears from the chest, bone marrow, or abdominal area; (2) coupling the clinical signs with a positive blood test for the presence of virus. This second method is done by only a few laboratories throughout the country, and will result in a delay in diagnosis of about one week, including handling and testing. A new and highly sensitive test has just been released which will be available either at local veterinary hospitals or at laboratories.

Many positive cats may harbor the disease from birth, but do not become clinically ill for many years. Cats known to be infected at parturition will sometimes not exhibit clinical signs of FeLV for as long as eleven years. The average age for infection break is at about four years, but the peak time is at two years of age.

As FeLV is a disease involving the immune system, the reader should check back to the general discussions on immunology (Chapter 17) for a more intimate understanding of procedures, immunities, and vaccinations.

It is important to realize that there are four immunologically different groups of felines involved in this disease:

1. The sick cat who has the virus present and can infect other cats.

2. The well cat who has virus present and who will eventually become ill and die of FeLV or who, because the virus is immunosuppressant, will expire of other related diseases (infectious peritonitis, for instance). Meanwhile, until the cat becomes obviously ill, it will contaminate the environment and cause infection of other cats.

3. The cat who can build an immunity to the disease but harbors the virus and sheds it. This is the most dangerous cat because it will remain clinically healthy all its life, but will transmit the disease to other cats.

4. The completely immune cat, who will not become a harborer of the virus for transmission or fall victim to the disease. This is the ideal animal. Approximately 44 percent of all cats fall into this category.

Only infectious transmission of the disease has been proven. There has been speculation that inherited transmission is possible, but there is no substantial proof to support the theory. Cats thought to have been infected by inheritance have actually received the virus from their infected mother across the placenta while they were still *in utero*. Infected but non-clinically ill queens may reabsorb or abort fetuses, and surviving fetuses are often born infected. Older kittens and cats become infected through communal feeding and watering dishes, litter pans, bites, fleas (transport hosts), and grooming tools.

In the laboratory the virus will grow in many types of cells, including human cells. Unfortunately, this has led to periodic articles in the press that have alarmed many cat owners. The facts at the present time indicate that FeLV cats cannot transfer the disease to humans. Owners of catteries with a high incidence of FeLV, veterinarians, and persons with cancer living in households with infected cats have all been tested for FeLV virus, and all tests have been negative. This research is constantly being updated. Because the virus will grow in human cells *in the laboratory* it has to be listed as a possible hazard by the cancer institutes but, we repeat, there has never been a known case of human FeLV virus cancer.

Controlling the disease is most important in multiple-cat households. It is obvious that any cat sick and suffering with the disease should be immediately euthanized for humane reasons. In single-cat households, only about 6 percent (overall) of felines are infected, so unless there is evidence of disease, routine testing is not recommended. But in multiple-cat households, if disease occurs, all cats should be tested. Only by the removal of disease-positive cats can the spread of the affliction finally be stopped. If there are "positive" cats and they are removed, a repeat test should be made at three-month intervals until all remaining cats are negative.

In catteries all cats should be tested and "positive" cats removed (as in the multiple-cat household) until the cattery tests negative. Once this has been accomplished, any cats that are breeders, if the cattery is not a closed breeding establishment and the queens are brought to other catteries for breedings, should be tested three months following exposure. Meanwhile, the queen should be isolated until tested. Any cats that are known to have been exposed should be tested also, and all cats who could be exposed to FeLV—such as stud cats servicing outside queens, and cats regularly entered in shows—should be tested yearly. At the present time, only such strict methods can keep a cattery FeLV-negative to the disease.

FeLV vaccines are just around the scientific corner. As you read this, both a killed and a modified live vaccine are being tested. Most likely the killed vaccine will be available first, as safety testing of a killed vaccine is much less time-consuming than the testing of a live vaccine. When vaccines do become available, we urge every cat owner to take advantage of them with alacrity. Vaccination and boostering will soon make the dreaded FeLV a disease of the past.

Fibrosarcoma Virus

Similar to FeLV virus, and probably a mutation of FeLV, the fibrosarcoma virus causes tumors, usually on the skin of felines. The tumors so formed metastasize (transfer) to the central organs. The virus constitutes a *possible* danger to ailurophiles, although no known transfer to humans has been recorded. It has been established that the virus can be transferred to canines and cause a fibrosarcoma in that species. Because of the cross-species transfer we must consider this disease potentially dangerous.

The lesions vary from very small, hard growths to large single tumors. Any skin growth should be diagnosed by a veterinarian. Fortunately the disease is rare, and one hopes that when FeLV vaccine is available, it will establish a cross immunity that will protect cats against this mutant virus as well as FeLV.

Infectious Feline Peritonitis (IFP)

IFP is a lethal, slowly progressive disease of felines, with a mortality ratio of close to 100 percent. The disease was initially recognized in 1963, and all subsequent research indicates that a virus is the causative agent. Though the disease has been transferred via infectious material taken from sick cats, the virus itself has not been isolated. Incubation of the disease can be up to five months. Not all cats contacted become infected. Actually, the method by which the infection spreads is not known at this time. But we do know that 50 percent of the cats that have died of IFP have also been infected with feline leukemia virus.

It may be possible that immunosuppressive disease (disease that lowers the general ability of the animal's body to produce immune bodies—antibodies—to fight infection), such as feline leukemia, greatly influences the cat's ability to withstand infection. This disease occurs mainly in young cats, although all ages of felines have been infected. Since we have not yet isolated the virus we do not know if carrier states, or subclinical infection, exist, or to what degree it is prevalent.

Clinically, the disease exhibits several facets. In the classical form the cat becomes slowly ill, its appetite varies, gradually becoming poorer until it is completely nil. Puss becomes listless, dehydrated, and emaciated, and usually displays a constant fever of 103 to 105 degrees Fahrenheit. During this period an exudate (discharge) builds in the abdominal cavity and occasionally in the chest cavity. Most cats survive for about a month, but there are some cases where the stricken cat has survived for more than three months.

Some cats exhibit a nonexudative form of the disease. Affected cats also show listlessness, lack of appetite, dehydration, and fever, but they may display eye lesions too, and nervous-system signs including muscle weakness, disorientation, and convulsions.

Diagnosis can be exceedingly difficult early in the disease when the symptoms are too general, and blood counts and blood chemistry tests are nonspecific. It may be possible to feel enlarged lymph nodes in the abdominal cavity, or to determine abdominal pain on palpation. However these signs, if present, could also indicate any infection draining to the lymph nodes, or feline leukemia, so the symptoms are not truly diagnostic. As the disease progresses and proves unresponsive to antibiotics and other therapy, the possible diagnosis of IFP becomes relevant. Once fluid builds in the abdominal cavity, the diagnosis becomes more definitive. Samples of fluid taken by hyperdermic tap will then confirm the presence of the disease.

There is a new immunological test available to detect the disease, but its accuracy has been challanged. It is the authors' opinion that positive results with this test, coupled with symptoms related to the disease, cannot be ignored.

Treatment is unsatisfactory. There have been reports that three cats survived the disease when treated with Tylocine and prednisolone (steroids), administered over a long period. These results have not been successfully repeated, and the course of the disease in other felines has remained unaltered by these drugs. It is possible that the three cats mentioned were self-cured by building immune bodies in the presence of the disease, but with the life cycle of the virus being unknown, this is mere speculation. Sick cats in multiple-cat households should be isolated and great care taken concerning handling and sanitation. Death is almost inevitable, and when suffering is apparent poor puss should be euthanized.

Rabies

Rabies is a dreaded viral disease affecting the central nervous system and then the brain of all warm-blooded animals. Once symptoms begin, death is the inevitable outcome, and there is no reprieve. Because this disease is a public health problem, state health departments and their programs have done much to help control or eliminate the disease in all pets. In natural surroundings the reservoir of infection is in the creatures of the wild, especially bats, foxes, skunks, and raccoons.

The virus, which is present in the infected animal's saliva, enters the victim usually via a bite wound. The virus then travels along the nerve trunk to the brain, after which the symptoms of this terrible disease develop.

Incubation time is usually two to four weeks, but can be as long as six months. The virus then courses along the nerves from the brain to the saliva a few days before the onset of clinical symptoms. Since the animal is infectious for only a few days before the beginning of clinical disease, observation of any animal that inflicts a bite upon another animal is necessary for ten days. If the offending creature dies during the ten-day observation period, its brain must be examined. Many states have definite laws pertinent to bite cases; if you or your pet are involved in a bite incident, check immediately with your veterinarian or the public health department to determine what course of action should be taken.

The first clinical sign of rabies is a behavioral change (the "anxiety" stage). Usually, the diseased feline will quit eating and drinking and seek a dark, quiet place to hide. Excessive salivation may or may not occur. Sometimes the cat will exhibit an increased sexual drive. It may wander blindly while seeking a retreat and will bite anything it contacts. After a few days, the cat begins to resent handling and will progress to the paralytic or the "furious" form.

In the paralytic stage the muscles of the head become paralyzed, the jaw droops, and salivation increases; the paralysis extends over the body area and the cat descends into a coma leading to death. Hydrophobia, another name for rabies, means "fear of water"—the appellation used because stricken animals develop paralysis of the throat and cannot drink.

The "furious" form is often called the "mad animal" condition. In this state the cat is aggressive, the expression is one of tenseness and anxiety, and the animal will attack moving objects, exhibiting no evidence of fear. Animals in the grip of this form of the malady are the vicious and deadly roamers that attack other creatures, even humans. As the condition progresses, incoordination and convulsions take place, followed by death.

There is no known cure for rabies, but this dread disease can be *prevented* by vaccination, and this method is recommended for any cat that is allowed its freedom outdoors and unattended.

Pseudorabies

This is also a fatal viral disease, occurring in cattle, pigs, sheep, rats, dogs, and cats. The disease was discovered by Aladár Aujeszky, a Hungarian physician and veterinarian, almost one hundred years ago. Dr. Aujeszky called the disease "Mad Itch," because the infected animals exhibited a severe skin irritation that caused them to lick and scratch the afflicted area incessantly. The virus is particularly virulent and will remain in the environment for more than a month. Strong disinfectants are needed to cleanse the surroundings.

The disease occurs worldwide. In the United States it is mainly a problem among swine in the Midwestern states, but it has been reported in most states throughout the country. Cats appear to be one of the less susceptible species.

The virus apparently travels via the nerves to the central nervous system. Virus has been found in the brain, spinal cord, skin, lungs, and several of the internal organs of stricken animals. The organism is shed in nasal secretions, urine, and blood. The incubation period of the disease is about one week, and once clinical signs begin death occurs within twenty-four to thirty-six hours.

The first signs of the disease are a change in the behavioral pattern of the diseased animal. The cat becomes depressed, hides, and usually cries almost as though in pain. Its appetite disappears completely, and occasionally vomiting occurs. The pharynx then becomes paralyzed, salivation becomes pronounced, and the cat is unable to swallow.

Unless death occurs very early, a pruritis ensues: the cat's skin irritation is so severe that it rubs, scratches, and licks, causing a rather large lesion. The temperature remains normal, but may become sub-normal before death. In severe cases, terminal convulsions occur. Diagnosis is based upon clinical signs and confirmed by virus isolation.

CHAPTER 19

Bacterial Diseases

Bacteria, popularly called germs, are a class (schizomycetes) of microscopic, non-spore-forming, morphologically simple, single-celled or noncellular, non-green vegetable organisms that can produce, through fermentation and putrefaction, a host of dangerous diseases with a high mortality rate in all living things. There are many varieties; most are nonpathogenic, and many are useful. Bacteria are classified in three basic groups: spiral-shaped, rod-shaped, and dot-shaped. Most pathogenic bacteria that invade the body produce toxins. Bacteria reproduce every twenty minutes. Luckily, other bacteria are waiting to feed upon them.

Feline Abscesses

Abscesses must be considered a disease rather than a "condition" of cats as they are probably numerically second to ear mites as a clinical entity. Because most abscesses are caused by bites, particularly bites from other felines, it follows that the roaming tom cat is most commonly affected.

The infections are caused by a variety of bacteria, some from the attacker's mouth and some carried inward from the skin of the victim. Cat and rodent teeth, which are sharp and puncture rather than tear, cause most abscesses. The attacker's teeth puncture the skin, which seals over within twenty-four hours, trapping the infectious germs inside where they multiply and create a purulent infection. The bacteria most commonly found are staphylococci, streptococci, and enterobacteria, or mixtures of these bacteria.

Often the bite the cat receives does not completely pierce the skin and a cellulitis, or locally infected area of the skin, occurs. The skin will weep with an infected discharge and become hairless, red, and raw. If the bite punctures the skin to the subcutaneous area, a pocket of pus forms, which we call an abscess. The pocket is walled off by the body, so as it builds, it will seek the surface and rupture through. If unattended, puss can slough off a large area of skin that has been destroyed by the infection beneath it. Some abscesses are incompletely walled off and will migrate and spread under the skin, causing extensive damage to subcuticular tissue and skin.

Treatment is uncomplicated if detected early. If you discover a bite on your cat that is less than twenty-four hours old, cleansing deeply with hydrogen peroxide and applying hot packs on the area will usually aid in the healing process.

Cellulitis (a diffuse inflammatory process within solid tissue) is treated with hot packs and appropriate antibiotics.

Abscesses usually must be lanced and drained. If the abscess is extensive, rubber drains may have to be put in place for several days. Keep the surgical area open and draining. Hot packs are also often used to keep the circulation open and the surgical area draining. Usually, local and oral antibiotics are recommended to control the infection.

Tetanus (lockjaw)

A specific bacterial disease affecting all animals, tetanus is caused by *Clostridium tetani.* The disease is relatively rare in cats. Tetanus develops in puncture wounds, because open wounds do not usually support the infection, which grows best in an environment free of oxygen.

Tetanus causes muscle spasms. The cat initially stumbles and moves stiffly; then the spasms increase and the animal is unable to stand. The body becomes rigid with tetanied muscles. Noise provokes the spasms, and finally the cat dies when the respiratory muscles become involved and fail to function.

Treatment is often futile after symptoms are advanced, but early detection may allow a successful conclusion. Antitoxins are used to destroy the toxins of the bacteria. Penicillin is specific to destroy *Clostridium tetani.* The wound should be opened and flushed with hydrogen peroxide.

Tuberculosis

This bacterial disease is also rare in cats. Felines generally are infected by the bovine type of TB from ingesting infected milk. With the control of tuberculosis in cattle in this country, the chance of transfer becomes less and less likely.

Most lesions occur in the gastrointestinal tract because the route of infection is via ingestion, but the more familiar lung lesions can also occur. Infected animals should not be treated. The condition is a significant public health problem, and recovery is most improbable, so the infected cat should be put down.

Pyothorax, pyometritis, and pyocystitis are bacterial conditions discussed in the chapters devoted to the systems in which they occur.

Infectious Feline Anemia (IFA)

IFA is caused by *Haemobartonellosis felis,* a species of organism classified as rickettsia. *Haemobartonella* is an obligatory parasite of the feline's red blood cell. It is seen under the microscope as small, round dots in the red blood cell. Incubation is from three days to several months when a clinical infection arises, but many cats can be carriers exhibiting little or no clinical signs. Under severe stress conditions, the carrier cat can exhibit a clinical case. The disease is also often seen when other infection is present, the new infection constituting the pressure necessary to overcome the balanced condition of cat-and-parasite premunity. The main pathology is the destruction of red blood cells, resulting in a greatly reduced red blood cell count. This condition may or may not be accompanied by a reduced white blood cell count. The parasite may not be visible in every blood smear, so, if suspected, your veterinarian may do a series of smears over a period of several days.

Transmission is by injection or oral routes. Cat fights are probably a main cause of IFA. It is possible that fleas, mites, and other insects are vectors (carriers), but while this has been suggested by many writers, it has never been proven. Intrauterine (within the uterus) infection can also occur.

The anemic cat is usually depressed and weak; it has stopped eating and lost weight, and exhibits pale mucous membranes. The urine is usually dark or even blood-tinged.

More than half the felines with uncomplicated infections will recover on their own and never exhibit the clinical picture drawn here. But many of these recovered cats become carriers. Once a true clinical picture is seen, treatment must be instituted and followed through to completion.

If the cat's blood level is below 50 percent before chemotherapy begins, it is often necessary to give transfusions to strengthen the patient. There are two recommended treatments for IFA. The first is wide-range antibiotic therapy with either tetracycline or chloramphenicol for about three weeks. The second, more effective treatment utilizes intravenous arsenic. This has been shown to produce true cures, while the former treatment seems to reduce the parasite and support the cat while it recovers. Only about 50 percent of all cats respond to antibiotic therapy. Many veterinarians combine therapies by giving the intravenous arsenic first, and then following it with antibiotics for three weeks.

Mycotic Diseases (systemic)

Most systemic mycoses (fungi) occur in hot and tropical areas, but in recent years more and more cases have been identified in all sections of North America. The importance of proper diagnosis becomes increasingly apparent to the reader with the realization that these infections can be spread to humans. In the animal kingdom, fortunately, cats have a low incidence of the infection.

Cryptococcosis

Caused by the fungus *Cryptococcus neoformans,* cryptococcosis is the most common of feline mycotic infections. Granulomatous (inflamed-tissue) lesions occur mainly in the lungs and brain, but most body systems can be infected. The lesions are raised, thickened growths of tissue and fungus, resembling tumors, or TB-like lesions.

The most common signals of the infection are nasal discharge and forced breathing. Incoordination results from central nervous system lesions, and blindness can occur, also due to lesions. The patient may live for several years with chronic, recurring attacks of illness.

Diagnosis is by direct identification of the fungus on slides made from the lesions or discharges from the lesions. Treatment in generalized cases is usually futile, and because of the public health hazard created by the infection, diseased cats should not be kept as household pets or in a cattery population. Recently, amphotericin B and Fluorocystein have been successfully utilized on limited cases.

Nocardiosis

The *Nocardia* fungus causes a nodular disease of the lungs. Care must be taken to differentiate this fungus from TB. Skin lesions can also appear. The condition is rare, but two species of *Nocardia* have been incriminated; *N. asterodex* and *N. brasiliensis.*

Coughing, heavy breathing, and enlarged lymph nodes are associated with a long-term, chronic illness and are the most prominent clinical signs.

Once again, treatment is futile and the animal, as a host, is dangerous to its owner.

Blastomycosis

Another chronic systemic and cutaneous disease in which suppurative granulomatous lesions are found in lungs, bones, and skin. The disease is found in the North American continent only. The granulomatous lesions are found in the skin, but mainly in the lungs, and the lung infection leads to the typical chronic coughing seen in other systemic fungi diseases.

Most cases are fatal, just as they are with the other systemic fungi diseases. The disease is exceedingly dangerous to man, so treatment should be discouraged and the recipient animal put down.

Maduromycotic Mycetomas

Several higher fungi cause granulomatous lesions of the skin in cats and other animals. These MM fungi can be found in the soil and on plants.

Most telltale lesions occur on the legs of the cat: the feet become swollen with suppurative ulcerated lesions.

Treatment is usually unsuccessful, but attempts are made with radiation therapy and surgical excision. Some of the antifungal drugs may also be helpful, but the cure is generally only temporary, with recurrences for many years.

Toxoplasmosis

Due to its public health aspects, toxoplasmosis is a disease that has received much publicity, and this publicity has been detrimental to the pet cat.

The disease (systemic protozoal disease) is caused by a protozoan, *Toxoplasma gondii,* and is widespread in nature, affecting all species of animals and birds. The protozoan lives inside the cells of the organs infected.

The clinical expression of the disease is rare compared to the actual infection rate. Serological testing for antibodies has shown that infection rates taken throughout the United States in different species, including birds, rats, sheep, dogs, and cats, vary from 10 to 60 percent. However, clinically ill animals are rare. In Hawaii, human infection rates (serologically tested) varied from 5 to 20 percent or more, depending upon the group tested. Yet during the same period the tests were made, only three clinical cases were identified.

The infected cat can show various clinical signs, and the symptoms reflect the organs infected. Granulomatous lesions caused by toxoplasia can develop in the lungs, liver, brain, intestines, and other organs. Common disease signs are pneumonia, encephalitis, diarrhea, and jaundice from hepatitis. Ocular drainage is common. Eye lesions of iritis (inflammation of the iris, the colored membrane around the lens), and retinitis (inflammation of the retina, the innermost area of the eye that transfers light images into nerve impulses to the brain), with generalized disease, are clues to diagnosis. Positive diagnosis is based on blood tests. The immune response is measured, and a repeat test is done a week later. If antibodies are rising rapidly, there is evidence of the presence of disease.

Occasionally, the protozoan can be found in blood cells or intestinal cells. Usually, the diagnosis is made from postmortem sections. Some cats exhibit only diarrhea as a symptom; but such cats, though they may be clinically healthy, might shed oocysts that can infect humans. These oocysts are not infectious for at least twenty-four hours after leaving the cat's body. This stage lasts about two weeks. Since clinical infection in humans is rare, the main danger lies in transplacental infection, causing birth defects in unborn children. We advise all women who are pregnant not to change the contents of the litter box, but instead to leave this chore to their husbands (a suggestion that is readily acceptable to wives—pregnant or not). The litter box should be cleaned at least once a day when there is a pregnant woman in the house, and the tray scrubbed with very hot or boiling water and antiseptics. We also advise pregnant women to wear gloves when gardening, for their garden may be a wandering tom's bathroom.

No other animal is infectious by stool contamination. The only way to catch toxoplasmosis from other clinically infected species of animals, and from non-disease-shedding cats, is by ingestion of their raw meat.

Treatment can be undertaken by giving sulfadiazine and pyrimethamine for about two weeks, during which time antibody production increases until a state of premunity exists, temporarily controlling the toxoplasmosis, which will often recur in the body indefinitely.

CHAPTER 20

External and Internal Parasites

Parasites are organisms that live in or on other organisms (known as the host), from which they obtain their nourishment.

Throughout your cat's lifetime it may have problems with internal parasites. Most commonly referred to as "worms," these parasites may cause diarrhea, vomiting, depression, loss of appetite, loss of weight, and general illness. Not all parasites are found in the bowel, and not all parasites are worms. We will first describe those parasites that are either truly worms or are present in the cat's bowel.

Throughout the ages, superstition and folk medicine have revolved more around worms than any other feline disease problem. People of different ethnic backgrounds have favorite herbal or home remedy worm expellants. Garlic is an often recommended eliminator of worms by peoples of Mediterranean races, but only an outrageous breath and the loss of a very few adult roundworms is the end result; the major portion of the worm population within the cat remains unaffected. Tobacco, another home remedy for worm eradication, is better smoked (or not smoked according, to the U.S. Surgeon General), and bracken tea is better consumed at teatime and served with a crumpet or a tart than used to attempt to worm puss.

The source of worms seems to be another mysterious subject to cat owners. It defies common sense to believe that your cat's worm infestation is due to the same milk or candy that you or your children have consumed, yet many people unthinkingly accept such unfounded theory. For a worm to come from candy, it would necessarily have to be created spontaneously—and the spontaneous generation theory became outmoded at the time of Charles Darwin. If the candy *was* wormy, and you ate it, we suggest an immediate appointment with your oculist, or your psychiatrist . . . or whatever!

Infection with worm parasites may occur in many ways: the body can become infested by ingestion of worm eggs, by penetration through the skin, or through prenatal infection from the mother queen. In many cases the infection is directly passed from cat to cat. But often the parasite's life cycle takes place in another animal or insect, making cat-to-cat transmission impossible.

EXTERNAL PARASITES

Fleas

The dictionary tells us that these most common ectoparasites of cats are any of numerous small, wingless, blood-sucking insects of the order *Siphonaptera,* parasitic upon mammals and birds.

These tiny vampires are not host-specific, and they will move from cat to dog and even to humans. Cat fleas carry tapeworms to felines, and may be vectors (carriers) of other diseases. Human fleas are known to carry bubonic plague, tularemia, and typhus. Cat fleas also cause damage to the host's hair coat and skin. Allergy to flea saliva is common, causing severe inflammation of the skin; subsequent scratching will open wounds that lead to skin infection. Heavy infestations of fleas in young cats can result in anemia due to blood loss.

The cat is usually infected by two species of fleas: *Ctenocephalus felis* and *C. canis.* Female fleas lay eggs on the cat, and in floor and furniture crevices. The female flea can live for two hundred days and lay about five hundred eggs during that time. Fleas are most active in temperatures of over 65 degrees Fahrenheit, coupled with high humidity. The eggs hatch a larva in two to ten days, and it is this form that feeds on fecal matter and blood from the adult fleas, and may ingest eggs of *Dipylidium* (a genus of tapeworm) from the hair of the cat. The flea then becomes a pupa and finally an adult flea. The process of becoming an adult usually takes about three weeks but may be delayed by low temperatures for up to one year.

Flea control is the responsibility of the owner. Both the cat and the premises must be treated. It is a continuous chore, as can readily be seen by studying the life cycle of the flea. Many of the dips and sprays available for canines are toxic to cats and should definitely *not* be used. Powders, sprays, and dips should be used only according to label directions, and only if manufactured particularly for felines. Most of these products have a fairly lasting effect on the cat, and should be used from five to seven days apart.

Flea collars will give lasting protection without constant owner involvement. Since the collar causes a cloud of medication around the cat, it does not keep fleas off the cat, but kills them during the cat's periods of resting and sleeping. Flea collars are generally not recommended for long-haired cats, who can have severe toxic reactions to them. Occasionally any cat, short- or long-haired, may indicate a local allergic reaction to the flea collar by developing a rash at contact points around the neck. When this happens, remove the collar immediately and use other flea control methods. Flea control products must be fresh to be efficacious; many over-the-counter brands do not last the advertised time, so check for dating. Good products are always coded and dated. If you are not having success with the flea control program you have initiated, go to your veterinarian and yell, "Help!"

Stronger products of flea elimination should be used on inanimate objects in the home that have become infested with fleas. Veterinarians, pet suppliers, and exterminators can supply you with foggers to rid the home of these seemingly immortal parasites.

A more comprehensive coverage of ectoparasites will be found in the section devoted to skin diseases in Chapter 27, "Musculoskeletal and Skin Ailments."

Lice

Lice on cats are very rare. The most common louse is *Felicola subrostratus,* tiny, tan, pear-shaped ectoparasites that attach themselves to the cat's body. They are so small that they can be carried by fleas and other insects. When owners rub their hands over the infested cat's body, the lice feel like grains of fine sand in the coat.

The parasite causes a ruffled coat, and the skin may be raw from scratching. The cat will lose weight, and appear debilitated from general irritation, nervousness, and loss of appetite.

To treat, use feline flea sprays and powders.

Mites

Acariasis is the infestation of mites. *Notoedres cati* causes cat mange, and is discussed under skin diseases. *Otodectes cynotis* is the ear mite of cats, and will be analyzed in Chapter 28, "Diseases of the Cat's Eyes and Ears."

Cheyletiella parasitivorax infests rabbits and sometimes cats. Usually, this mite causes no clinical signs, but occasionally a dandruff-like condition appears. Brushing the cat's coat over a piece of paper will reveal the mite as a small yellow insect. Treatment is with powders or flea sprays.

Myiasis

Botflies, *Cuterebra* (species) larvae, often attach themselves to the cat's skin during the summer months. The owner might see a small (1 to 3 mm.) hole in the cat's skin with a mild amount of drainage present. This is the breathing hole of the larva, and if you watch it closely and carefully, you will note the movement of the larva. If left untreated, the pocket will abscess and the larva will rupture out. The area around the larva must be carefully incised and the larva removed by your veterinarian. The larva will be plump and up to 1 inch in length and, if crushed during removal, a severe allergic reaction can occur and the host cat could die. The cavity where the larva lived must be cleansed and disinfected thoroughly.

Screwworm maggots of the *Callitroga americana* blowfly will attack cats. This parasite most often occurs in the Southern sections of the United States. The attack usually centers on the perianal (around the anal) area of weak or sick cats. The larvae must be removed and the area cleansed.

INTERNAL PARASITES

Some parasites use transport hosts to carry them from cat to cat. The transport hosts are simply vehicles by which the parasite travels. Each parasite has its specific life cycle, involving one or more methods of producing infection. In this chapter we will treat each parasite separately and describe its life cycle.

Whip worms.

Your veterinarian is the only one who can tell you if your cat has parasites. Several methods can be used to check for parasites. A small stool sample, and a description of anything you may have observed to make you think your pet has worms, are necessary. One worm check is not absolute. Often it is necessary to do several, because some varieties of internal parasites produce very few eggs, and others do not produce eggs daily.

Your veterinarian may do a direct smear test. This can be done with a thermometer if no stool sample has been brought. This method is satisfactory if the result is positive, but the procedure is very inaccurate and produces a high percentage of false negatives. Flotation or centrifuging, however, results in a concentration of eggs (if present), and greatly improves the efficacy of the test. In these methods the stool is mixed with a supersaturated solution of sugar or sodium nitrate. The mixture is allowed to stand, or is spun in a centrifuge. When the eggs of the parasite float to the top of the solution, a small amount is skimmed off and examined under the microscope. In most cases, the purpose of the examination is to identify the worm eggs rather than the parasite itself. The veterinarian can pinpoint the exact parasite infesting your cat and select the proper drugs for treatment.

There are many drugs available for worming. Each has a limited field in which it is efficacious. We must definitely advise you against selecting a worm medicine off the shelf of a pet shop or feed store, and worming your cat indiscriminately without knowing which intestinal parasites are present. Preparations are sold that advise the buyer to worm every thirty days. This is not only poor medical procedure but also dangerous to your cat's health. There is no reason to believe that puss is constantly pathologically infected by parasites. The difference between the cost of selecting over-the-counter medicines without proper medical counsel, and the veterinarian's charge for his advice, which is dispensed with the proper medicine, is not worth the loss of professional expertise. You could also leave your cat with a lethal parasitic infection if the drug you selected and administered did not touch the parasites your cat hosts. Further, worming procedures can be dangerous or toxic to your cat, and your veterinarian may advise that the cat be hospitalized for the worming.

However, the prevention and control of parasites, and the breaking of the cycle of infection, are actually in the hands of the cat's owner. There are three basic modes of attack: eliminating parasites in the environment; preventing contact with infected areas; and worming infected cats on the instructions of your veterinarian.

Queens should be checked for parasitic infection and treated before planned breeding times. Litter trays should have their contents changed every twelve hours and the trays scalded until your cat is parasite-free. If infection recurs, outdoor areas used for toilet purposes should be treated chemically with salt solutions or pesticides. Sodium borate applied at the rate of 10 pounds per 100 square feet will reduce larval and egg inhabitants of the soil. Carrier pests, such as fleas, must be controlled, especially to keep the incidence of tapeworm infestation down. Be certain to bring a small sample of your cat's feces when you take it to the veterinarian for the yearly examination and vaccinations. Also report any parasites you have seen in the feces or observed under the cat's tail, as some signs of parasites (see "Tapeworms," page 210) are not picked up in routine stool checks.

As we discuss the different parasites, we will describe their modes of infection and their life cycles, as well as their effect upon public health. Most cat parasites do not affect humans, but there are important exceptions and these should be understood. Proper care can eliminate any fear you may harbor of becoming infected.

All cats recovering from a parasitic infection that has caused illness should be carefully watched and cared for. Extra nourishment, vitamins, or special nursing may be needed to rebuild your cat's health.

Roundworms

Three species of ascarids (roundworms) infect the cat: *Toxicara canis, Toxicara cati,* and *Toxicaris leonia.* All three parasites inhabit the lumen (cavity or channel) of the small intestine, and cause digestive upsets and unthriftiness. Kittens are more severely affected than adult cats, who often build an immunity to the parasite. Kittens will become pot-bellied, emaciated, and exhibit anemia when infected. Migrating larvae of the worm can cause liver or lung damage at times, leading to pneumonia. Adult cats, however, seldom exhibit symptoms any more drastic than restlessness or mild weight loss.

Roundworms.

Infection occurs mainly through ingestion. A cat, licking its paws to clean them, may be carrying worm eggs from the litter pan on its feet, or from a highly contaminated outdoor area from which it has just returned. Puss ingests the worm eggs as he licks his paws and thereby becomes parasitized. Prenatal infection also occurs through migrating larvae in the queen, passing the placental barrier into the unborn kitten.

The normal feline ascarids *(T. cati* and *T. leonia)* do not migrate, but develop in the bowel wall as larvae and reenter the bowel lumen when they grow to adults. *T. canis,* the dog and cat roundworm, produces larvae that penetrate the bowel wall, enter the bloodstream, and travel via the liver to the lungs. While in the blood they are capable of crossing the placental barrier to the unborn kitten. Some of the larvae are destroyed, but some become dormant, and if this happens in a queen, the larvae later become active when she is pregnant and invade the kitten fetus.

From the lung, the larvae may be coughed up, and either vomited out or swallowed to continue their life cycle in the cat's intestine. The adult worm is 1 to 4 inches long, white and slender, with tapered ends. The life cycle takes approximately ten days in a cat. Since only *T. canis* have the ability to cross the placenta, prenatal infection is far less frequent than in the canine species.

People contaminated with *T. canis* worm eggs via ingestion can become a dead-end host. The larvae migrate through the body organs, but do not become adult worms. Cases of this happening are exceedingly rare. In sixteen years of veterinary practice, the junior author has yet to see or hear of an actual case. Simple cleanliness is the key to prevention, so wash your hands well after changing the litter tray.

Diagnosis of roundworm infection is by a simple fecal examination. Since these worms are treated with very mild eradicators (unless there is a combined infection with other parasites or it is a very severe case), your veterinarian will usually give you the proper medication to use at home. Two or three wormings at ten- to fourteen-day intervals usually rid cats of the infection, and unless there is a continual environmental contamination, the cat will remain worm-free. Piperizine compounds are the simplest and least toxic of the medicines used today to eradicate roundworms, and will be dispensed by most veterinarians for this purpose.

Hookworms

The hookworm most likely to infect your cat is *Ancylostoma tubaeforme;* it has worldwide distribution. *Ancylostoma braziliensis* and *Unicinaria stenocephala,* which are mainly hookworms of dogs and wild animals, also can infect cats, but less commonly than *A. tubaeforme.* Hookworm infection is more common in the summer than in the wintertime, and therefore less common in the Northern regions of the United States.

Like the roundworm, ingestion is the most common way for a cat to become parasitized. Transfer hosts, such as beetles and mice, can also carry the worm to the cat. Lastly, the larvae in the ground may penetrate the cat's skin, causing infection. When penetration happens, the larvae travel by way of the bloodstream to the lungs to be coughed up and swallowed, and to continue their development in the intestine. Migrating larvae can cross placental membranes (as with round-worms) and infect the fetuses of pregnant queens.

Hookworms.

Hookworms (though not as common as roundworms) also infect the small intestine of the cat, where they attach to the intestinal wall. The worm ulcerates the lining of the intestine and sucks the blood of its host. Even when it moves to a new site the old area may continue to bleed, unquestionably causing an undesirable blood loss. The cat may begin to cough, show weight loss, abdominal pain, and produce a dark, soft, and tarry stool. The blood count can drop far enough to cause anemia. Kittens, heavily infected, can die suddenly from loss of blood.

Ancylostoma larvae can penetrate the skin of humans, causing a skin condition known as cutaneous larval migrans, but as with round-worms, such infection is quite rare.

Diagnosis of a cat for hookworms is made by stool examination. The eggs are present in the stool and can be identified during a routine flotation. If hookworms are suspected, several specific checks may have to be done to confirm the diagnosis, for the eggs are not as plentiful as they are with roundworms. Adult hookworms are very small, white or red-hued with blood, and hairlike, measuring only 10 to 20 millimeters in length; they are therefore seldom seen by the cat owner.

Treatment and supportive treatment are equally important. Several drugs are available to eradicate the worms, both injectable (DNP) and oral (Task Tabs). Many of the older drugs will eradicate the parasite, but they are liver-toxic and should be avoided, especially for the cat under stress. B complex and B_{12} vitamins, especially with liver and iron, give good supportive treatment by helping to provide the products needed to restore normal blood levels. If the infection is severe and the cat becomes anemic, it may be necessary to give a blood transfusion before treatment.

The eggs and larvae can exist in the environment for more than a year, but the larvae are sensitive to sunlight and both are susceptible to freezing and drying out. Plenty of sunlight plus a program of careful and rigorous disinfecting should cleanse infected premises.

Stomach Worms

Several species of the genus *Physaloptera* infect the stomach of cats. An uncommon infection seldom seen or diagnosed in felines, they specifically inhabit the stomach area and cause a poor coat, unthriftiness, vomiting, and soft stools. They attack the stomach wall, creating small ulcerations to the surface. When coughed up they look like roundworms, 1 to 4 inches long. The tail of the male worm is coiled; the eggs can be identified by the usual flotation methods. Infection is usually through insect and rodent transfer hosts. Treatment is simple and consists of the use of piperazine compounds (as with roundworms). Control is achieved mainly by controlling the transfer hosts.

Threadworms

Another uncommon parasite of the cat is the threadworm, the *Strongyloides* species. These worms either penetrate the skin or enter the cat when the infective larvae are swallowed. They can be free-living and, in the cat, may cause little or no disease. In heavily parasitized kittens, coughing and ocular discharge can occur, accompanied by minor digestive disturbances.

Diagnosis through fecal flotation does not produce the visual egg within the microscopic field as with the other worms so far discussed, but rather a larval worm form. Treatment with thiabendzol is quite effective, and usually no supportive therapy is necessary.

Tapeworms

This worm is the most common small intestinal parasite of the adult feline, and there are several types that commonly affect cats. Each type has a life cycle that differs from that of the other tapeworms, but in all cases an obligatory intermediate host is involved. A part of every tapeworm's life cycle is spent in the intermediate host, and because of this, the cat cannot reinfect itself.

Tapeworms vary in length and have multiple segments or proglottides, each of which contains a set of reproductive organs that produce eggs. In the bowel, the segments break off and are shed whole in the stool: they look like pieces of rice. They are white when fresh, but turn brownish as they dry up. Some segments when dry cling to the hair at the base and undersides of the cat's tail and can be seen there. When

Tapeworms.

the segment dries up, eggs are released to continue the life cycle. Owners usually see and report the presence of the segments to their veterinarians. Repeated stool examinations (flotation) are usually negative unless infection is very great because eggs are only released when the segment is destroyed in the bowel, and most segments are passed whole.

When the eggs are swallowed by the intermediate host, they hatch and form different types of cysts (larval forms) in the intermediate host's body. The cat ingests the intermediate host, or the parts of its body containing cysts, and thereby becomes infected.

Tapeworms cause less clinical disease than most other common parasites. Chronic diarrhea and loss of general condition will occur with large infestations, or more commonly with the larger tapeworms. Either a slight loss or a great increase in appetite can also result.

Following are descriptions of five types of tapeworm:

Taenia taenaeformia (T. hydatigena). This tapeworm is found worldwide. The intermediate hosts are most commonly rats and mice, though rabbits, squirrels, and muskrats can also harbor the cysts. The cysts form in the host's liver, and ingestion of the raw, infected liver by the hunter cat causes infection. The adult worm can be up to 2 feet long.

Dipylidium caninum. This is the most common feline tapeworm because the flea is the intermediate host. Swallowing an infected flea completes the life cycle. It follows that good flea control of the cat and its premises can eliminate the problem.

Rarely are humans infected. They are never infected from their cat, but only from swallowing an infected flea, a practice seldom indulged in by most people. This tapeworm is less than 1 foot long. The flea larva on the cat's body ingests the worm eggs shed into the feline's coat from segments that have been caught in the hair near the tail and have dried out. The adult flea develops the cysts in its ovary.

Treatment will be discussed under general tapeworm eradication, but it must be concurrent with flea control of the already infected cat.

Taenia pisiformis. A common parasite of the country cat, the cysts of

T. pisiformis are found primarily in the mesentery (a fold of the peritoneum) of the rabbit. Other rodents can also be carriers. Almost 100 percent of the rabbits in a given area can be infected. In the cat, the worm will grow up to 16 inches in length.

Diphyllobathrium latum. Two intermediate hosts are required by this tapeworm. The first host to contain the cysts is the small crustacea (a class of chiefly aquatic arthropods—shrimp, crabs, barnacles, and so on) which form the food of freshwater fish. The fish consume the crustacea, and become the second intermediate host, and the cysts become larvae that invade the fish body, especially the liver. Eating infected raw fish, or fish liver, causes infection and development of the tapeworm in its final host. Cats, dogs, and even man can become infected in this fashion.

This parasite is limited to the Northern United States and Canada in this hemisphere, but can be common in man where raw fish is eaten. The worm can grow as long as the intestinal tract of the final host allows. Treatment is not always successful, as with other tapeworms, because this worm is resistant to specific tapeworm drugs.

Echinococcus granulosa. These are very small tapeworms that use the gut of the sheep and cow for intermediate hosts. They are not common in this country, but are frequently found in Australia, New Zealand, and those Continental countries where raw intestines are fed to cats and dogs. When the egg is swallowed by a human, it can cause hydatid disease (cysts) in the gut, leading to a fatal ending.

In Australia and New Zealand, government laws prevent the feeding of raw inner organs to animals, but such laws are difficult to control on remote farms where animals are frequently slaughtered.

Tapeworms are treated with various drugs. The older types, such as arecoline, essentially paralyze the worm. They cause severe bowel contractions and thus elimination of the parasite, but they can be very dangerous to the host, and should never be used on very young kittens or very old cats.

Yomasan and Scolaban kill tapeworms. The worm is seldom seen after treatment of the host with either of these drugs, for the cat digests it as it disintegrates. Scolaban is the most effective eliminator, but both drugs are excellent and relatively safe to use. Worming must always be accompanied by a rigid control program, and control means the removal of the intermediate host—an insoluable problem in the predacious hunter cat. Many cats need routine wormings to keep the infection levels low.

Flukes

Flukes are very rare parasites in this country, but there are several varieties that can occur. They usually utilize two intermediate hosts: small snails and fishes. The adult fluke is found in the gall bladder, bile ducts, or liver of the cat.

The following are fluke varieties:

Opisthorchis felineus. This fluke is sometimes found in Canada but is mainly a European and Asian fluke.

Amphimerus pseudofelineus. This is an American fluke that is very rarely reported.

Platynosomum fastosum. This fluke is carried by lizards rather than fishes, and is found mostly in Florida, Puerto Rico, and the Bahamas, as well as in the Far East.

Fasciola hepatica. This fluke is found throughout the world and is not host-specific. It can cause great losses to the sheep and cattle industry, but it rarely infects cats.

Troglotrema salmincola. This variety carries a rickettsia organism. The fluke infects salmon, and the rickettsia gives rise to what is commonly called "salmon poisoning" in the Pacific Northwest. Lynx, raccoons, dogs, and other carnivores can be affected, but domestic cats are a questionable host.

Protozoa

These minuscule parasites are phyla comprising the lowest animal forms and consisting of microscopic, unicellular organisms:

Coccidiosis. This is a protozoa infection causing watery, mucoid bowel movements. The cat becomes weak, loses its appetite, and suffers weight loss. The intestinal tract becomes inflamed, and whole blood can be found in the diarrheic evacuation. In kittens, invasion by coccidiosis parasites can result in a fatal clinical disease from depletion.

Adult felines may be carriers but rarely indicate a clinical disease. The condition is most common in pet stores and catteries.

Isospora bigemina, Isospora felis, and *Isospora rivolta.* These are a trio of coccidia that specifically infect the feline species. The eggs of each can be found in the feces through a routine fecal examination, but carriers of the infection may show no eggs.

Treatment is with sulfonamides, or nitrofuazone, but despite such treatment the disease usually runs a course of about two weeks. Cats that are unable to build an immunity to the infection can relapse for a considerable length of time. Control is accomplished through strict sanitation.

Toxoplasma gondii. See Chapter 19, page 200.

Giardia canis and *Giardia felis.* These protozoa can cause diarrhea in felines, but this is usually quite rare. Flotation methods of identification habitually miss the parasite, which can best be seen in the microscopic field through the use of wet smears of the feces. Treatment is with a specific sulfonamide.

Entamoeba histolytic. Causing amebic dysentery in kittens, this protozoan commonly affects primates, but is rather rare in cats.

Respiratory Parasites

These include:

Aelurostrongylus abstrusus. This is the lungworm found in cats, and it is distributed in the United States. Snails and slugs are intermediate hosts, but infection in felines probably occurs through ingestion of transfer hosts such as rodents. The adult worms live in branches of the cat's pulmonary artery.

The infected cat may exhibit coughing during the migration stage of the parasites from stomach to lungs. Afterward, pneumonia, fever, and hard breathing are in evidence, and lung sounds may be altered. Heavy infections of *A. abstrusus* will result in eventual death.

Diagnosis is difficult and the condition is not common. If suspected, larvae may be found in direct smears or by the flotation method. Treatment involves good care and nursing. Several drugs are available, including Dithrozanine and Methyridine, the drugs of choice, which directly attack and kill the parasite.

Capillaria aerophila. All carnivores can be infected by this lungworm, but it is not common in cats. Foxes are the most prevalent host. The worms live in the trachea and bronchioles, and an infected cat may cough or show other respiratory distress. Secondary pneumonias are common. The eggs of the worm can be found in the sputum or feces of the diseased cat but are difficult to demonstrate. The disease is generally self-limiting, and good nursing can result in a complete cure.

Blood Parasites

These include:

Haemobartonella felis (IFA). See Chapter 19.

Babesia felis. This is a tick-transmitted disease that is found mainly in African cats. The red blood cells are attacked, and the clinical picture is much like that of infectious feline anemia.

Dirofilaria immitis. The heartworm of dogs has been reported in cats. The incidence is not frequent, and usually the cases are identified on postmortem only. Occasionally, the baby larvae will appear in the bloodstream, making antemortem diagnosis possible, but usually the condition is sterile. The clinically ill cat will evidence the signs of congestive heart failure.

At present, it is not necessary to do routine heartworm examinations or to use medications to prevent the disease. But future alterations in the incidence of heartworm disease may modify this.

Urinary Parasites

Capillaria plica. This worm can be found in the bladder and kidneys of cats, dogs, and foxes. The lining of the bladder becomes thickened and inflamed. Sometimes, but rarely, it will be found in the pelvis and kidneys. The eggs are discovered in the urine, and there is no known treatment at the present time.

Ocular Parasites

Thelazia californiensis. Most commonly found in the Far Western states in this country, thelaziasis is probably transferred to mammals by flying insects, especially the deer fly. The worm, which is about ½ inch long, is found under the cat's third eyelid, and causes irritation and exudation. Treatment consists of physical removal of the worm.

CHAPTER 21

Toxicities and Poisons

Poisons are substances (liquid, solid, or gaseous) that, upon ingestion, absorption, application, injection, or development within the body, by reason of an inherent, deleterious property, tend to destroy life or impair health through their chemical action.

The three most common ways in which poisons invade a cat's body are by ingestion, inhalation, or absorption through the skin. The cat is normally a fastidious eater and will seldom consume tainted food or a poisonous substance. The greatest exception to this general rule is antifreeze poisoning, simply because the liquid leaking from a car radiator is sweet and pleases the cat's palate.

Many of our decorative houseplants may contain toxic substances, yet can be somewhat attractive to the curious cat, who will often chew on the leaves. Some parasitic dips used for dogs are mistakenly bought for cats and may poison puss via absorption, or through licking the insidious substance on his coat. Many of our wonder drugs, sedatives, and even vitamins, which do so much for the health and relief of suffering in cats, can, if overdosed, cause toxicities and even death.

There are several general methods of attacking toxicities. Cutaneous contamination should be washed off as quickly as possible. If the substance burns the skin, vegetable-oil bandages can be used. Vomiting can be induced for recently swallowed poisons. One-half to one teaspoonful of hydrogen peroxide given orally will induce regurgitation within ten minutes. Repeat the dose within ten minutes if there is no reaction. How well the junior author remembers Ipecac: as a child his mother thought that any illness could be vomited out. Even the name still produces nausea. One-quarter teaspoonful of Ipecac, however, works well on cats. Gastric lavage (the washing out of the stomach with water or a saline solution) will flush out poisons. One or two teaspoons of charcoal can be added to a lavage. Charcoal is a neutralizer for many poisons.

The balance of this chapter describing poisons will be presented in chart form to make it easier for the reader to follow. It must be remembered that many of the symptoms are very general, affecting most often the central nervous system or the gastric system. It is important to match availability of the toxic agent in toxic proportions and proper symptoms, before one decides on a poison diagnosis.

When your cat has ingested poison of any kind, do not become hysterical. Calmly and clinically evaluate the situation and attempt to quickly apply the necessary treatment. Then rush puss to your veterinarian. We must stress that in all cases where the owner can presumably treat the poisoned pet with success, time is of the essence. The quicker the remedy can be supplied to the cat, the greater its chance of recovery.

AGENT	SOURCE	SYMPTOMS	TREATMENT
Acids	Chemicals and household preparations	Vomiting	Egg albumen or vegetable oil, milk of magnesia
Alkalis	Cleaning preparations, lye	Colic and vomiting, alkalosis	Wash mouth with vinegar or water, oral vegetable oil, or egg albumen, followed by vinegar
Alpha chloralose	Eating contaminated rodent	Stumbling, followed by hyperexcitability and convulsions, finally coma	Supportive, until kidneys detoxify
Arsenic	Herbicides, insecticides	Acute—stops eating, weak, gastroenteritis, and death Subacute—same but less severe	Vomiting or gastric lavage early; dimercaprol (BAL) injected in advanced cases
Aspirin	Administered	Affects blood and liver; gastroenteritis	IV fluids and nursing

AGENT	SOURCE	SYMPTOMS	TREATMENT
Barbiturates	Overdose	Anesthesia	Remove source; stimulants if necessary
Benzoic acid	Food preservative (safe in normal amounts)	Aggressive, hypersensitive, salivation	Remove source
Benzyl benzoate	Miticide preparations	Gastroenteritis and hyperexcit-ability	Don't use on cats
Carbamates	Plant and animal insecticides	Low toxicity, tremor, saliva-tion, diarrhea	Pralidoxine
Chemicals:			
Aerosols, naphthaline, phenol, resorcinol, hexachloro-phene	Coal-tar preparations and mothballs	Skin irritation, salivation, weakness, convulsions, paralysis, and death	Egg albumen, vegetable oil, milk, then lavage; treat shock and coat intestines
Ethylene glycol	DeIcer or antifreeze	Causes crystal deposits in brain and kidneys, apprehension, depression; atoxic; partial paralysis, coma, and death	Lavage, IV 10% calcium gluco-nate, support kidneys
Chlorampheni-col	Overdose	No appetite, depression	Remove source

AGENT	SOURCE	SYMPTOMS	TREATMENT
Chlorinated hydrocarbons	Pesticides	CNS signs, kidney and liver damage	Wash exterior, lavage if ingested, phenobarbitol, quiet and dark
Dichlorvos	Flea collars	Dermatitis in sensitive animals, systemic toxicity	Remove collar
Grisofulvin	Administered in normal or overdose	Birth defects, low fertility	Don't breed while on treatment
Hexachloro-benzene	Seed coating to prevent fungi	Ataxia, tremors, weakness, paralysis, and death	Lavage
Iodoform	Skin preparations	Toxic if ingested; depression	Don't allow to lick
Kerosene and fuel oil	Household	Gastroenteritis, circulatory collapse, convulsion, and coma	Wash skin; vegetable oil followed by sodium sulfate
Lead	Pesticides, paint, plaster, newspapers	Anemia with gastroenteritis and/or convulsions	Sedative and calcium EDTA

AGENT	SOURCE	SYMPTOMS	TREATMENT
Mercury	Contaminated fish	Long buildup, part paralysis, tremors, and finally convulsions	Dimercaprol (BAL)
Methylene blue	Urinary antiseptic overdose	Hemolytic anemia (blue urine and feces), depression	Remove source
Nicotine	Tobacco and insecticides	CNS signs, respiratory paralysis, and death	Lavage and support control; past 4 hours will usually survive
Opiates	Administered	Spasms, death, especially with morphine	Confine in dark
Organo-phosphates	Pesticide dips, flea collars, worm medicine, ingested, inhaled, or absorbed	Tremors, salivation, diarrhea, convulsion	Atropine; may need oxygen
Phenylbuta-zone	Overdose	No appetite, dehydration, depression	Remove source
Plants—Common dry plants:			
Bittersweet		Gastroenteritis	
Caladium (crown of thorns)		Salivation	Remove source
English ivy		Vomiting, heavy breathing, coma	Remove source
Hydrangea		Gastroenteritis	Remove source

AGENT	SOURCE	SYMPTOMS	TREATMENT
Laurel, rhododendron, rose-bay azalea		Vomiting, watery eyes and nose, drooling, convulsions	Remove source
Mistletoe		Cardiovascular collapse	Remove source
Oleander		Cardiac glycoside causes heart arrhythmus, abdominal pain, convulsion, and coma	Potassium chloride and atropine
Philodendron, dieffenbachia		Salivating, liver and kidney damage, nervous signs, 50% mortality	Remove source
Poinsettia		Vomiting, delirium, and death	Usually too late to treat
Plants—Flowers:			
Lily-of-the-valley, foxglove		Heart irregularities	Remove source
Lupine, tobacco, delphinium		CNS signs	Remove source
Nightshade, casterbean, precatory bean		Gastroenteritis	Remove source
Plants—Flower bulbs:			
Narcissus, hyacinth, jonquil		Gastroenteritis	Remove source
Plants—Fungi:			
Mushrooms	Wild—are poisonous to man and beast	Vomiting, salivating, and coma	Lavage, remove source

AGENT	SOURCE	SYMPTOMS	TREATMENT
Plants—Shrubs:			
Yews, box hedge, daphne, wisteria seeds		Gastroenteritis	Remove source
Rat Poisons:			
ANTU (off market)		Lungs and heart; death	No successful treatment
Na fluoracetate and fluoracetimide		CNS signs, gastroenteritis, and cardiac involvement; death	Vomiting—but usually too late to treat
Thallium (off market)		CNS and/or respiratory signs; with chronic cases, skin lesions	No successful treatment
Warfarin	An anticoagulant; cat must have had multiple doses before affected	Bleeding	Vitamin K
Zinc phosphide		Loss of appetite, colic, coma, and death in 48–72 hours	None successful
Reptiles, Bufos:			
Lizard, rattlesnake, coral snake, water mocassin, spider, scorpion, bufo toad, gila monster	Fields, garden	Salivation, vomiting, CNS, uncoordination, and death	None specific; atropine, and maintain animal with fluids and nursing

AGENT	SOURCE	SYMPTOMS	TREATMENT
Stilbestrol	Overdose	Causes blood dyserasias	Remove source
Strychnine	Oral, from pesticides and deliberate poisoning	Start minutes to hours after ingestion: convulsions, CNS signs	Early vomiting; later put under sedation and maintain with IV fluids
Turpentine	Household	Nausea, colic, bloody urine; restless, unsteady, coma, death	Lavage with sodium bicarbonate, oral liquid petroleum
Vitamin A	Overdose, if raw liver diet	Cervical bony bridging of spine, weakness, no appetite	Balance diet
Yellow phosphorus	Highway flares, rodenticides	Salivation, heavy breathing, convulsion, liver florescence	Wash mouth, lavage stomach

CHAPTER 22

Diseases of the Respiratory Tract

The cat's respiratory tract begins at the nose and ends in the lungs. There are two nasal passages, which open into the pharynx, the back of the throat. From the pharynx there are three more exits: the mouth (forward), and the esophagus and trachea posteriorly.

Incidentally, though you have already been exposed to much of this litany in Chapter 15, "Feline Physiology," it seems wise to review briefly the pertinent bodily sections we discuss in each of these chapters on disease. You will then be instantly cognizant of the location of the physiological part discussed and its relationship to the other parts of the cat.

So, to continue the respiratory system, we leave the common area of the pharynx and enter the trachea. From here on, the system is continuous and dependent on each succeeding part. In front of the trachea, if the cat's nose becomes blocked, it can breathe through its mouth and aerate the lungs; but any blockage occurring as we proceed toward the lungs from the trachea will obstruct all the structures beyond the blockage. The larynx is short, only a bit over 1 inch long. From the larynx we enter a long tube called the trachea, which traverses the neck into the chest cavity, where it divides into primary bronchi.

The primary bronchi supply different lobes of the lungs. The bronchi then branch into secondary bronchi and finally into bronchioles. The bronchioles connect with alveolar ducts in the lungs, which terminate in the small sacs, called alveoli, that make up the lung tissue. It is across the cells of the alveoli that oxygen and carbon dioxide are exchanged with blood.

The lungs lie in the thoracic cavity, with the heart and the primary blood vessels of the body. Both the lungs and the cavity are covered by a sheet of pleura. The entire chest area is under negative pressure —in other words, a vacuum, allowing the lungs easy expansion during the act of breathing. Should this vacuum be lost, from leakage in a lung or puncture of the chest wall, the lungs would then have to laboriously attempt to expand against a positive pressure caused by the entrance of air into the chest area.

There are several ways to examine the chest. The normal respiratory rate of the cat is between 10 and 30 respirations per minute. We can, therefore, count the respirations and watch the character of the breathing (mouth breathing, forced, too deep, excessive abdominal movement, and so on), recording any abnormalities. Your veterinarian will further examine the chest by listening through a stethoscope for abnormalities. He may tap the chest wall to listen for density changes, or tap into the chest with a needle and syringe to withdraw and examine suspected and offending fluids. Finally, more sophisticated examinations can be accomplished with bronchoscopes and X-rays.

Rhinitis

This is an inflammation of the mucous membranes of the nasal cavity. Viruses, bacterial infections, foreign bodies, tumors, allergy, and trauma can cause rhinitis.

The affected feline will display blocked or partially blocked nasal passages. Unilateral blockage usually indicates a physical cause, such as a grass seed (foreign body), trauma, or tumor. Bilateral blockage can be due to a virus, or caused by bacteria, an allergy, or a tumor. There is usually a discharge—clear, if no infection is involved, to purulent, depending upon the type of infection. The cat will often mouth-breathe because of the blockage. Loss of appetite is common since puss cannot smell his food. Temperatures vary depending upon the cause.

Veterinary examination and treatment are necessary to differentiate between the various causes of the disease and to treat the true cause.

Laryngitis

Though laryngitis is commonly connected with other respiratory infections, it is also frequently caused by overzealous calling by the tom or queen searching for a mate. Boarded cats, especially Siamese, will often return home hoarse with laryngitis. Usually, tincture of thyme will cure the amorous, vocalizing puss. Laryngitis associated with infection requires identification and veterinary treatment of the primary cause.

Pneumothorax

The movement of air into the chest cavity resulting in a loss of the natural vacuum is called pneumothorax. Most pneumothoraxes occur as the result of trauma (a wound or injury). Broken ribs or objects penetrating the chest wall are prime causes. Broken ribs may also tear a lung, or pressure on the chest due to a blow can rupture a lung, and both may result in a leak of air into the chest cavity. Occasionally, a lung abscess or tumor may rupture, also causing a leak.

If the tear in the wall is small, it might heal itself in a few days, but usually any tear requires surgery. A tear in the lung may seal as the affected piece of lung collapses; most of the lung will again become functional. If too much air enters the chest, the negative pressure may have to be restored and maintained by draining the chest of the accumulated air, thus allowing the lung free expansive movement.

Chest X-rays are usually taken after accidents, if the chest appears involved, to see whether a slow leak in the area is present. The feline must be kept from indulging in all exercise, and be given antibiotic coverage to prevent infection that can enter via the trapped air.

Pleuritis

Pleuritis is an inflammation of the covering of the thoracic cavity, lungs, and heart. The condition can be either dry or moist. The causes of pleuritis are many and varied. Penetrating wounds, extension of general bacterial and viral infection, and migrations of *Aelurostrongylus abstrusus* (see page 214) larvae, are the most common causes. Many different bacteria, and most of the upper respiratory viruses, can be involved. Most of the viruses reach the pleura by extension inhalation from the original site of infection. Bacteria such as streptococci, staphylococci, and E. coli can reach the pleura either by inhalation or via the bloodstream.

Stricken with pleuritis, puss usually shows an increasingly painful respiration, sitting carefully and resting his chest on the floor with both elbows extended. Coughing will finally result, and generally a fever is present. If the condition advances from a dry to a moist pleuritis, large amounts of fluid can accumulate in the chest. This fluid will inhibit lung expansion and put pressure on the large blood vessels leaving and entering the heart, as well as the heart itself. The fluid must be analyzed to differentiate it from fluid produced in a ruptured thoracic lymphatic duct; leukemia (see "Feline Leukemia," page 189); and pyothorax; or from a transient fluid, one that can be produced as a result of other diseases that alter the blood pressure, allowing some noncellular fluid to escape into body cavities and to be reabsorbed when the condition is controlled.

Pleuritis is treated with antibiotics and good nursing. The cat should be kept inside in a warm environment, and its food and water intake encouraged so that it does not become weak or dehydrated.

Fluid accumulations in the chest should be drained out, a chore for your veterinarian.

Pyothorax

When pus accumulates in the thoracic cavity, the condition is called pyothorax. It is rather a common condition in cats, caused by various pus-producing bacteria, and it can follow a pleuritis or occur as a primary condition. The symptoms in the afflicted cat are much like those of pleuritis, but more dramatic. Depression is severe and the cat moves very little, the lung sounds disappearing in the reservoir of suppuration in the chest.

A cat in this condition should be hospitalized and carefully watched. The pus should be removed from the chest to relieve pressure on the lungs and to enable the cat to take in oxygen. Some cats, stricken with this disease, will have to be supplied with an oxygen-rich environment, such as oxygen cages and incubators with an oxygen supply, so that they can absorb enough oxygen through their damaged and inflamed respiratory system. The junior author has drained chests of cats in this condition, and found a reaccumulation of up to 3 or 4 ounces within twelve hours, indicating that constant monitoring is absolutely necessary.

The cat is treated with systemic antibiotics, and often needs antibiotics flushed directly into the chest. Sometimes a protolytic enzyme is used to facilitate the breaking up of the purulent material. Intravenous fluid therapy is necessary as most stricken felines will dehydrate rapidly, the result of fever combined with lack of eating and drinking. As the fluids in the chest diminish, and appetite and thirst return, we can count puss happily over his crisis.

Chylothorax

Chylothorax is caused by a rupture of the thoracic lymphatic duct, which then dumps a fatty, milky solution into the chest cavity. The rupture is usually caused by a wound or injury to the chest. Infections and tumors may also weaken the duct and cause leakage, and sometimes spontaneous rupture occurs for no known reason.

The clinical signs are similar to those encountered in other illnesses where fluids invade the chest area, except that the cat's temperature usually remains normal. Testing of the fluid will specifically identify the condition. Correction of the condition is surgical: the thoracic duct rupture is located and ligated.

Tracheitis

Tracheal inflammation is generally an extension of upper respiratory disease or bronchial disease. Inflammation of the membranes of the trachea causes coughing, which can often be elicited by palpating the trachea. Antitussive cough remedies and cortisones will relieve the cough, but the major treatment must be directed at the primary cause of the inflammation.

Bronchitis

Inflammation of the bronchi and bronchioles is usually secondary to upper respiratory disease, but can be primary if air containing an irritating substance is inhaled. As the condition persists, bacteria can invade the irritated membranes and cause purulent or moist infection.

Some cats in which this condition occurs will become chronic if not treated quickly and successfully. Constant irritation causes thickening of the bronchioles and loss of elasticity. This chronic, noninfectious condition is known as bronchiectasis. X-rays will show the permanently thickened bronchioles and confirm the condition.

The symptom expressed by the cat is a cough, but early in the condition breathing problems are rather slight. As the untreated illness progresses, the cough becomes moist and productive, breathing is more difficult, and the chest becomes evidently painful. Broad-spectrum antibiotics are used and, if the condition is unresponsive, the discharge must be grown in the laboratory and the offending bacteria identified so that a suitable drug can be selected to effect a cure. Antihistamine preparations are given to reduce irritation, dry the secretions, and dilate the bronchioles.

Pulmonary Edema

Edema is the accumulation of fluids in the bronchioles and tissues of the lungs, which can be relieved by a chest tap. It is secondary to diseases that change blood pressure and lymphatic drainage. Heart disease can cause chronic edema. Allergy reactions (anaphylaxis) and insect bites can cause severe and deadly edema.

Pulmonary Emphysema

This disease occurs when there is a rupture of the alveoli in the lungs. The rupture causes the coalescing of several small saccules at the end of the bronchioles into a larger sac with less surface area. The loss of surface area results in a reduced capacity to transfer oxygen and eliminate carbon dioxide from the blood, which is the main function of the lung.

The condition is usually chronic and results from pneumonia, bronchitis, or asthma. The cat remains normal and may only evidence a cough when exercised. As the condition worsens, the breathing becomes exaggerated, but puss will look well and continue to eat and drink normally. Upon examination, however, your veterinarian will detect fine, crackling sounds through the stethoscope.

The condition is permanent (unless it is an acute allergic state), and is treated with drugs that will improve aeration of the lungs.

Pneumonia

When inflammation affects the lung tissue of your cat, pneumonia results. The causes of pneumonia embrace a wide range of invaders, including inhaled foreign material, migrating and primary parasites, lying on one side too long during other illnesses, or injuries and congestion due to heart disease. The inflammation predisposes the cat to infectious pneumonias. The primary cause must be treated to relieve the lung inflammation.

Infectious pneumonia is caused by fungi, viruses, and bacteria. The fungi involved are those discussed under mycotic diseases, and include cryptococcosis, blastomycosis, and nocardiosis. Viral pneumonias are extensions of the upper respiratory viruses. The common bacteria in pneumonia are staphylococci, streptococci, *Escherichia coli,* and *Pasteurella,* but *Proteus,* pseudomonas, and *Bordatella* are also found. Tuberculosis can cause a pneumonia, by a cat's drinking raw milk of a TB-positive cow, but strict controls have made this cause rare.

Bacterial pneumonia is probably the most common form, with the possible exception of viral pneumonia. Both are treated with wide-range antibiotics: bacterial because of the many types of bacteria involved, and viral to protect against invading bacteria in the already inflamed lung.

Fungal causes need special laboratory testing. If a fungal cause is suspected, X-rays will exhibit the typical pattern and support the suspicion. The material from the lungs should then be examined directly for fungus.

Asthma

Feline asthma is a respiratory disease characterized by its sudden onset, accompanied by heavy breathing and forced expirations. Some cats exhibit coughing and cyanosis (blueing of the mucous membranes due to lack of oxygen) when most severly affected. The cause is unknown.

Diagnosis is often only arrived at through response of the cat to therapy. Some felines exhibit an increase of eosinophils (white blood cells common in parasitic and allergic-type diseases) in the blood. X-rays may also help by showing a suggestive pattern of increased bronchovascular marking.

If the condition is suspected, epinephrine or cortisone therapy is used. When the cat responds, the diagnosis is confirmed. Cortisone therapy is continued for several weeks, after which the cat will remain normal for an undetermined length of time, until another attack occurs.

Cancer

Cancer of the chest is very common. The lungs are the collecting area for secondary cancer from many primary sites throughout the body. Leukemia can cause a primary chest condition, and the lungs are targets for several primary types of tumors.

Cancer of the respiratory tract in cats usually begins with respiratory distress, and examination will rule out probable infectious causes. X-rays will show the presence of dense lesions taking over the lung tissue. Positive diagnosis and differentiation of the type of cancer is only possible by examining the invading lesions directly.

Diaphragmatic Hernia

This respiratory tract ailment is almost always the result of severe trauma, such as a car accident. The diaphragm is a muscle that divides the respiratory cavity and the abdominal cavity. The rupture, or partial rupture, will cause a loss of the lung vacuum and allow the migration of abdominal organs into the chest cavity.

The condition is a surgical emergency, especially if the chest area has been invaded by abdominal organs. These organs must be placed back in the abdomen and the integrity of the muscle (diaphragm) restored.

CHAPTER 23

Diseases of the Digestive System

The digestive system of felines starts with the mouth, containing the teeth, the tongue, and the opening of the ducts of the salivary glands. A description of the teeth and tongue of the cat, with their utilitarian purposes, can be found in Chapter 15, "Feline Physiology." The salivary glands add moisture and digestive enzymes to the food the cat ingests. The dorsal surface of the mouth is covered by the hard palate, followed by the soft palate, a judicious arrangement.

The cat's mouth opens into the pharynx, which contains the nasal openings and also the entrance to the esophagus. The esophagus begins at the neck and transverses the neck and chest cavity, opening into the stomach just behind the diaphragm at the front section of the abdominal cavity. Digestion begins in the stomach and continues in the intestinal tract, which is about 6 feet long. It is divided into a small intestine about 5 feet in length, and a large intestine about 1 foot in length. (In comparison, man's small intestine is 20 feet long, and the large 5½ feet long.) At the junction of small and large intestines is the cecum, a small sac that, in man, ends in the appendix.

The small intestine is divided into three sections—the duodenum, the jejunum, and the ilium. The sections are histologically different and perform diverse jobs in the process of digestion. The large intestine is mostly colon, ending in a short rectal and anal opening.

The abdomen also contains the liver, which surrounds the anterior part of the stomach and lies against the diaphragm, and the pancreas, which is situated along the duodenum. Both organs are involved in digestion.

Symptoms of disease of the digestive system are loss of appetite, bad breath, jaundice, vomiting, diarrhea, constipation, and/or abdominal pains.

MOUTH DISORDERS

Eosinophilic Granuloma (rodent ulcer)

This disease is a condition in which an ulcer forms, usually on the upper lip. Similar lesions may also occur on the tongue, lower lip, or even the legs, but these locations are rare. The cause of the lesion is unknown. Invariably, a lesion forms on the upper lip before being present anywhere else. The lesion must be differentiated from a cancerous growth as it will resemble a carcinoma, but rodent ulcer is not malignant. Scrapings of the ulcer often contain eosinophils, a type of white blood cell, hence the name *Eosinophilic granuloma.*

Until quite recently treatment has often been frustrating, as lesions have tended to recur. Classical treatments have been to inject the area with cortisones, which gave dramatic but short-lived results, or to resort to surgical excision, which also too often resulted in recurrence of the ulcer. Very recently a new drug, used primarily for birth control in dogs and cats (and for skin cancer in humans), has been shown to have both dramatic and lasting effects with a low-dose, continual control program.

The drug, megestrol acetate, has been effective in a number of unrelated skin conditions of cats. Medication is given every other day until the condition improves, then weekly until it is cleared up, followed by medication every other week indefinitely to prevent recurrence. The condition may recur if the drug is stopped after several months, as several cases we know of have reverted, so it is best to keep puss on a low dose, or to reinstate the low drug dose immediately upon recurrence. The drug's method of attack on the lesions of any of the skin conditions is unknown.

Stomatitis

Inflammation of the inside of the mouth is a common ailment of cats. It is not a specific disease, but can have many causes. A great many pathogenic bacteria invade the mouth. They include staphylococci, *Proteus,* pseudomonas, and the fungiform bacilli. *Candidi sp.* fungus will also occur in the mouth. Ulcerations of mouth and tongue will

take place from upper respiratory virus. Foreign bodies piercing the
mouth can cause abscesses. String attached to food or a toy can wrap
around the base of the tongue. If your cat is struggling and pawing at
its mouth, look under the tongue when you check the entire mouth
area.

The main clinical signs are fasting (even though the desire to eat is
obviously present), drooling, and bad breath. Treatment consists of
locating the primary cause and proceeding accordingly.

Trench Mouth

No, this oral illness is not confined to humans. In cats it is a mixed
bacterial infection of the feline mouth. Spirochetes and fusiform
bacilli are usually present with various other forms of bacteria. The
gums are inflamed and raw, often with ulcers scattered over the surface. The infected areas have a film covering the gum tissue, and the
teeth accumulate heavy tartar deposits.

Treatment is with antibiotics, often supplemented with vitamin B
complex. All eating and drinking bowls must be thoroughly cleaned
daily.

Dental Disease

The normal dental formula for the cat is:

Upper: three incisors, one canine, three premolar, one molar.
Lower: three incisors, one canine, two premolar, one molar.

The above represents only one-half of the jaw for both upper and
lower, and therefore has to be doubled. There are variations in number
that are normal, but usually only in premolars or molars. The adult
incisors begin to erupt at four months of age, and a cat will have a
complete set of permanent teeth by six months of age.

The cat does not suffer from cavities as its human companion may,
but rather its teeth problems relate to inflammation of the bone, gums,
and ligaments supporting the teeth. This is known as periodontal
disease. Along with inflammation of the gums there is a tartar increase.
These deposits push the gums farther and farther back. The result is
loose teeth, inflamed gums, bad breath, and finally infection of the
jawbone. The teeth must be scaled and the gums underrun or fresh-
ened before the condition causes bone infection (osteomyelitis) and
bone destruction.

The cat will fracture teeth. Teeth broken off horizontally usually cause no problem, although if a tooth turns black, it should be removed. If the fracture extends vertically, toward or into the root, it should also be removed.

ESOPHAGEAL DISEASE

Diseases of the esophagus in cats are relatively rare. The more common problem is obstruction: foreign bodies will block or partly block the esophagus and cause inflammation of the esophageal lining. Small balls, and other objects of this size, will cause total obstruction, while fish hooks, needles, and other sharp objects will cause partial obstruction, penetration, severe inflammation, and sometimes rupturing of the esophagus. Correction is surgical.

Other obstructions are caused by bands of material that were, in fetal life, blood vessel connections for the blood to bypass the heart, and that have degenerated around the time of birth. Persistent right aortic arches cross the esophagus and will obstruct it. Again, correction is surgical.

Lastly, cancerous growths can obstruct or irritate the esophagus. Benign growths can be removed, but malignant growths are terminal.

The only other esophageal problem of any significance is dilation of the esophagus. The organ loses its muscle tone and becomes flabby and dilated. Although the condition's causes are unknown, we do know that it may occur in related individuals, and therefore we must consider that it has some basis in genetics.

STOMACH DISORDERS

Hairballs

The most common stomach problem of cats is hairballs. In the daily grooming process, cats swallow hair, which mats into masses in their stomachs. Many of these hairballs pass into the intestine and cause constipation, while others will be vomited instead. Treatment consists of laxatives. During heavy shedding times and with long-haired cats it may be necessary to use a laxative prophylactically. Mineral oil is efficient but often too strong. A dab of Vaseline on the nose daily during these times will be licked off and ingested, and will usually work to ease elimination. Most veterinarians can supply you with a cat laxative, flavored and easier to administer if you so desire.

Gastritis

There can be many different causes for the inflammation of the stomach known as gastritis. Foreign bodies, such as bones and hair balls, may irritate the stomach lining and cause inflammation. Food poisoning, bacteria, drugs (especially aspirin), and heavy metal poisons will all cause gastritis.

The initial sign of gastritis is vomiting of the stomach contents; the cat may also have a fever if the condition is infectious.

Treatment is to identify the primary cause and treat it specifically, and also to control the vomiting. If regurgitation is excessive, dehydration and loss of stomach electrolytes may take place, and intravenous fluids, incorporating the lost electrolytes, may become necessary.

Pylorostenosis

At the end of the stomach is a valve, the pyloric valve, that connects the stomach to the first part of the intestinal tract. This valve can spasm and cause vomiting. If the condition becomes persistent, the valve muscle must be surgically cut in order to allow the passage of food.

DISEASES OF THE SMALL INTESTINE

As we saw with the esophagus, obstructions can occur in the small intestine. If the object causing the blockage cannot be moved by enemas, surgery will be necessary. A special word here to warn all cat owners about needles and thread. Long threads are extremely enticing to kitty, and she will play with them for hours. But, if swallowed with a needle attached, the needle can migrate in and out of the intestines, literally sewing them together. The result is a very serious and difficult surgical problem, with multiple areas of local peritonitis. Please, store all your sewing equipment carefully away from your cat. You may joke about this but it is puss whom you will have in stitches.

Volvulus (twisting of the intestine), Intussusception (telescoping of the intestine)

These are both severe intestinal catastrophes that are caused by increased intestinal motility from parasites, foreign bodies, and other intestinal disease. They present surgical problems, and must be identified and corrected rapidly or death of sections of the intestine, followed by death of the stricken cat, will take place.

Enteritis

Enteritis, an inflammation of the small intestine, has many causes. Perhaps the most common, until we can achieve nationwide vaccination in 90 percent or better of our cats, is feline distemper. Many varieties of bacteria have been identified in enteritis: *E. coli*, *Salmonella* sp., *Clostridium perfinges*, and *Bacillus piliformis* (Tyzzer's disease) are among the more commonly found. Of course, parasites cause enteritis as a common symptom. Eosinophilic enteritis, which is believed to be a disease in which the cat becomes "allergic" to its own cells, or "allergic" to milk, will cause enteritis.

The feline that has an infection causing enteritis will exhibit loose bowel movements that may contain mucus or blood. Usually puss will run a temperature that can reach 105 degrees Fahrenheit, and exhibit depression, loss of appetite, and rapid dehydration.

Treatment consists of antibiotics to kill the bacteria, compounds to solidify the feces and slow the bowel motility, and also, if necessary, forced fluid intake. If the cat refuses to drink, it may need to be hospitalized and given intravenous fluids.

Malabsorption

Malabsorption, or the inability of the cat's small intestine to absorb nutrients, may be a part of many small intestine diseases and conditions. Pancreatic disease and liver disease—followed by allergy, intestinal inflammation, and neoplasia—are the most common causes of malabsorption.

Many cats with this condition are bright and have a good appetite unless concurrent infections are present. The feces are liquid or soft and contain undigested food products, especially fats, which can be identified through laboratory tests.

Treatment is based upon diagnosis and treatment of the primary cause plus replacement of digestive enzymes, bile salts, and vitamins, and a high-quality protein and low fat diet.

DISEASES OF THE LARGE INTESTINE

The large intestine consists of the cecum, colon, and rectum, and has few problems. Once again, blockage by foreign objects and tumors, intussusception (the small intestine slipping into the large), and penetration of sharp objects can occur in this area. Severe, unrelieved constipation can stretch the bowel and cause an enlarged colon that becomes flaccid (a condition known as megacolon). Surgery is indicated in all the former cases and sometimes in the case of severe constipation. If the colon is flaccid, it may be necessary to keep the cat on laxatives until function returns—if it does.

Prolapse

Prolapse of the colon and/or rectum through the anus is uncommon, except in Manx cats who may have poor innervation of the anal muscles. These cats will require surgery, which may make it necessary to "tie down" the intestine and narrow the anal ring with a pursestring suture. The cat is then placed on a soft diet and laxatives for one to two weeks, until the anal suture is removed.

Colitis

Inflammation of the colon has many etiologies, just as enteritis does. Mycotic colitis usually occurs because of antibiotic overdosing, which kills off the normal intestinal bacteria that compete with and control fungi, allowing them the opportunity to multiply and become the dominant growth in the colon. Feline distemper virus and bacteria, especially *E. coli*, are common causes of colitis.

Necrotic colitis is a specific entity in which several areas of the colon are involved and may slough, causing blood-streaked, watery feces, and a very high fever. The causative agent is unknown, but various authorities attribute it to feline distemper and *E. coli* bacteria. The affected feline has soft to watery evacuations, often tinged with whole blood which, because of its nearness to the end of the intestinal tract, has not had time to mix with the feces. Poor puss usually has many bowel movements during every twenty-four-hour period, but body temperature remains normal or is only slightly increased.

Treatment consists of identifying the cause and treating it accordingly; plus the use of a low fiber diet and coating medications.

DISEASE OF THE PERITONEUM

The peritoneum is the serous membrane lining the abdominal and pelvic cavity walls and covering the contained viscera, the two layers enclosing a potential space, the peritoneal cavity. Both external penetration into the abdominal cavity and internal penetration (usually caused by sharp foreign bodies) will introduce bacteria and cause peritonitis. Clinically, the cat is very feverish, loses all appetite, and indicates no desire to move. Palpation of the abdominal area will indicate great pain there. Fluid develops in the abdominal cavity.

Treatment is by wide-range antibiotics, removal of the abdominal fluids, and culture of the abdominal fluids to identify the causative bacteria.

The condition must be differentiated from infectious peritonitis (see page 192). Supportive treatment consists of intravenous drips in order to maintain hydration and to feed the cat. Surgery may be necessary if there is organ rupture or any crushing due to automobile trauma. These crush syndromes often do not show up until several days following the trauma to the cat.

DISORDERS OF THE LIVER

The liver must be included in a discussion involving the digestive system because it not only serves as a main organ in gathering venous blood and sending it to the heart, but also takes products from the digestive process into the blood and sends bile salts and other digestive helpers to the bowel. It is a main detoxifying organ.

The liver can be infected by many systemic diseases such as infectious peritonitis, peritonitis, toxoplasmosis, and secondary spread of cancer, as well as primary cancer and heart disease. Damage to the liver causes digestive upsets and ascites (fluid in the abdomen).

Cirrhosis of the Liver

This is a replacement of normal active liver tissue with thick fibrous scar tissue. It is common in human alcoholics due to constant insult from the alcohol. In our nondrinking cats, the cause can be parasites, infection, heart disease, and any condition that impairs the normal flow of blood to the liver.

Clinically, the stricken cat shows mild digestive disturbances. As the condition increases, anemia followed by jaundice occurs. The liver function is greatly impaired, and pressure causes the "leaking" of the fluid part of blood, which accumulates in the abdomen due to the inability to cope with the normal flow to the liver. This is called ascites.

Diagnosis is based on a manual examination of the grossly enlarged liver through the abdominal wall, combined with X-rays and liver function tests.

High-quality protein diets, replacement of bile salts, and support of the digestion are the only approaches to treatment, plus the treating of any concurrent condition that may be involved (such as heart failure).

Necrosis

Death (necrosis) of the liver tissue is due to infection and toxic agents, especially poisons and worm preparations. The symptoms are much like those for cirrhosis, and diagnosis is mainly through liver function tests, as the liver is not enlarged.

Treatment is supportive, as it is with cirrhosis, and includes the removal of all toxic agents, plus the treating of any concurrent infection.

Cholelithiasis

This condition is one of stones in the gall bladder. The symptoms that appear—vomiting, diarrhea, depression, lack of appetite, and possibly jaundice—are all similar to the symptoms displayed by other liver problems. Pain may also be present. The causes of this condition are not generally agreed upon by the medical profession.

Diagnosis is based upon identification of stones in the gall bladder by X-ray. Treatment for the condition is surgical, but the condition is not at all common in cats.

Tumor

The liver is a popular place for tumors to occur. They may be primary or metastatic from general cancer such as feline leukemia. Since most liver tumors are malignant, the condition is usually terminal.

DISEASES OF THE PANCREAS

The pancreas is an exocrine gland that empties enzymes for digestion into the first part of the small intestine. It contains the endocrine glands, and the islets of Langerhans, which a client once thought were small tourist isles off the coast of Spain but are actually a part of the cellular structure of the pancreas that controls the body's insulin output. A long-term inflammation of the pancreas can cause temporary or permanent damage to the islets of Langerhans, and so cause diabetes. Exocrine glands have ducts running directly to the areas they supply, while endocrine glands are ductless and rely on the blood-vascular system.

Acute Pancreatitis

This is a disease of sudden onset caused by the digestion of this organ by enzymes. The cat begins to vomit, loses its appetite, and has diarrhea and severe abdominal pain, often with ascites.

The disease is diagnosed by clinical evaluation followed by specific laboratory tests to determine amylase and lipase levels. These are the two primary enzymes of the pancreas. X-rays may also be of value in diagnosing the disease.

Acute pancreatitis should be treated in the hospital. The cat is taken off all foods and placed on intravenous drips, painkillers, antibiotics, and antisecretory drugs to relieve the pancreas.

Chronic Pancreatitis

This may result from an attack of acute pancreatitis or it may come on as a slow, insidious disease. The cat will show little or no pain, periodic vomiting, grayish greasy stools, and gradual loss of weight. Treatment is with pancreatic supplements and vitamins.

CHAPTER 24

Diseases of the Urinary Tract

Often referred to as the genitourinary or urogenital system because of the close relationship to the reproductive organs, the urinary tract (or system) is formed in the body by the kidneys, the urinary bladder, the ureters, and the urethra.

KIDNEY DISEASES

The kidney consists of three main sections:

1. The glomerulus, a capillary blood vessel that acts as a filter of the body's blood;
2. The nephrons and collecting ducts, which segregate the filtered products, returning those needed to the body;
3. The pelvis, which receives the filtrate from the many ducts like a large cistern, and sends the filtrate (urine) to the bladder.

Any and all systems can become infected concurrently. Acute renal disease can be caused by bacteria of various types, viruses, and chemical agents. Nephritis, an inflammation of the kidneys, is known in man by the more familiar name of Bright's disease.

Common among the bacteria attacking the kidney are *Escherichia coli*, streptococci, staphylococci, and *Proteus* species. Virus kidney disease is usually associated with generalized viremia; for example, leukemia virus may attack the kidneys, at the same time causing general disease within the cat. Arsenic, mercury, lead, bismuth, and thalium can cause acute renal disease, but they are uncommon.

The three most common chemical agents can be guarded against. First, several of the antibiotics are nephrotoxic. They include the sulfonamides—neomycin, gentomicin, polymicin, kanamycin, and amphoteracin. These drugs, which are safe and effective agents in the hands of a veterinarian, can cause acute kidney damage if given in too heavy doses; therefore, they should *only* be used under the supervision of a veterinarian.

Second, carbon tetrachloride, an antique worm medicine still available at pet stores, is severely kidney toxic. It should definitely be avoided since there are safer and far more effective medicines available today.

The third chemical agent to guard against is antifreeze. Leaking car radiators containing antifreeze are a danger to household pets. The liquid is sweet and attracts cats, but even small amounts of the mixture can cause acute renal failure and death.

The kidney-diseased cat will exhibit depression, lack of appetite, vomiting, and occasional diarrhea. Early in the acute disease, a kidney shutdown may occur, and very little urine is produced. The feline becomes dehydrated from lack of water intake.

As the cat recovers, or the disease progresses to a chronic condition, the water intake increases and becomes excessive, followed by extreme urination. The kidneys lose their ability to concentrate urine, and the urine gradually approaches the density of plain water. The cat's appetite is poor and it remains dehydrated and depressed, with occasional regurgitation in the clinical stage.

Chronic Interstitial Nephritis (CIN)

Recurring attacks of kidney disease from different agents, or a continuous attack which progresses to chronic, eventually scar the kidneys, leading to a condition known as chronic interstitial nephritis (CIN). When this happens, the working parts of the kidney are replaced with scar tissue, resulting in lowered function until there is not enough true kidney to keep puss in a normal physiological balance. CIN is a common cause of death in aged felines whose kidneys have survived many years of coping with intermittent disease problems.

Treatment for the acute case is to identify the causative agent and then to attack it specifically or remove it from the environment. Bacterial disease is, of course, treated with antibiotics. Viruses are usually treated by attacking the general viremic disease (see Chapter 18, "Infectious Viral Diseases"). Toxic agents are dealt with by removing the agent and giving supportive treatment and detoxifying agents (see Chapter 21, "Toxicities and Poisons"). Supportive treatment, especially the use of intravenous fluids, is very important and requires hospitalization.

If an acute case is cured quickly, a minimum of kidney scarring will occur, and the cat may function normally for the rest of its life. But repeated attacks and disease that progress toward CIN will finally result in end-stage kidneys (kidneys so scarred that there is not enough of the functional organ left to support life).

Uremia

A cat can function on less than one total kidney. But, as damage proceeds, the kidney is unable to handle the wastes, especially the nitrogenous wastes. The blood urea nitrogen (BUN) rises and the cat becomes toxic and goes into uremia—a condition of poorly functioning kidneys in which the toxic products cannot be removed from the blood. Three laboratory tests are done to find out how bad the uremia is and to provide a prognosis. Urinalysis is primarily utilized to find how high the protein is; to establish the presence of blood, acidity, or the basicity of urine; and to determine the specific gravity and presence of crystals, bacteria, and blood cells. As the specific gravity approaches water, we know the kidneys are losing their ability to concentrate. Protein is normally only a trace, and blood should be absent. The urine should be acid, and no bacteria, or high numbers of red or white cells, should be present.

The normal BUN level is 10–30, and increases above 40–50 are significant. Above 80 is very dangerous, and indicates that the cat is extremely toxic. Creatinine (a nitrogenous compound excreted in the urine, the level of which, in the blood, may be used as a measurement of kidney function) is normally less than 1 but rises during the disease. This provides a better indicator of prognosis than BUN, as felines with creatinine levels of 2 to 4 usually do quite well, while cats with levels over 7 usually succumb to the disease. The uremic feline is thin, dehydrated, and has bad breath and teeth that become loose in the gums. The gums are often covered with a brownish slime.

The life of a CIN cat can be prolonged and the animal enabled to function normally with dietary help. Diets that produce low nitrous wastes are the best approach. Proteins are the worst offenders. Therefore, only proteins of the highest biological value should be fed. Very lean meats, chicken, eggs, cottage cheese, and milk (all of high biological worth) will provide the necessary protein, but should only represent a portion of the complete diet. The rest of the diet should consist of foods such as wheat bread, vegetable oils, high carbohydrate foods, fat desserts, and macaroni or pasta-type products. Vitamins should also be supplemented, especially vitamin B complex. There are specially prepared prescription diets available through your veterinarian that are balanced and easy for you to feed.

These diets will not stop kidney disease or prevent it, but they will help the diseased kidney to function until it becomes an end-stage kidney, at which point the only help is to replace it. Unfortunately, kidney transplants are not a solution at this time in veterinary medicine, though they may be possible some time in the near future. Expense and the problem of finding a suitable donor are the stumbling blocks, yet some day such a transplant may be done as routinely as a hysterectomy is today.

Congenital Renal Diseases

These include:

Renal hyperplasia. This condition, arising from a defective formation of the kidneys, results in fewer functioning nephrons. Hence, an early uremia can occur.

Aplasia. Aplasia is the complete lack of development of one or both kidneys. Cats can function normally with one kidney, so a single aplastic kidney may not be discovered until the cat dies. There is no known treatment for complete aplasia of both kidneys, but with one normal kidney, the cat can be maintained on a special diet for varying periods of time.

Polycystic kidneys. These are kidneys in which much of the functional tissue has been replaced with cysts of varying sizes. The junior author has seen polycystic kidneys where only a thin cover of functional tissue remained over organs that were the size of cantaloupes.

DISEASES OF THE URETER

Misplaced ureters occur occasionally. The ureter, which carries the urine from the kidney to the bladder, may insert too far into the neck of the bladder; as a result, the urine bypasses the bladder and is constantly dripped out of the animal.

Rarely do we see a presentant uracus. This is the tube that runs from the fetal bladder into the placenta. If the tube does not close at birth, the kitten will drip urine from the navel. Surgical correction is simple and successful.

DISEASES OF THE BLADDER

Cystitis

The causes of cystitis, inflammation of the bladder, may be either bacterial or viral. Some cats form small bladder stones called uroliths, which cause a noninfectious recurring cystitis (see "Urolithiasis," below).

Bladder infections often need therapy for extended periods. An antibiotic is given for primary or secondary bacterial infection, and can be given in combination with urinary antiseptics, which will also help to sterilize the bladder. Many infections will result in the normally acid urine becoming alkaline. To control these infections, it is most important to acidify the urine.

The cat with cystitis will spend more time than normal in the litter box. It will produce urine each time, but the amounts will be below normal. The urine passed may be odiferous and possibly blood-tinged. The cat will lose its appetite and become depressed. Puss may also begin making mistakes around the house because he can't reach the litter box in time to relieve himself of the burning feeling of the urine produced in an infected bladder.

Cystitis requires veterinary care. Laboratory work may be needed to identify the causative agent if initial therapy is not successful. If possible, bring a urine sample with your cat when you visit your veterinarian.

Urolithiasis

This feline disease abounds with out-of-date and incorrect information. Let us first define the condition: It is a cystitis (inflammation of the bladder) in which small bladder stones (gravel) are formed. These small stones are the uroliths. Both male and female cats can suffer from this condition, but due to anatomical differences, female cats can pass the uroliths while in male cats they often plug up at the tip of the penis, producing the blocked-cat syndrome. Obviously, the disease is more dramatic and dangerous to male cats. Female cats are often diagnosed (wrongly) as having recurring infectious cystitis, when they are actually undergoing recurring cystitis with urolithiasis.

Knowledge of the disease's cause has increased over the last few years. Three viruses have been linked to urolithiasis, but to date only one has (experimentally) produced the disease: picornavirus. The extent of possible interaction between the the viruses is unknown. Before the discovery of virus involvement, urolithiasis was linked with many antique theories. Dry cat food was blamed, but there is no real evidence that it is at all involved. Dry food is widely fed and therefore an easy target since most felines who have uroliths consume some dry food. Actually, the cat can find the minerals, proteins, and other products that are components of uroliths in any diet, and can even store them in its own body. Being aware of these facts we can rule out diet as a primary source of uroliths, and probably even as a contributing factor. Early castration was also blamed, the theory being that the cat's urethra would have had greater development if allowed to mature before castration. But the disease occurs statistically in as high a percentage of entire males as in neutered males. Vitamin A deficiency has also been incriminated, even though vitamin A–deficient cats are clinically unknown, so the involvement of vitamin A in the disease is difficult to justify.

Clinically, the owner will notice the afflicted cat spending a great deal of time in the litter box straining to eliminate. The feline with urolithiasis will pass little or no urine and, if any is passed, it is often blood-stained. A cat with cystitis without uroliths will also spend extra time in the litter box, but will produce a greater amount of urine each time. The straining of the blocked cat is so intense that many owners imagine their cat is constipated. Gently feel the lower abdominal area by pressing in on both flanks. In the blocked cat you will feel an enlarged ball, often the size of a grapefruit, which is the distended bladder. When the cat blocks completely, the situation is an acute emergency and you must consult your veterinarian immediately.

With blockage, the cat becomes depressed and dehydrated; it quits eating, and will become toxic, being unable to rid its body of urine waste. If the condition is not corrected in time, the bladder will rupture and death will ensue.

Initial treatment is to relieve the bladder of its obstruction, followed by the use of fluids to correct dehydration. Antibiotics are administered to clear any infection that would be primary or secondary. Most of these cats need hospitalization so that the urine output can be monitored until the patient is functioning normally. Many cats need a catheter left in place until perineal inflammation recedes. Most patients are given antibiotics for several weeks, and are usually placed on a urinary acidifier because some uroliths and infections thrive in an alkaline condition, normal urine being acid.

Control of the condition is not very satisfactory. Some felines have one attack and become well after veterinary care; but many cats have recurring episodes. High water intake will help to wash out the uroliths, and salting food can aid in increasing water intake. Antibiotics and acidifiers are helpful with recurring symptoms of a pending blockage. Many veterinarians utilize the acidifiers as a long-term therapy, the object being to keep the urine acid, thus, one hopes, lowering the rate of recurrence.

Puss may go through a recurrence within days, or remain normal for several years, but the chronic blocker will eventually die as a result of a ruptured bladder, toxicity, or kidney damage, unless surgical control is undertaken.

Surgical intervention will provide the male cat with the ability to pass the uroliths, but it does not stop their formation. The cat's penis is narrow at the tip and widens as it approaches the bladder. Surgery consists of dissecting back the wider area and moving it forward after amputation of the narrow tip. No control is lost by this procedure. The opening thus formed will be as large as the female passage so that the uroliths can be passed out, as they are by the female feline. Any entire males are castrated at the time this surgery is done. Surgery is definitely the most effective procedure for controlling chronic cases.

On occasion, a cat, whether male or female, will form over-large bladder stones that cannot possibly be passed through any opening. In such cases, the surgeon must invade the bladder and remove the offending stones.

Many cat owners find the cost of surgery difficult to justify. But recurring attacks, with several after-hour emergency calls, will cost more than surgery, and leave both cat and owner no closer to a conclusion of the condition. Following surgery, normal control programs of antibiotics, urinary acidifiers, and/or increased fluid intake are usually continued.

CHAPTER 25

Diseases of the Circulatory System

Briefly, the circulatory system consists of a pump—the heart—blood vessels carrying blood to and from the heart, veins and arteries, and the lymphatic vessels.

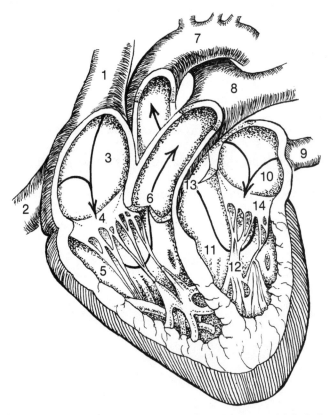

Cutaway view of the feline heart: (1) superior vena cava, (2) inferior vena cava, (3) right atrium, (4) tricuspid valve, (5) right ventricle, (6) pulmonary valve, (7) arch of aorta, (8) pulmonary artery, (9) pulmonary vein, (10) left atrium, (11) left ventricle, (12) papillary muscle, (13) aortic valve, (14) mitral valve. Arrows indicate the path of circulation in the heart.

The heart is a four-chambered pump, which receives blood from the body, pumps it to the lungs for oxygenation, and then back to itself for redistribution to the rest of the body.

The veins, with the exception of the pulmonary vein, carry non-oxygenated blood to the heart: blood received from the pulmonary vein (from the lungs) is oxygenated blood. The arteries leave the heart, branching out and carrying oxygenated blood to the body tissues, except for the pulmonary artery, which carries nonoxygenated blood to the lungs.

Blood leaves the left ventricle (the fourth chamber of the heart) via the aorta (the great artery) and is delivered to lesser arteries until it distributes oxygen, carried in the red blood cells, and nutrients, to all the body tissues. At the end of the arterial system there are vascular beds (called capillary beds), which pick up the exhausted blood and deliver it to the venous system, which returns it to the heart. Most venous blood from the posterior body is filtered through the liver and enters the posterior vena cava. The anterior and posterior vena cava join at the right atrium (first chamber) of the heart.

The blood is then passed to the right ventricle and is contained in the chamber by the tricuspid valve between the first chamber and the ventricle. The pulmonary valve opens and the blood moves out by the pulmonary artery. The blood filters by the lungs, collecting oxygen, and this newly oxygen-enriched blood is returned via the pulmonary vein, which enters the heart through the left atrium. The mitral valve between the atrium and the ventricle opens, allowing the blood to move through the ventricle and from there through the aortic valve to the rest of the body. As you can readily see, the journey of the blood through the bodies of all mammals including you and your cat is a complicated process that continues without pause throughout a lifetime.

DISEASES OF THE HEART

Until a few years ago, it must be confessed, very little was known about feline heart disease. Congenital heart conditions are rare in the cat as compared to the dog. Since the cat tends to regulate itself better, it can tolerate these diseases with greater ease than can the dog. The normal limits and patterns of cardiac conditions in the cat differ from those found in other more widely studied animals, so it will be several years more before good and pertinent clinical knowledge can be imparted to all veterinarians. But it is important that veterinarians do EKG's (electrocardiograms) on every cat with heart disease to aid in

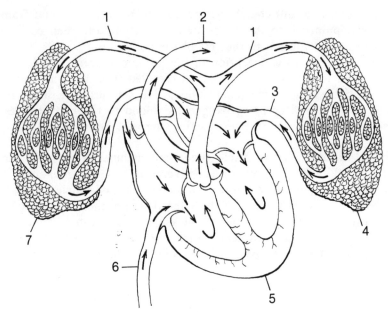

Heart and lung circulation: (1) pulmonary artery (to lungs), (2) arch of aorta, (3) pulmonary vein (return from lungs), (4) left lung, (5) heart, (6) inferior vena cava, (7) right lung.

diagnosis. Other methods at their disposal for examining the heart include inspection, palpation, stethoscopic examination, electrocardiograms, X-rays, and laboratory tests.

Heart disease can be congenital or acquired. There are two groups of congenital heart disease: one displays defects within the heart; the other is susceptible to outside attacks. Congenital heart disease within the heart exhibits five syndromes (a combination of symptoms resulting from a single cause and constituting a distinct clinical picture):

Pulmonic stenosis: a narrowing of the opening between the right ventricle and the pulmonary artery. The narrowing prevents the full force of blood from entering the lungs.

Aortic stenosis: the same type of narrowing. But it occurs between the left ventricle and the aorta, thus slowing the exit of blood to the body.

Atrial septal defect: an opening in the wall between the right and left atrium. This opening shunts some blood from right to left without passing through the lungs.

Ventricular septal defect: an opening in the wall between the right and left ventricles. Again, some blood is shifted between ventricles, or even backflows in the shunt from left to right.

Tetralogy of fallot: the most complex congenital defect. This condition is a syndrome of four separate defects: pulmonary stenosis, ventricular septal defect, an aortic artery override of the ventricular septal defect, and thickening of the right ventricle, which occurs because of back pressure from the other defects.

To correct each of these congenital diseases surgery is necessary, and in most cases heart-lung bypasses are needed. Private practitioners seldom possess the equipment necessary to perform such surgery; they simply do not have the funds available to purchase a machine worth many thousands of dollars to be used only once every several years. So if surgery is necessary, these congenital heart defect patients will usually end up at veterinary schools, large funded institutions, or some better-endowed central veterinary hospitals.

In the case of pulmonary stenosis, it is possible to use surgery that does not require the heart-lung machine, but does need a veterinarian who has had advanced training in this area. If no surgery is done, then on the rare occasion that secondary congestive heart failure occurs, it should be treated with drugs (see the treatment for feline cardiomyopathy described below).

There are two main circulatory system ailments that are external from the heart: patent ductus arteriosus and persistent right aortic arch.

Patent Ductus Arteriosus (PDA)

The ductus arteriosus is a channel that should have closed within a few weeks of birth. Before birth this shunt connected the pulmonary artery with the aorta, thus bypassing the lungs. But when the shunt remains open, blood continues to be sent past the lungs, the heart enlarges, and permanent damage is done. Damage will begin by the time the kitten is three to four months of age. Less than 10 percent of such cats reach the age of four years, and damage along the way is permanent. Surgical treatment, while rather difficult because of the area being worked on, can be done by any general veterinarian experienced in surgery. The small shunt must be isolated and closed off. If no permanent damage has occurred, the heart will revert to a normal electrocardiogram as soon as the shunt is closed.

Persistent Right Aortic Arch (PRAA)

This occurs when, during fetal development, the fetal fourth aortic arch arises from the right rather than the left side. This arch, coming down from the right, passes on the opposite wall of the esophagus, thus pairing with a ligament on the left side to cause a constriction. There is no heart disease, but as the arch degenerates into a cord after birth, the cat begins to vomit and the esophagus in front of the cord is dilated. The condition often does not become clinical until the kitten is presented with solid food. Again, correction is surgical. Removal of the ligament is not difficult, and given time and a soft diet, the esophagus will usually return to normal or near normal.

Feline Cardiomyopathy

Of the acquired heart diseases, this is the most common, accounting for 95 percent of the disease affecting the heart muscle in felines. The condition is seen more often in Persians than in any other single breed.

The condition occurs in two primary forms: either a floppy type of muscle known as congestive; or a thickened, hard muscle known as hypertrophic, which narrows the ventricular openings. While these syndromes can occur as primary conditions, 95 percent of cardiomyopathies occur as secondary conditions, and 70 percent of the total are hypertrophic.

Secondary cardiomyopathy can be just myocardial from virus infections, or combined valvular and myocardial from infections and diabetes mellitus. Hypertrophic cardiomyopathy is secondary to renal disease, high blood pressure, and chronic anemia. Neoplasia (tumors) may also cause myopaths.

Diagnosis is through stethoscopic examination, X-rays, and electrocardiogram. The feline is generally afflicted with heavy breathing, poor appetite, and lethargy. Early in the disease the cat may adjust to the malady, and unless a noticeable change in the heart's sounds is present, the disease may be missed. About 40 percent of these cats exhibit aortic thrombosis and become paralyzed, and sometimes sudden death occurs.

Treatment with digoxin in hearts undergoing congestive failure is begun at a low level, not in large introductory doses since felines are particularly sensitive to digitalis derivatives. This is considered a slow digitalization process. If we are dealing with a hypertrophic heart, propranol is the drug of choice, with or without digoxin. If the lungs become congested, treatment will include diuretics to dry out the lungs and low sodium diets to prevent water from building up. Finally, if aortic thromboembolism occurs, heparin (an anticoagulant drug) or surgery must be instituted.

While many hypertrophic cases respond well, the congestive cases often die within weeks in spite of treatment, and aortic thrombosis reduces the prognosis of hypertrophic cardiomyopathy.

Valvular Endocarditis

This is associated with bacterial infections in the cat. Often the source of the infection comes from one of many abscesses that cats get (particularly the out-on-the-town tomcat). The bacteria are taken to the heart, where they attack the valve and cause small, gray, nobby lesions. Treatment is with antibiotics.

Heartworm

Today veterinarians are discovering more cases of heartworm in cats. Most of these cases are seen upon postmortem, and they have not infrequently been the main cause of death. Most cats are dead-end hosts with no heartworm sexual cycle produced in their hearts. Thus, while the heart is being damaged, none of the normal diagnostic methods of finding the larvae work because the larval stage, by which diagnosis is made in the dog, is usually absent in the cat. Some few cats will produce larvae, and they can be diagnosed and treated, and should be put on a preventative medication. At the present, only dogs need heartworm prevention as a routine procedure. But if the parasite establishes itself in the cat, we may have to start a preventative program for felines.

Aortic Thrombosis (blood clot)

This condition occurs in the aortic vessel near the distal end of the aorta in the pelvis. Sometimes it may affect the femoral vessels in the hind legs. The thrombosis often results from heart damage. The patient generally exhibits hind-end paralysis, lameness, and pain as the main disease symptoms, but the central nervous system can also become involved, and sudden death may occur.

There are two methods of treatment. The first is medical treatment with injectable heparin and oral aspirin. If these fail, surgery is performed, usually as a last resort, since the disorder often recurs.

DISEASES OF THE BLOOD

Anemia

Anemia is a deficiency of quality or quantity in the blood. Usually, the term refers to a decrease in the number of red blood cells (erythrocytes), or a reduction in hemoglobin content. Lacking the ability to move oxygen from the lungs because of one of these defects, the body will suffer from lack of oxygen. The blood count is the most efficient measurement of blood cell availability.

Most acute feline anemias are due to a rapid blood loss from an accident. Ruptured hemorrhagic tumors, and large cuts or wounds, will cause acute blood loss, but most cuts will coagulate, and few tumors are hemorrhagic. The sudden loss of over 25 percent of the body's blood will cause shock, weakness, and death. When bleeding internally, puss will exhibit pale mucous membranes, cold gums, and subnormal temperatures; but, unfortunately, these same signs also can indicate shock from any cause. The simplest way to diagnose internal bleeding is a hyperdermic tap into the chest and/or abdomen. The most important laboratory test is the packed cell volume, which informs the veterinarian of the percentage of blood loss. Treatment consists of administering blood expanders, or whole blood, accompanied by repair or bandaging of the wounded area.

Chronic Anemia

Chronic anemia is a sluggish blood loss from slow-bleeding lesions in the body, vitamin deficiencies, or partial bone marrow depression. Causes of these disorders are injuries, poor diet, toxins from poison, bacterial invasions, and parasitic assault. Once again, blood counts supply the main clue to the problem, but this time there is no history of sudden trauma. Chronic anemia is also caused by a host of general diseases such as distemper and leukemia. Packed cell volume, platelet counts, diet inspection, fecal and general health tests, must all be accomplished to identify the reason.

Treatment is accomplished by removing or treating the cause. Parasites must be removed, blood replacement is necessary, toxins must be eliminated or treated, and needed vitamins should be supplied. The majority of chronic anemia patients may have as little as 25 to 30 percent of their normal red blood cell count before becoming very ill, and are often brought to the veterinarian in this state. All basic treatments must be followed up with mineral and vitamin therapy, as well as high proteins to help supply the building blocks for blood.

Aplastic Anemia

This anemia creates a complete depression of the bone marrow. The most common cause of bone marrow depressions are toxins, but distemper and neoplastic disease can also cause complete marrow depression. Blood counts will indicate anemia and/or low platelet counts, while bone taps will give conclusive evidence of the complete absence of active bone marrow.

Treatment is directed at removal of the toxin, if one is present, and supportive doctoring. Blood transfusions or blood expanders can be very helpful. Testosterone or metabolic hormones may help to build new cells by stimulating the bone marrow. The drug prednisolone will help to release, and control, continuous bone marrow depression.

Intravascular Anemia

This is caused by three main diseases: autoimmune disease, reaction to methylene blue dye, and haemobartonellosis.

Autoimmune diseases are caused by the sensitivity of a cat to its own red blood cells. The cells are destroyed, and the packed-cell volume falls. Special tests indicate the presence of the disease. The condition is treated with very high doses of prednisolone, which are gradually reduced until a control dosage is reached.

Methylene blue dye is often administered as part of a urinary medical treatment. Cats who react adversely to the dye will exhibit a packed-cell volume as low as 15 percent. If removal of the drug is accomplished in time, the red blood cells will usually regenerate.

Haemobartonellosis (infectious feline anemia) was discussed in Chapter 19, "Bacterial Diseases."

Iron Deficiency Anemia

This is mainly generated by mineral-deficient diets. Iron is the most important mineral in the production of red blood cells, though copper and cobalt are also important. Iron-poor diets are the chief cause of mineral-deficient anemias; to prevent this type of anemia, be sure to give your cat a diet rich in iron and vitamins.

Hemophilia

There are many types of hemophilia, attributable to the absence of various factors from the blood. It has been called the "bleeder disease," because it is a condition characterized by impaired coagulability of the blood, and a strong tendency to bleed. Most cases are exhibited early in life, and the luckless cats are unable to enjoy their legendary nine lives or even one normal life, for they are destined to die early.

The disease is hereditary, and sex-linked. The females are the carriers of the abnormal gene, but the male exhibits the disease. Toms seldom live past castration or "fighting time," while the clinically unaffected female lives on to pass to her progeny the dread gene.

Lymphadenitis (or lymphangitis)

The two most prevalent diseases of the white blood cells are leukemia and lymphadenitis. Leukemia has already been discussed in Chapter 18, "Infectious Viral Diseases."

In lymphadenitis, the lymph vessels normally drain all tissues, and carry offending materials to the white blood cells in local lymph nodes (lymphocytes). But sometimes infection will be halted and surrounded by the lymphocytes, causing lymphatic vessel and node infection and swelling, or lymphadenitis. Treatment consists of taking cultures to find out what antibiotic will work against the bacteria.

CHAPTER 26

Disorders of the Nervous and Endocrine Systems

Disorders of the nervous system occur in three separate or combined areas: the brain, the spinal cord, and the peripheral nerves (consisting of the nerves and ganglia outside the brain and spinal cord). These last form the autonomic nervous system that performs without conscious control, and they govern the glands, the cardiac muscle, and the body's smooth muscles. Definite tests can be made to locate disease in the peripheral nerves. Spinal reflexes will help to establish the sites where lesions or injuries have occurred in the spinal cord. In brain disease, the cerebrospinal fluid can be tapped and pressure read, cultures for germ growth done, and the cell structure read. These procedures will indicate certain pertinent changes to the brain and spinal cord with as much authority as will a blood count for other conditions.

There are tests for cranial nerves that indicate eye muscle defects, blindness, deafness, eating difficulty, balance, head tilt, and many other anomalies. X-rays are also used, sometimes with special dyes injected into the spinal area. These tests must, of course, all be done by an expert. All the information must be pieced together, then a completely informed diagnosis can be made of the area of damage or disease.

DISORDERS OF THE BRAIN AND CENTRAL NERVOUS SYSTEM (CNS)

Head Injuries

Blows to the head from falls, fights, and car accidents cause most feline skull injuries. Inside the skull the brain can become concussed, torn, bloody, swollen, and usually, as an accompanying part of such injuries, it can suffer increased intracranial pressure.

The injured cat is usually put into an oxygen environment. Corticosteroids are administered to reduce swelling, and osotic diuretics (such as mannitol) are used. The patient is usually taken off food and put on maintenance intravenous fluids. If bacterial contamination is suspected, wide-range antibiotics with a predilection for the CNS (central nervous system) are given. Unless grossly out of place, skull fractures usually heal well.

Brain Infections

Bacteria are the most common cause of brain infections, though such infections are rare. They are usually accompanied by nasal discharge, internal ear infections, bone infection, or a circulating blood infection. Several viruses, such as Newcastle's disease (affecting birds and poultry), have been used experimentally to cause brain infection, but are not known to occur naturally. But the use of these viruses indicates that the brain can probably be invaded by numerous viruses not yet discovered. The commonest fungi to affect the brain are *Aspergillus fumigatus* and *Cryptococcus neoformans*.

The broad spectrum antibiotic chloramphenicol is the usual treatment for bacteria. For fungi, amphotericin, an antifungal antibiotic, is used. Supportive treatment for all three causes—bacteria, viruses, and fungi—depends upon the severity of the disease. If the cat is unable to eat, it must be fed intravenously. Temperature should be monitored, and the environment controlled.

Toxoplasmosis

The protozoan disease toxoplasmosis occurs rather commonly in the brain but shows little or no clinical brain disease.

(See Chapter 19, "Bacterial Diseases.")

Hypoglycemia

This is an uncommon metabolic illness usually associated with pancreatic tumor. The cat is weak and trembling, and shows excessive salivation. As the blood sugar drops, convulsions occur. To confirm the presence of an insulin-secreting tumor, food is withheld for twelve hours. The cat is fed L-lencine, after which a drop of 50 percent in the blood sugar level of affected felines will be noted. If a tumor is not present, the hypoglycemia may be a hereditary defect, and feeding several times a day may maintain the blood level.

Thiamine Deficiency

This deficiency causes hemorrhage and swelling of the brain. The cat's head weaves, muscle tremors occur, stumbling is frequent, and the eyes are dilated. Righting reflexes disappear, circling starts, and behavioral changes take place. Some kinds of raw fish have a high thiaminase content (thiaminase is the enzyme that breaks down thiamine), resulting in Chatek's paralysis, a thiamine deficiency. Changing from a raw fish diet will result in a cure of all but the most extreme cases.

Feline Ischemic Encephalopathy

This is a cerebral scarring, which results in a loss of blood supply to the scarred areas of the cerebrum. The signs of the disease are acute upon onset, nonprogressive, and point to the cerebrum. The cat usually displays dilated eyes, with apparent blindness. There can be severe depression and some difficulty in walking; also some cats will have convulsions, and between these periods of disturbance, they will circle aimlessly. Personality patterns will change.

Within a few days the cat will improve, and then go on to a normal or near normal recovery. Some cats, after recovery, will retain the circling routine, or personality change, and/or blindness, any of which may make the pet no longer acceptable to the family, but in general the prognosis is optimistic. The only treatment is with corticosteroids, given to reduce brain inflammation as in any intracranial injury. The cause of this disease is unknown.

Inherited Metabolic Diseases

A chart of inherited metabolic diseases in cats follows. These will be named and the incidence charted, with the basic pathology, but they will not be individually described. Basically, they are all progressive and degenerative disorders of the central nervous system, which usually begin as muscle tremors and advance to complete motor disability.

All of these diseases are transmitted as recessive inherited genes, but only when the double recessive is present is the clinical picture produced. When the cat carries a lone recessive gene, there is no clinical indication of the disease. Such carriers are exceedingly detrimental to the breed and should be found and eliminated from any breeding program. If infected kittens occur, there is no doubt that both sire and dam are carriers. For these poor kittens there is no treatment.

Toxicities affecting the brain are described in Chapter 21, "Toxicities and Poisons." Note also that queens who harbor the feline distemper virus, whether from disease or from having been given live vaccine at the time when they were carrying kittens during pregnancy, can birth kittens with cerebellar hypoplasia. The condition becomes apparent a

DISEASE	BREED	PATHOLOGY	AGE	SIGNS
Feline globoid cell leukodystrophy	Domestic	Demyelination of globoid cells	5–6 months	Progressive motor disability
Feline sphingomyelin lipidosis (Niemann-Peck disease)	Siamese	Vacuolation of nerves	2–4 months	Same as above
Feline metachromic leukodystrophy	Domestic	Demyelination	2 weeks	Same; rapidly to convulsions
Feline CNS glycogenosis (Pampe's disease)	Domestic	Neural accumulation of glycogen	Young adult	Nonspecific
Feline GM$_2$ gangliosidosis (Sandhoff's disease)	Domestic	Vacuolation of neurines	8–10 weeks	Tremors, uncoordination, and paraplegia
Feline GM$_1$ gangliosidosis	Domestic and Siamese	Vacuolation of neurines	10–16 weeks	Same as above

few weeks after birth when the kittens indicate a complete lack of ability to function or move normally.

Stroke

The stroke is a syndrome that has not yet been conclusively identified in man or animals. Clinically, the syndrome does exist, as a cerebrovascular hemorrhage, or occlusion. Circling, head tilt, eye abnormalities, reflex abnormalities, depression, coma, or convulsions may all occur. Cats recover much more rapidly than do humans, and within a week may go on to apparent recovery. But, as with man, some may die. Cats are treated with corticosteroids and complete rest.

Tumors

Tumors occur in the brain of the cat with some regularity. Most are not operable due to an equipment need that cannot be fulfilled. Nonmalignant brain tumors proceed slowly in felines, and the cat can be helped to a more normal existence by treatment with corticosteroids and anticonvulsants.

Epilepsy

Of all the diseases already described that cause convulsions, perhaps the most familiar to the reader is epilepsy. This is a brain disease in which the body reaches a state of excitement through a stimulant that would normally be received by the brain and controlled by it. The uncontrolled stimulation triggers the convulsion.

The condition is believed to have a hereditary background and first occurs usually when the cat is two to three years of age, though cases younger and older than this have been observed. It is treated with epileptic drugs if the convulsions occur with any frequency. In cases of convulsions that occur with a time lag of six months or more between attacks, it may take fully half of the cat's life to balance the correct dosage of drugs to be given.

SPINAL DISORDERS

Spinal Lesions

The initial group of lesions are very similar to those we have listed under brain infections with viral, bacterial, protozoal, and fungal causes. They have essentially the same clinical signs, and the same diagnosis and treatment would apply.

Trauma

Trauma, a wound or bodily injury produced by violence, is similar to the earlier lesions—but there are some differences. First, X-rays as a clinical tool are much more definitive than in lesions produced by virus, bacteria, and so on. Second, gunshot wounds rather than natural phenomena often cause the trauma, and if the spinal vertebrae are broken or dislocated and the spinal cord has broken, the cat will never recover. If the cord is stretched or pressured, surgical correction should begin at once. A delay of even a few hours can make a vast difference in the chances of recovery.

(See also the discussion of spinal-disc disease in Chapter 27.)

Hypervitaminosis (A)

Cats fed excessive amounts of raw liver will receive too much vitamin A. This causes an ankylosis (abnormal immobility and consolidation of a joint) of the vertebrae and joints, particularly in the neck. The cat will evidence pain, abnormal gait, and wasting of the muscles.

There is no treatment other than a change of diet. The damage is irreversible.

DISORDERS OF THE PERIPHERAL NERVOUS SYSTEM

This system consists of the nerves that go to the red muscles of the body and perform with conscious control. They are usually damaged through trauma. To diagnose the nerve involved, the nerve or muscles it animates are stimulated. If there is no response we know the nerve is damaged, and damaged nerves may take as long as six months to recover. During this time, treatment is directed toward minimizing the damage to the limb or area affected through the use of corticosteroids. After six months, if there is no natural response to treatment, the useless limb is amputated to keep it from constant damage and infection. Some owners, if puss is very dear to them, will avoid the surgery and have special protective boots made for the injured leg.

Today there is a method that can give far better results, though it is expensive and time-consuming. Each leg has extensor muscles and flexor muscles, and rarely is more than one muscle group affected by the disease. The surgical technique is to borrow a tendon from the muscle group not affected and to transfer it to the main tendon of the affected group. The leg is then placed in a cast for four to six months with periodic cast changes. During this time, the new tendon retrains itself to operate the affected muscles.

The junior author has had the opportunity to treat one such case which resulted in a very happy conclusion. The patient was a dog who, despite numerous fractures and severe nerve damage, has now regained approximately 75 percent of the normal use of the leg involved and shows no chronic cuts or bruising due to inability to control the limb. The solution is worth trying as long as the owner has both the patience and the necessary funds.

Neoplasia (tumor)

Tumors of the spinal nerves are neurofibromas or neuromas. The tumor mass may be palpable. Prognosis depends upon whether or not the tumor is easily reached and if the condition is nonmalignant.

Myasthenia Gravis

This condition is a weakness of the voluntary muscles due to the inability of the nerves to send action potential to the muscle fibers. Treatment is with drugs that will stimulate the acetylcholine production needed to cross potential from nerve to muscle. The dosage necessary may be too high to be maintained; prognosis therefore depends upon the cat's reaction to the drug used.

Neuritis

Neuritis is an inflammation of any nerve. Treatment, if there is no infection present, consists simply of corticosteroids and rest.

DISORDERS OF THE ENDOCRINE SYSTEM

The endocrine system is a group of unrelated glands which contain no ducts, but the secretions of which travel via the blood system. The secretions of these glands have one thing in common—they are involved in body metabolism.

The parathyroid glands consist of two pairs of glands. One pair is partly buried in the thyroid gland. This gland regulates blood calcium. When the blood level of calcium drops, more calcium is absorbed from the kidneys. If there is no excess calcium, the hormone then mobilizes calcium from the skeletal system. This system is aided by vitamin D and calcitonin, another hormone common in primitive fishes and still present in animals. (Calcitonin is a polypeptide, thought to be a secretion of the thyroid gland, which lowers both calcium and phosphate in the plasma.) As the calcium level rises, the hormone rate falls, keeping a normal balance.

Hyperparathyroidism

Hyperparathyroidism is caused by abnormal parathyroid glands that secrete excessive hormones. There are two types of overactive parathyroids: primary hyperthyroidism and secondary hyperthyroidism. In primary hyperthyroidism the gland, for no known reason, produces excess parathyroid hormone (PTH). Calcium continues to be mobilized from the bone, and small, partial fractures occur due to decreased bone density.

Nutritional secondary hyperparathyroidism is an increase in the PTH due to nutritional imbalances, and/or due to renal problems. The situation is most common in Siamese and Burmese cats, but it occurs in all breeds. The condition is known as osteogenesis imperfecta, juvenile osteoporosis, or (less technically) paper-bone disease. The basic causes can be one or more of the following: low calcium, high phosphorus, low vitamin D. When these dietary problems are present, the amount of PTH increases, the bone becomes calcium-depleted, puss becomes weak, and fractures occur without any known injury.

The type of diet that causes this condition is an all-meat diet, especially beef heart, which can bring on the disease in about one month.

Treatment consists of supplying the correct diet and an improvement in mineral supplements until the cat is well. Sometimes anabolic agents are necessary to encourage recovery.

Secondary hyperparathyroidism can also be caused by renal disease. With kidney damage, phosphorus levels increase because they are not able to be filtered through the kidneys and, as a result, calcium levels fall. This causes the PTH to mobilize bone from the body, which creates a type of adult rickets. The bones become soft and rubbery, and when the disease affects the jaw it is commonly called rubber jaw. As the condition increases, since there is no real call for calcium, much of the excess calcium is deposited in the muscle tissue. Correction of this anomaly is to treat the kidneys with proper kidney diets, and to supplement the calcium loss until a balance is achieved.

Hypoparathyroidism

This is a condition caused by damage to the parathyroid gland, which reduces the PTH. The hormone reduction causes loss of control of the calcium content of the blood. The hormone lack fails to pull calcium into the blood, and the blood level falls. The drop of blood level has no effect on the PTH; therefore, the blood level descends until a tetanus caused by lowered blood calcium (calcium tetany) occurs. Treat the sick cat with high vitamin D and calcium supplements, but keep the phosphorus content of the diet low.

Thyroid Gland

The cat's thyroid gland is seldom disturbed. The main problems here are growths, benign and malignant, and goiters. Most conditions take place in the older cat, and only hypothyroid disorders have been shown to be a problem in felines. Thyroxine levels in the blood fall and then the symptoms appear. The condition is most characterized by a loss of hair on the hind legs and the abdomen. The coat over the rest of the body becomes short and coarse, and the affected cat fat and lethargic.

The treatment for hypothyroidism is L-thyroxine, sometimes supplemented with male or female hormones. Therapy will last about three to six months, until control is completed. Often, medication must continue from then on.

Islets of Langerhans

When a deficiency reduces the production of insulin in the area of the islets of Langerhans, diabetes mellitus occurs. The islets of Langerhans function in the pancreas as a separate system, but if the pancreas becomes inflamed, it may put pressure on the islets and cause transitory diabetes mellitus.

The disease's incidence is higher in male than female cats, and the frequency of the malady is about one or two cases in every one thousand felines. The cats most affected are those of middle age or older.

The most prominent signs of the illness are increased thirst and urination. Both blood sugar and urine sugar are increased, usually above 200 mg/ml (milligrams/milliliters) of sugar, although lower readings still indicate diabetes, which often needs only dietary change for control. The liver enlarges and becomes fatty, and lastly the lenses of the eyes may become cloudy with cataracts. Treatment is through dietary control and injections of insulin. The injective process must be monitored with glucose urine dip sticks. The insulin dosage should just keep the urine in the positive range; although some cats may be difficult to monitor with urine tests, and need blood tests for accuracy.

The Pituitary Gland

The pituitary gland is the main control over several other glands. It is located in the skull just under the brain. The gland itself is controlled by the thalmus in the brain, and works with the adrenal gland's cortex and the thyroid gland to control their secretions. It also affects sperm and egg production through FSH (follicle stimulating hormone). Among other hormones from the pituitary glands are the growth hormone, pituitary luteinizing hormone (to preserve pregnancy), and oxytocin, which stimulates the process of birthing.

Abnormal growth of the pituitary gland will become much advanced before there is a clinical effect. Then, as the tumor spreads to the surrounding brain, the symptoms begin. The cat may become either obese or quite thin; it will become frightened and hide, and it may become blind; and because of the controls connected to the thyroid and adrenal glands, symptoms indicating damage to these organs will also appear. Since pituitary damage is usually tumorous, the condition will progress until death occurs.

The Adrenal Gland

The only adrenal gland disease in felines as yet known is the deposit of large amounts of minerals in the gland, which would, because of their invasive nature, be expected to cause hypoadrenal gland problems; yet they do not. The reason for the deposits is unknown, and they are usually found only during postmortems.

CHAPTER 27

Musculoskeletal and Skin Ailments

There are few problems of the musculoskeletal system in felines. Cats have not deviated as greatly from the original evolutionary type as have the varieties of dogs. Fitted for a feral lifestyle, the *Felidae* family, during the process of evolution, has developed a structurally perfect anatomy, reaching the end physical composition necessary to fit its natural role. The most noticeable changes in our domestic cats (man-made through selection) are the loss of the tail in most Manx cats, the bobtail in the Japanese bobtail, and the shortened foreface of the Persian and Himalayan breeds.

CONGENITAL MUSCULOSKELETAL PROBLEMS

Polydactylism

The most common congenital problem is polydactylism (an increase of digits). This inheritable anomaly has been adopted by a certain group of cat fanciers who want to produce the polydactyl cat, which sports the extra toes as a breed identification. There can be two or three extra thumbs displayed; usually these extra toes cause no problems. But if three toes are crowded into one area, there is often not enough room for the proper expansion of all the nails, and some of them may curve back and grow into the foot unless diligently clipped.

Hip Dysplasia

Although the condition of hip dysplasia may be present in the cat, the weight of the feline body is so distributed that the dysplasia very seldom damages the hips enough to cause symptoms or clinical deformity. The condition is one in which the head of the femur does not fit properly into the pelvic socket in the hindquarters, causing eroding and malformation of the femur head and the pelvic socket, and at times lameness and pain.

The condition is treated initially with painkillers. In animals the size of a domestic cat, this is usually enough. But if the condition continues to be painful, surgery is necessary and the pectineal muscle can be cut to relieve pressure on the joint. Finally (though this is rarely done), the hip joint can be removed and refashioned into a muscle joint.

Patellar Luxation

This malady is more common than hip dysplasia in felines. The luxation (dislocation) may be congenital or traumatic. The breeds most commonly affected are the American silver tabby and the Himalayan. The condition, since it appears to be a genetic recessive, is seen far more frequently in all purebreds (where inbreeding may occur) than in the common house cat.

As with hip dysplasia many cats, because of their light weight and body balance, need no repair. If mild repair is necessary, a new and stronger ligament can be made on the lateral side of the leg, since the knee luxates medially. If this is not considered enough support for the knee, a transplant of the tibial crest off the tibia bone, with the lower patellar ligament attached, is moved to the lateral side, pulling the patellar back to a normal line.

ACQUIRED MUSCULOSKELETAL PROBLEMS

Osteomyelitis

Osteomyelitis is an infection of the bone. Since bite wounds are quite common in cats, bone infection is also very prevalent. If an abscess resists treatment, X-rays of the area should be taken and, if present, osteomyelitis can be identified. While most abscesses respond to drainage and antibiotics, infections deep in the bone need special wide-range antibiotics, such as chloromycetin. Cultures may be necessary to properly pinpoint the correct antibiotic to use. The area of infection should be opened, drained, and flushed with antibiotics and antiseptics.

Spinal Disc Disease

This disease is not a common ailment of cats. Between each vertebra is a small, disclike cushion that protects the area. If one of these discs ruptures upward into the spinal cord, the cat can become paralytic or ataxic (uncoordinated). Subsequently, the disc will calcify and lose its flexibility. If the initial attack produces pain but no paralysis, it is reasonable to treat the animal medically with painkillers and corticosteroids. But if the cat has repeated attacks or is completely paralyzed, surgery may be the only answer.

Two types of surgery are used: the scraping out of the involved discs; or, a better procedure, removal of the top of the backbone to allow the spinal cord to float up above the ruptured discs.

Spondylosis

The bridging of one vertebra to another on the ventral surface of the backbone is called spondylosis. When the bones are in the process of bridging, the pain may be appreciable, but once the bridge is firm the pain will almost entirely cease, though the cat's back will lose some of its flexibility.

The condition is treated with painkillers, and especially with anti-inflammatory drugs such as butazolidin and cortisones.

Cancer

Cancer of the bone is far more common than muscular cancer. The most prevalent tumor is the osteosarcoma, which usually occurs at the end of the long bones. This tumor is deadly and should be removed as soon as it is identified. All bone tumors are dangerous and should receive swift surgical intervention. Any cat that lives more than six months past the time of surgery will probably live out its normal life span.

Cerebellar Hypoplasia

Incomplete development of the cerebellum is caused by a viral disease, especially feline distemper, during the fetal development stage.

Most affected cats cannot coordinate their bodies, heads, and limbs. The condition is usually recognizable when the kitten is about six weeks of age. Postmortems show a small cerebellum with a normal-sized hind brain and forebrain.

Gangliosidosis

This is the only muscular disease of any real importance to cat fanciers. The condition is inherited as a recessive trait, and is caused by an accumulation of ganglioside (muscular disease) in the cerebral cortex. The disturbance in the cortex causes uncoordination of the muscles, beginning at about two months of age and progressing until about eleven months, when a sudden downhill course develops and the cat succumbs very quickly.

SKIN AILMENTS

To reiterate, the skin is the cat's first line of defense. Covering its entire body, it prevents disease from entering the other systems. The hair coat insulates and protects puss against hot and cold temperatures. If the skin becomes damaged, or the cat's coat thins as a result of disease, these important protections fail, the feline's resistance is dangerously lowered, and local skin infections result.

Ectoparasites

See Chapter 20.

The Manges

Mange is caused by mites—small ectoparasites that affect the skin. Four mange mites are noted here; ear mange, more commonly called ear mites, will be discussed in the chapter to follow.

Demodectic mange. The demodectic mite is rarely found on cats. When it is, it causes a scaly, spotty lesion. General disease has not been found. The condition will usually resolve itself, but it can be helped by specific creams and lotions.

Cheyletiella mange. See Chapter 20.

Notoedric mange. These mites cause the most common mange of cats. The mange affects the head, ears, neck, tail, and legs. The areas affected become irritated and crusty, and the cat is very itchy and scratches incessantly at the infection. The traumatized skin often becomes secondarily infected with bacteria. Treatment is with sulfur preparations, but these are not always successful, and malathion, which is relatively nontoxic to cats, is excellent. Treatments must be repeated at intervals for one or two months.

Myiasis. See Chapter 20.

Pyoderma

This is a bacterial infection of the skin. It can be primary and generalized, causing small pustules all over the skin, or it can be secondary. If secondary, the bacteria invades skin that has already been irritated by another, unrelated skin disease. The condition can also be localized, due either to an abscess or to cellulitis from punctures and bites. Classification is also predicated upon the section of skin affected. Impetigo is a superficial infection; ecthyme is a deeper infection; while folliculitis involves the hair follicle. Severe pyoderma of the follicle and skin glands is called furunculosis; and even more complicated are carbuncles. Finally, acne is a pyoderm combined with follicular plugging, which occurs mainly on the cat's chin and lips.

Most of these infections are caused by staphylococci, but streptococci and other bacteria have also been identified. Treatment involves the use of staphylocci-specific antibiotics. Since not all of these are as efficacious as desired, laboratory tests must often be used to identify the best antibiotic to use. Baths with bacterial soaps are sometimes resorted to, as are applications of local bactericides and creams. Vaccines made directly from the cat's infection have been a necessary treament in some cases. Carbuncles must often be surgically debrided. If the infection is secondary, the primary, unrelated skin disease must also be treated.

Ringworm

This is not a worm but an infection by a fungus that affects the skin. It is known as a dermatomycosis. Most of such infections are caused by *Microsporum canis*, but *Microsporum gypseum* and *Trichophyton mentagropytes* have also been found.

The lesions usually begin on the cat's head and forequarters, appearing as small, round, bald, and scaly areas. Most are only about ½ inch in size, but they can become much larger. The hairs break off and, as the disease progresses, the lesions become covered with white scales. If untreated, the disease will spread over the cat's entire body. Some animals display no visible lesions, only a dry coat. These latter cats are the carriers and are particularly dangerous to catteries, as they may introduce the infection without knowledge of the cattery owner.

Diagnosis can often be done by your veterinarian on just the typical clinical appearance. But if there is any doubt in identifying the infection, skin scrapings will discover the responsible spore or fungus. The fungus may also be grown on a special culture for positive identification. Some ringworms are fluorescent under ultraviolet light, but others are less so or not at all.

The disease is dangerous since it is communicable to humans. If your cat has been diagnosed as being infected, examine your hands and forearms, which have the greatest contact with puss, for small, round, red areas. If you find such areas, you know that you now share something more with your cat than just love.

Treatment (for your cat) is both systemic and local. Cats with one or two small lesions should be given local treatment. Grisofulvin, a systemic fungicidal drug, should be given on a daily basis or in massive doses on a weekly basis. Fungicidal baths with iodine soaps, or other fungicidal soaps approved for felines, are effective. Local treatment is accomplished with daily applications of creams specific for fungal disease.

Seborrhea

Seborrhea is an abnormal keratinization of the skin. Normally the skin flakes and is replaced at an orderly rate; in the cat with seborrhea, this rate of flaking increases and the cat becomes scaly, with an abnormally dry or oily coat. The disease can also occur in cats that are weakened and run down from other disease. Treatment is with coal-tar shampoos, specific lotions, and increased nutritional supplements.

Miliary Dermatitis

This is a condition typified by a skin that is covered with small pupules and a thin coat, especially along the dorsal surface. The cat usually displays some irritation and will scratch and rub the affected area. Many causes have been advanced, but responses to therapy and pathological studies have ruled out most of them; in all probability the cause is a type of hypersensitivity (allergy). In any case, the response to therapy has been limited and the condition tends to recur even during treatment. We can best call it a condition of hypersensitivity with unknown secondary factors involved.

Historically, the condition has been treated with cortisones, antibiotics, and skin baths, with varying results. Recently a new drug, megestrol acetate, has been shown to control not only this condition but also many other skin conditions to which puss is heir and which are also of unknown origin. The drug is given every other day until the cat has improved, then the dose is reduced gradually to a very small amount every two weeks to control the condition. This may have to be continued for the rest of the cat's life, or the disease can return. Since megestrol acetate is also a birth control pill, it cannot be used for active breeding queens.

Castration Alopecia

Hair loss due to a lack of male hormone after castration occurs rarely in the altered male. When it does, it is a nonirritating baldness, bilateral under the tail and/or on the back of the thighs. Treatment is with small amounts of testosterone.

Hair Chewing

This is a common condition seen in all cats and specifically in Siamese and Burmese. The cat licks and chews the hair from the area of the abdomen and the inside of the upper legs. The areas it chews become moist and raw. The cause of this performance is not known. Treatment with cortisones and soothing creams has been traditional, but always with poor results. Recently we have found that this is another condition that responds favorably to megestrol acetate, probably for the same reasons that miliary dermatitis (see page 275) responds to the drug.

Skin Allergies

Allergies are as common in our pet animals, including our cats, as they are in pet owners, and they manifest themselves in many ways. In cats they cause watery eyes, sneezing, heavy breathing (respiratory allergies), diarrhea and vomiting, or gastric allergies (the majority of which are due to diet). Most common of all are the skin allergies. These can be divided into two types: contact allergy and noncontact allergy.

Contact allergies occur when the cat's body comes in direct contact with the allergy, and the lesion is found only in the contact area. Typical is the flea collar dermatitis that manifests itself as a circular lesion around the cat's neck.

In noncontact dermatitis (allergic) the cat gets the allergen on its skin, swallows it or inhales it, and the disease appears as a general itchiness of the skin. The cat licks, scratches, or rubs the offending areas, until they become raw and the hair falls out and scabs form. The most common areas of infection are those most easily reached by puss: the back and legs. One of the most prevalent allergies is caused by flea saliva, and the allergic cat is greatly irritated by even a single flea, its bite causing a large area of inflamed allergy reaction. Almost any material containing a protein has been demonstrated to cause an active allergic reaction in some cats. These protein materials include such varied substances as wool, grasses, leaves, trees, foods, insecticides, cotton, kapok, dust, molds, and animal hairs.

It is even conceivable that your cherished cat may be allergic to you. It has always exasperated the junior author as a veterinarian to receive a request to put some poor cat to sleep because the owner is allergic to it. We have often wondered what the reaction would be if we suggested the opposite to the above deplorable action, when asked the solution to the puss that is allergic to its owner. But, seriously, if any owners are allergic to their cats, a few drops of mineral oil rubbed over the coat daily will seal in the dander and relieve the owner's suffering, and perhaps allow a continued happy relationship between owner and cat.

Control of allergic dermatitis is not difficult in the majority of cases, but the owner must understand that this is a *control*, not a cure. First, if the cause of the allergy is obvious and can be removed, do so at once. For instance, fleas can be removed and should be strictly controlled on all cats, not just those allergic to flea saliva. Second, puss should be put on an allergy medication, usually cortisones or antihistimine-cortisone combinations. The medication is reduced over a period of several days to weeks, until the lowest dose that prevents symptoms is reached. The medication is then given as long as the allergy season is active for the individual cat, which could be several weeks to several months, and sometimes throughout the entire year. If the allergies are still present when the medication is withdrawn, the condition returns. Many veterinarians treat cats displaying such symptoms with a long-lasting injection of cortisone rather than daily medication. These injections can last from two to six weeks, depending upon the individual cat's reaction. Cortisones given in high doses, or over longer periods of time, can cause side reactions. The long-lasting injections only affect the body for seventy-two hours, although they control the disease for many weeks, thereby reducing the side effects. Finally, depending upon the condition of the skin, lotions, creams, skin baths, skin moisteners, antibiotics, and nutritional supplements can be used to help effect control.

If none of these medications and supportive treatments controls the disease, and medication dosage needs to be administered longer and stronger, it may be necessary to have the cat skin-tested to identify the allergies positively so that vaccines can be manufactured for them. This is an expensive operation and, though very successful on some cats, may show poor results in others. The procedure is resorted to because prolonged, high doses of cortisone can cause permanent damage to the adrenal glands, and it is best to reduce to an acceptable level, or completely eliminate, the use of cortisone.

Skin Tumors

Tumors of the skin are common on felines, and are of both benign and malignant types. Many kinds of tumors occur. Often your veterinarian can make a reasonably correct diagnosis from their appearance alone, but a certain diagnosis can only be achieved through surgical biopsy. Treatment (if necessary) is by surgical removal.

Hormonal Skin Disease

Secondary hair loss is common in the presence of hormonal imbalance. Hypothyroidism, estrogen imbalance, diabetes, and testosterone deficiency can all cause nonirritating hair loss. Treatment consists of isolating and attacking the basic condition.

CHAPTER 28

Diseases of the Cat's Eyes and Ears

From the huge and powerful lions and tigers to our small domestic cat, the eyes of the family *Felidae* have evolved with special adaptations to survive in their special world and fulfill their roles as primary predators. Both the eyes and the ears of felines (aided by the vibrasse) play most important parts in the body's receptor system. Indeed, without the high sensitivity of these organs, the *Felidae* could not fill their ecological niche and endure as successful predators.

The feline's large eyeball has a frontal position and a big cornea that permits exceptional vision. Though the cat cannot move its eyes too rapidly, it compensates by utilizing quick side-to-side head movement. The large cornea, pupil, and lens allow better than normal vision in reduced light. The retina (the light-reception area at the rear of the eyeball) is specially adapted to double the stimulation of the visual image. These anatomical adaptations endow the cat with its unique ability to hunt and to protect itself against other predators, including man.

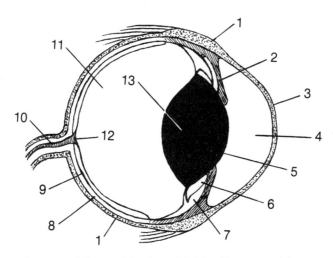

Horizontal section of the eye: (1) sclera, (2) iris, (3) cornea, (4) aqueous humor, (5) lens, (6) suspensory ligament, (7) ciliary muscles, (8) choroid, (9) retina, (10) optic nerve, (11) vitreous humor, (12) blind spot.

CONGENITAL ABNORMALITIES
OF THE EYES

(Note that unless specifically stated, the following eye abnormalities cannot be treated or corrected.)

Microphthalmia (undersized eyeball)

This is the most common feline eye defect. It may be bilateral or unilateral. The eye may be normal in structure but undersized, or it may have numerous anatomical abnormalities of the inner structures. Usually the orbit also fails to develop. The result of small eye and orbit may turn the eyelids inward (entropion), causing irritation to the eye surface. There is usually some sight deficiency.

Congenital Glaucoma

Congenital glaucoma is an enlargement of the eyeball due to increased pressure from fluids inside the eye. The fluids are deprived of their normal flow because of incomplete development of the circulation channels. Primary, or congenital, glaucoma can be controlled for a time but it usually remains progressive.

Anophthalmia

This is the congenital absence of an eyeball. The orbit is filled with a fatty tissue, and the lids usually are underdeveloped.

Lagophthalmos

A defect that can be congenital or acquired, lagophthalmos is characterized by lids that cannot cover the eye. Injuries that damage the nerves controlling the lids, or cause scars that prevent the lids from extending over the eyeball, will cause acquired lagophthalmos. The eye must be treated with artificial tears to prevent dry eye, which will result in corneal irritation if allowed to persist.

Acquired lagophthalmos may rectify itself. Congenital defects are more of a problem and may result in the loss of an eye due to dry irritation leading to ulceration and destruction of the organ. Surgery to enlarge the lids so they cover the eyes will help to rectify the situation.

Esotropia (cross eyes)

Another of nature's abnormalities, this defect is particularly prevalent in Siamese cats, but it apparently causes no vision problems.

Strabismus (inability to focus both eyes at the same time)

This problem can be congenital or acquired from nerve damage due to trauma, and usually results in puss squinting with the eye that is out of focus. Temporary suturing of the eyelids of the focusing eye will often allow the other eye to strengthen and re-position, especially when the condition is acquired.

Congenital Nystagmus (involuntary bilateral movement of the eyes)

Most nystagmus is side to side. The condition is unrelenting. Some nystagmus is due to vestibular disease, or trauma to the head, but congenital permanent nystagmus is occasionally seen.

Coloboma

The congenital absence of a part or all of the eyelid has been named coloboma. The condition is caused by pressure from the fetal membranes during embryonic development and is not inherited.

The absence of parts of the lid may keep the eyelids from covering the eye, or may allow hairs to scratch and irritate the eye. The chronic irritation eventually leads to kerititis or cornea inflammation (see page 285). The kerititis can be treated medically but will recur unless plastic surgical correction is done.

Coloboma of the uvea is a cleft defect of the iris, ciliary body, or the choroid.

Entropion (inversion, or turning inward, of the eyelid margin)

Most cases of eutropion involve the lower lid only. The condition is normally congenital and inherited, and is most common in Persians and Himalayans. Congenital entropion is normally bilateral. On occasion, the condition can be acquired from injuries and inflammations leading to swelling or scarring. The inverted lid causes irritation of the eye surface (the cornea) and results in a kerititis leading to ulceration.

Correction of the condition is by surgery. A portion of the skin below the margin is removed and the edges brought together. This tenses the skin and rolls the lid outward to a normal position.

Ectropion

Ectropion, the opposite of entropion, is the eversion of the eyelid. The condition is congenital and inherited but is rare in cats. Mild irritations are the result of ectropion. Once again, the correction is surgical.

Epiphora (overflow of tears from the eye)

This is caused either by overproduction of tears, or by a blocking of the drainage apparatus that conveys the tears to the nose. The Persian cat with its flat face and protruding eyeballs is particularly prone to the condition since facial anatomy hinders the drainage of tears. The tears spill over the face, causing a stain from the inner corner of the eye down the face.

Symblepharon

A congenital formation of adhesions between the conjunctivae of the eyeball and the eyelid, this condition is corrected by surgical separation.

Congenital Conditions of the Uvea

The uvea is the vascular area of the eye and consists of the iris, ciliary body, and the choroid.

The following conditions may occur:

Aniridia. This is the rare congenital absence of the iris.

Albinism. Here there is the absence of pigment in the iris. The iris appears pink in color. Multicolored irises also occur, especially in white cats. The multicolor appearance is from partial unequal loss of color.

Persistent pupillary membranes. These are strands of tissue arising from the iris and extending over the pupil. They do not interfere with vision and seldom need treatment.

Ectopic lens. This is a condition of the shifting or luxating of the lens from its normal position. The condition can be congenital or acquired following degenerative diseases of the eyeball. The luxated lens may cause glaucoma. Removal of the lens is often necessary, depending upon the position of the luxation. Only a veterinary ophthalmologist can confirm, recommend, and treat these conditions.

Progressive Retinal Atrophy

This disease can be either genetic or acquired. The genetic condition occurs in all cat breeds, but is more commonly found in Persian and Siamese cats. The acquired condition is caused by a diet of commercial dog foods that are normally deficient in taurine, an aminosulfonic acid essential for felines but not for canines. The cat so fed will often become normal if the diet is switched in time to a good cat food.

The first signs of the disease are night-blindness and diminished optical reflexes in reduced light. The receptors in the retina degenerate, and gradually the cat's sight progresses to total blindness. There is, at the moment, no effective treatment for congenital degeneration.

DISEASES OF THE EYES

Horner's Syndrome

A lesion along the cervical (neck) sympathetic nerve chain—caused either by trauma or by tumors—this disease results in a drooping of the upper eyelid, protrusion of the nictitating membrane (third eyelid), swelling of the conjunctiva, and constriction of the pupil of one eye.

If the condition has been caused by trauma, it is treatable with eye drops that imitate the lost sympathetic nerve functions.

Ankyloblephzoon

Kittens normally open their eyes ten days after birth; this is a condition in which the eyelid margins remain closed beyond that time. If not opened by twelve to fourteen days, the eyes should be teased open by the owner with wet, warm (not hot) cotton applications, and gentle finger manipulation. There is usually an accumulation of water behind the eyelid, which will be relieved when the eye is opened.

Dacryocystitis

Dacryocystitis is an infection of the lacrimal tear sac. The area can be treated by using wet heat and by expressing the sac opening, which can also be flushed out. Occasionally, the flushing will reveal a small seed or some other foreign body lodged in the opening to the lacrimal sac, which should be carefully removed with a small forceps. If the area abscesses, the abscess should be lanced, flushed, and treated with antibiotics.

Inflammation of the Conjunctiva

The conjunctiva is the mucous membrane that lines the eyelids and is reflected upon the white section of the eyeball. Inflammation of the conjunctiva can be caused by bacteria, virus, trauma, chemicals, or foreign bodies; the discharge that occurs depends upon the causative agent. Usually the condition begins with a mucous discharge regardless of the cause, and progresses, if untreated, to a reaction of pus when bacteria invade the eye.

Some viruses and bacteria can become constantly present in a cattery, causing chronic eye infections. *Chlamydia* is characteristic of this type of infection. *Parasitic conjunctivitis* is caused by *Thelazia californiensis*, a small worm that is prevalent in the Western United States. The parasite is found under the cat's eyelid. Physical removal and treatment of the irritation it has caused relieves the condition.

Treatment usually requires the application of antibiotic drops or ointments applied several times a day. Sometimes corticosteroids are used to reduce inflammation, and systemic antibiotics are also applied if there is a severe purulent infection.

Follicular conjunctivitis is due to hyperplasia of the lymphoid tissue of the conjunctiva. If there is no concurrent bacterial infection, antibiotic ointments will have no effect, but corticosteroids are frequently used. Moist heat should be applied several times a day. If the eye becomes dry, artificial tears are dropped into the eye to prevent further damage.

Prolapse of the Third Eyelid

This condition is generally bilateral, but may be unilateral as with Horner's syndrome. Many causes have been identified, including drugs (such as tranquilizers), poor nutrition, trauma, and secondary general infections, but a large number of cases are classified as cause unknown. Treatment is to remove or deal with known causes. Many cases resolve themselves.

Kerititis (inflammation of the cornea)

The cornea is a clear surface composed of five layers that covers the pupil. The fluid-filled anterior chamber is under the cornea; then comes the iris, which acts as a shade over the lens that is the inner border of the anterior chamber. Superficial kerititis is usually due to an injury or an irritation followed by infection. Entropion can cause kerititis because of the irritative rubbing of the cornea by the eyelashes.

In the course of this condition, the surface of the cat's eye becomes dull and aggravated in appearance, and small dotlike abscesses may be present. Continued irritation and concurrent infection will gradually wear away the surface, causing ulcerations. New blood vessels may invade, appearing as a red lacework across the cornea, after centering at an ulcer site.

Treatment of simple kerititis involves the use of antibiotics topically and sometimes systemically. If the anterior chamber becomes inflamed, atropine is utilized to keep the iris moving to prevent adhesions. Corticosteroids may be used only if the condition is superficial and there are no ulcerations.

Corneal ulcers are treated with antibiotic ointments or drops applied frequently every day. Systemic antibiotics are commonly administered, but cortisone ointments are contraindicated.

Treatment for ulcers must be vigorously pursued or the ulceration may penetrate the anterior chamber, resulting in the loss of the eye.

Uveitis

The uvea of the eye consists of organs inside the eye, near the eye lens. These organs include the iris and the vascular layer of the eye. They supply nutrients to the eye and regulate the fluid in the eye's anterior chamber. Infections of this area are called uveitis, and cause the cat to constrict the pupil and show sensitivity to light. The fluid in the eye often becomes cloudy with fibrous material and inflammatory cells.

Uveitis can be associated with several systemic diseases, including toxoplasmosis, cryptococcosis, blastomycosis, and infectious peritonitis.

Treatment consists of systemic antibiotics. Atropine ointment or drops are used to keep the iris open and to prevent adhesions of the iris to the lens. Corticosteroids are often applied to reduce eye pain. If the uveitis is an extension of kerititis, the primary kerititis must be treated. If the treatment is unsuccessful, the resulting painful eyeball may have to be removed.

Glaucoma

Glaucoma is an increase in the pressure inside the eyeball. When the eye is normal, there is a balance of inflow and outflow of the aqueous secretion. Blocking of outflow will increase the pressure inside the eye. (See also "Congenital Glaucoma," page 280.)

The blocking outflow of secretion occurs in uveitis, trauma to the eye, and luxation of the lens. These conditions cause secondary glaucoma. Correction of the primary condition will open outflow channels and resolve the condition. The eye swells, becomes inflamed, and the sight is impaired.

Treatment involves drugs to increase outflow of the secretion. Treatment of the primary cause is essential in secondary glaucoma. Any glaucoma that persists for an extended period will result in permanent destruction of the eye and call for removal of the offending and painful sight organ.

Cataract

Cataract, uncommon in cats, is an opacity of the lens that prevents the transmission of light to the retina. As the opacity develops, sight becomes poorer and poorer. Many years may be involved in the development of cataracts, and the condition is bilateral. The cat's eyes should be carefully monitored, and when blindness results, surgical removal of the lens should be done. This will return sight to the eye with only the loss of ability to adjust focal length.

Finally, the lens can have congenital cataract. This usually involves a small area of the lens often seen with spider-web-like extensions. The condition is nonprogressive and usually has minimal effect on sight since it is similar to having a dirt spot on your glasses. Congenital cataracts are occasionally found in kittens. They are usually small, focal, and nonprogressive.

Eye Tumors

As in any other body system, benign and malignant tumors can occur in any area of the cat's eye. Those occurring on eyelids and the skin around the eye can be very dangerous, and professional help should be sought if abnormal swellings or ulcerations of the skin are present. Tumors in the eye will cause symptoms similar to other eye inflammations and can therefore be a cause of uveitis, glaucoma, and blindness. These tumors are often primary, and removal of the eyeball will usually stop the spread of malignancy.

CONGENITAL EAR DISORDERS

The only significant congenital ear problem in cats is the deafness exhibited by blue-eyed white cats. The greater percentage of cats of this color (or lack of color) are deaf. This anomaly has been discussed at greater length in an earlier chapter. The deafness is caused by a single dominant gene. These deaf white cats adjust very well to their disability, but it is best not to allow them to wander in high-traffic areas where they will not be able to hear the sounds of oncoming traffic.

DISEASES OF THE EARS

The external ear, the pinna, is a thin area of cartilage covered with soft skin. Vascularization is abundant and, therefore, when the ear is lacerated, it bleeds profusely. Tears must be cleaned, disinfected, and sutured with the finest cosmetic suture material.

Hematoma

Sometimes no break in the skin will be visible but the ear will bleed between the cartilage and the skin. This is a hematoma, the result of a ruptured blood vessel. Sudden trauma, or constant shaking of the head and ears (usually due to the presence of ear mites), will cause blood vessels to rupture. Hematomas must be drained surgically and continuously to prevent deformity of the ear. Though puss will not die of a hematoma, natural healing causes internal scarring and crumbling of the ear structure, which will result in total ear deformity and blockage of the aural canal.

Squamous Cell Carcinoma

This most common ear tumor is a malignant cancer of the pinna, a disease more prevalent in white cats than in others. The tumor is one that usually invades locally rather than throughout the body (metastasis). Radiation therapy will arrest the growth, and if it is discovered early, cropping of the ear well beyond the lesion will result in a surgical cure. All treatments should be done before the tumor becomes too large, or before it changes character and begins to invade other areas of the body.

The pinna of the ear is one of the prime sites for ringworm (Microsporum canis) and feline mange (Notoedres cati). Both were discussed in Chapter 27, under skin ailments.

The external ear canal begins at the base of the pinna. It is funnel-shaped and vertical for about ½ inch, and then turns ventrally inward

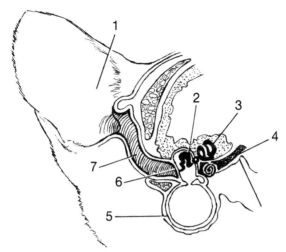

Ear: (1) pinna, (2) ossicles, (3) bony labyrinth, (4) auditory nerve, (5) tympanic bulla, (6) membrane (tympanic), (7) auditory canal with external opening.

to the eardrum (the tympanic membrane). Because of the 80-degree angle at the bottom of the vertical canal, it is almost impossible to damage the eardrum when cleaning the ears of an awake cat. You may go as deeply as gentle probing will allow without injury to puss's ears.

Ear Tumors

Tumors in the ear canal are not common. Adenocarcinoma (a malignant tumor) is the only ear tumor seen with any frequency by veterinarians. Polyps are much more prevalent and can be surgically removed.

Mites

The ear mite, *Otodectes cynotis,* causes the most common infection of the external ear canal. It is a tiny eight-legged insect that lives and breeds in the ear canal of cats and dogs. The junior author often informs clients that mite infestation is a "social disease," since it constantly recurs in the outdoor cat who "runs with the wrong crowd." Direct contact passes the mite on to another host. The mite's main habitation is the ear canal, but it can also be found in the hair around the ears, and often in the tail, which lies against the ears of a cat sleeping in the curled position.

The mite causes a thick black discharge that may become so copious it will block the ear canal. This material should be broken down and softened with light mineral oil or special wax dissolvers, then gently removed. The ear should be treated with specific mite-eradicating products obtained from your veterinarian. Treatment must be continued for a minimum of fourteen days and often as long as thirty days. The cat's coat should be treated concurrently with a flea spray or powder to destroy mites present in the hair.

Ear Infections

Ear infections, *Otitis externa,* usually are an extension of ear mite infestation in the cat, but they can also occur as a purely bacterial or yeast infection. They are treated by cleansing and the use of antibiotics, both locally and internally. If ear mites are present, combination ear lotions are available that treat both the mites and the infection.

If an infected and neglected ear is not professionally treated, it can become thickened with proliferating cartilage and coarsened skin until the canal becomes so narrow that infection cannot be controlled and air is all but blocked out. The resulting tiny blocked canal remains moist, irritated, and infected. When this stage is reached, it is often necessary to remove the outer surface of the vertical canal until the ear is open and only the horizontal ear canal remains. Such surgery can be avoided if an owner is alert to ear maladies, and takes care to control and treat them properly.

Otitis Media (infection of the middle ear)

The middle ear consists of three bones—the mallens, the incus, and the stapes—all of which transmit sounds to the inner ear. The eustachian tube connects the chamber to the nasal pharynx. Usually, infection of the middle ear happens as an extension of *Otitis externa,* when rupture of the eardrum allows the infection to spread. The most common and constant sign of the presence of the infection is rotation of the cat's head toward the infected ear. External canal infection is usually present, and the condition will sometimes produce convulsions. Some cats respond well to antibiotic treatment, and often proteolytic enzymes are utilized to break up the purulent material. Cortisones are used (but only with antibiotics) to reduce the inflammation. Response may be poor because the area has no drainage. Drainage can be initiated by surgical interference, but still not all sections of the ear can be reached by any one method. Response to treatment for this condition can be discouraging, despite all methods used.

Otitis Interna (infection of the inner ear)

The most common cause of this infection is a further extension of *Otitis externa* and *Otitis media.* When the inner ear becomes infected, the cat's balance is disturbed and it tends to circle toward the infected ear with a pronounced head tilt in the same direction. Nystagmus, the involuntary movement of the eyes back and forth, is often also present.

Too frequently these cases do not respond to treatment. Surgical drainage of the inner ear and antibiotic treatment may help, but the prognosis is poor.

Vestibular Disease

This is a specific ailment of the inner ear that occurs during the hot and humid months of the year. The disease has a dramatic onset. The owner may suddenly find puss confused and full of clinical symptoms within hours of having appeared completely normal.

Vestibular felines show a total loss of equilibrium; the head is held cocked at an angle, and the animal turns severely in one direction. The combined loss of equilibrium and the head tilt influence the cat to roll in a corkscrew gait, causing it to become frightened and confused. The animal digs into whatever surface it can and yowls in fear. Nystagmus is common in cats with vestibular disease.

The cause of the disease is a disturbance of the vestibular nerve (the eighth cranial nerve), though the initiating reason for the inflammation is not known. The disease does not appear to be communicable, and cases are sporadic and seasonal.

Most cases respond to treatment after several days to a week. The cat begins to walk normally and to regain its balance, but the head tilt remains to the very end of treatment, sometimes becoming permanent. Total recovery may take up to a month. Treatment is nonspecific; the use of anti-inflammatory drugs, with antibiotic coverage, is standard but may not be valid. At the present time we can offer nothing more exact. Perhaps the most important rule is to confine and protect the cat until normal equilibrium is restored.

CHAPTER 29

The Geriatric Cat

The science of gerontology is the study of the aging process in all its aspects. Aging is basically a succession, in animals, of physiological and tissue changes. These changes are influenced by environment, past and present, former illnesses, organ damage resulting from former diseases or lack of proper nutrition during the cat's lifetime, and hereditary predisposition. Like people, some felines become "old" years before other cats of the same age do. We have frequently seen twelve-year-old, or even more elderly cats, that are in a physical and mental state far better and more youthful than other cats as much as four years younger. Yes, old age affects the mental as well as the physical being in animals, and senility eventually occurs in cats as in all other animals, including man.

In recent years, geriatrics has become an increasingly important area of veterinary practice, keeping pace with this specialized field of human medicine. Knowledge of geriatric problems is growing daily, due to increased research and more involved public interest. It is indeed gratifying to the veterinarian to be able to approach the problem of the aged cat with the ability to help puss instead of merely thinking of the old fellow as expendable. To meet this new challenge, a different approach must be taken with the elderly feline patient. We are faced with two different situations: the old well cat, and the sick geriatric feline.

At some time during your pet's later life, during a routine examination or vaccination, your veterinarian will suggest that puss is not getting any younger and it would be wise to indulge in some routine testing to determine his condition. This means that your veterinarian has identified your pet as elderly and that, as such, it can be expected to have had some definite internal changes that must be recognized. The routine examination suggested at this time will help you to begin to build a new set of facts about your aging cat that are its physiological and mental norms.

Geriatric examinations may vary, but they usually involve a blood count, various blood chemistries (particularly kidney and liver function tests), and a urinalysis. The examination could also include an electrocardiogram, a bone marrow test, and X-rays, for the initial workup may lead to different medical areas. From the information derived, certain precautions can be taken, treatments can be started if necessary, and a variety of facts about your pet as a senior citizen recorded and stored. Depending upon the resulting data, certain tests may need to be repeated every six or twelve months.

The real problem in this area is the sick geriatric cat who has not been recognized as being elderly and for whom there is no basic information. If, for instance, the veterinarian knew that your cat had poorly functioning kidneys, had been given supportive treatment, and had been rebalanced in its own environment, then when the cat became sick, it would be easier for the veterinarian to define the effects of the illness. A cat strange to the veterinarian, old, sick, and evidently in partial kidney failure, is difficult to evaluate and still more difficult to treat. Time is lost while attempting to define the parameters of the patient's normal state, while the familiar geriatric cat can have immediate, special treatment started to keep its body lifeline balanced.

It becomes obvious that in diagnosis, treatment, and prognosis, the veterinarian must make a total evaluation of the geriatric feline patient.

Just as with humans, many of the diseases and problems of the young are much less important in the aged. Parasites are rarely a problem except for tapeworms, and then only if the cat is still a hunter, or the owner does not practice good flea control. Most older cats have increased immunity to the diseases seen frequently in younger cats: simple contact and survival, as well as vaccination programs, have accomplished this. We do not mean to imply that a cat of advanced age cannot ever suffer from these diseases (we have had a twelve-year-old Siamese succumb to "distemper," confirmed by postmortem), but to explain that with advancing years the balance shifts.

Simple infections, on the other hand, become more dangerous in the old cat. Toxic products of bacterial infection are more difficult for the aged feline body to handle, and dehydration due to loss of appetite and normal thirst during a viral or bacterial infection becomes more dangerous much more quickly in the old cat than in the young one with healthy kidneys.

EXAMINING THE GERIATRIC CAT

The general appearance of the elderly cat will indicate several changes, depending upon the advancement of the aging process; and different clinical signs will become obvious. Muscular atrophy is common, and difficulty in walking and general mobility, due to arthritis and muscle depletion, is often seen.

The senile cat's sight and hearing should be evaluated. It will often exhibit confusion when removed from its familiar surroundings or environment. Sight and sound may be normal, but the older cat's response to the stimuli brought to its brain may be slow. It may not recognize a potential enemy (such as a dog) as quickly as it would have a few years before. Puss may yowl in confusion—an act never performed in the familiar surroundings of home. Remember that even though senile, your pet can function normally at home, where it will give and receive pleasure as a family member just as it has done for so many years before becoming old.

The skin of the older feline may become thicker, and the hair or coat rather sparse. Skin tumors are seen more often on an older cat, and hormonal skin conditions are found with some frequency. Medicated shampoos, fatty acids, and commercial moisturizers can all help the skin. Ectoparasite control is extremely important, and specific treatment for hormonal skin conditions will have to be prescribed by your veterinarian. To moisturize a dry coat and skin, use Alpha Keri bath oil (a people product)—one capful added to a pint of water, mixed well, and sprayed on grandpa or grandma cat several times a week, using the same technique as one would apply to moisturizing plants. Regular shampoos can be irritating to an older cat's skin, so only a neutral shampoo such as coconut oil shampoo, or a medicated, mild shampoo specifically formulated for felines, should be used.

Bad breath is common in older cats, and even their best friends won't tell them. But you can help your pet surmount this social barrier by having its teeth cleaned of tartar deposits and any rotted teeth removed. Gingivitis, an inflammation of the gums, is fairly common and can be caused by infection or vitamin deficiency, especially lack of vitamin B complex. Some mouth odor is due to other general diseases, such as kidney failure, and needs specific diagnosis. Mucous membrane color may be changed due to toxicity, anemia, or disease. Ulcers can appear from toxic products in the body, or poor condition.

The ancient cat may develop throat tumors, or it could become a habitual snorer due to an elongated soft palate. A flabby soft palate can be shortened to eliminate this condition. The eyes should be examined for sight ability, pressure changes (glaucoma), and infection. Evaluation of the chest is done with a stethoscope. The sound of harsh breathing, or the presence of enlarged heart perimeters, may call for X-rays to aid in diagnosis and prognosis.

The abdomen is examined by palpation. Small, hard kidneys may be felt, indicating existing nephritis. A pendulous belly may be due to simple muscular breakdown in that area, or (more seriously) to fluid accumulation indicating either heart or liver disease. Liver enlargement or tumors can often be felt. Flaccid intestines as a result of loss of physical tone could cause changes in elimination. The pelvic area is checked for constipation, tumors, and general muscle-tone loss, all of which can make defecation difficult.

Organ changes all indicate the need for varied tests to define the extent of damage, the ability of the animal to survive, and to indicate the necessary treatment. In the female cat, pyometritis is a condition that is more commonly seen after she reaches approximately seven years of age. Pyometritis is a purulent infection of the uterus, and the only treatment is immediate surgery.

Following the physical examination, blood tests may be done to better define the internal environment of the cat. A blood count will indicate the state of the red and white blood cells. A lowering of the red cell count results in anemia. This red cell loss, coupled with the loss of certain white blood cells and platelets, may indicate inactive bone marrow. A count of white blood cells can also reveal the presence of bacterial or viral disease, and indicate whether or not the body is fighting the invading malady.

BLOOD CHEMISTRIES

Blood urea nitrogen (BUN) measurement shows the increase of nitrogenous products and denotes the inability of the kidneys to rid the blood of these products; the result of this inability is kidney disease. The level of creatinine (the nitrogenous product that forms in the muscles in small amounts, passes into the blood, and is excreted in the urine) also increases in kidney disease. A creatinine level of 7 or above generally indicates that puss does not possess enough functional kidney to warrant treatment. SGPT (serum glutamic pyruvic transaminase) is an enzyme that denotes tissue breakdown, especially liver necrosis. Alkaline phosphatase is increased in liver and bone breakdown. Blood sugar increase will identify diabetes. Amylase (an enzyme) will help to show pancreatic disease. Gel digestion tests may also be done with amylase diagnosis. Cholesterol is an indication of liver and thyroid malfunction.

A urinalysis is one of the most important tests to run on a geriatric feline patient, for it will check the functional ability of the kidneys. If a urine sample cannot be caught, a hypodermic needle, pushed through the abdominal wall and into the bladder for a sample withdrawal, is no more painful than any other injection. Change in stool color or consistency should also be noted.

TREATING THE GERIATRIC CAT

Treatment of the geriatric feline is directed at improving and maintaining the internal environment of the body. Muscle atrophy must be retarded and rebuilding promoted. Digestive processes must be watched carefully, for a few days of diarrhea or vomiting can deplete an old cat twice as quickly as they will a young animal. Eating habits must be monitored to be certain that the cat consumes all the dietary food elements necessary to its needs and condition.

Diet is actually the primary approach. The senses of taste and smell diminish in the older cat, adding to the problem of keeping food intake regular; and all edibles in the diet must be of high quality and easily digestible. The elderly cat's appetite is less than that of an active younger cat, and its ability to utilize food is inferior. Therefore, even though it has spent most of its life on cheaper diets, your cat should, in its old age, be switched to better quality rations so that it can utilize a higher percentage of the food intake. Dry foods contain a good deal of fiber and should be cut back, while high protein, flavorful foods should be increased. Dairy products, such as milk and cottage cheese, are highly digestible for old cats, and contain little waste.

The older feline also has a greater need for specific vitamins and minerals, and to fill this need special geriatric vitamin supplements are available. Some of these are mixed with digestive enzymes to help puss to utilize his food, while other supplements contain added hormones to support diminished hormone production. Your veterinarian should choose the supplement, as some combinations may not be suitable for your particular pet.

Special foods are made for some problem cats. Owners of cats that have liver, kidney, intestinal, and heart problems can devise specially prepared diets that lessen the effects of these conditions on the old cat's body. Kidney diets have fewer nitrogenous wastes for the kidneys to metabolize; liver diets are lower in fats; intestinal diets are relatively fiber-free; and heart diets are low in sodium. All of the special foods are easier for the geriatric feline to digest.

Anabolic agents (aids in the constructive phase of metabolism, in which the body cells synthesize protoplasm for growth and repair) are particularly helpful. They promote the better use of food and also tissue buildup. These agents also stimulate bone marrow and appear to have an effect on attitude as well, though the latter is probably secondary in importance to their tissue-building responses. Your veterinarian may suggest a series of special injections of one of these agents, often followed by oral administration for an indefinite period.

The geriatric puss also needs a more regulated environment. Keeping the animal in a habitat where the temperature is constantly controlled helps. Regular grooming care is necessary, for the older cat is not the adept and frequent self-groomer that the younger cat tends to be.

Finally, do not forget to bring your old friend for his regular veterinary examination every six months to a year. Watch for urinary or digestive changes that may indicate need to seek continuing veterinary advice. In every way possible, allow faithful old puss, who has been your companion and friend for many years, to enjoy his old age with the grace and dignity he deserves.

CHAPTER 30

When Your Cat Dies

This is a chapter we found exceedingly difficult to write. It is not instructive, nor is it interesting; it consists merely of a few words of compassion that we wished to share with you, for we too have known the deep melancholy of such loss.

All things have a beginning and an end, and with living creatures the beginning is the initial life spark, and the end is inevitably death, the completion. We are conscious of the fact that this must be, and so we should accept an end to life with more equanimity; but because it is so final, so barren of hope, we never do.

Cats do not possess imagination or the ability to reason, so when your cat dies it is not, to puss, a frightful or traumatic experience; it is simply a ceasing to be. But to you, the friend and owner of puss, it is a traumatic occasion, and it is you who supply the grief and mourning, because you clothe your cat with human attributes. But this philosophy is based upon a false premise. Certainly you loved your cat and shared a rapport that almost bridged the species gap between you. What you must understand is that the association you shared was precious because it was a treasured and compassionate link between two very different species, from which both derived great pleasure.

There is an emptiness left when puss is gone, a vast hurt that, at the moment, seems to be a wound that will never heal. But it will, we promise you, if you give it time. Meanwhile, to fill some of that inner void left by absence, arrange to acquire another cat. No, it will not be disloyal to the cat who has passed away and whom you loved so dearly. The new kitty will never become a substitute for the old cat; that could never be, and we know it. This newcomer is an entirely different individual who will, so very often, help you to remember the old cat, and in time the new cat too will find its place in your heart.

Our love for our cats, and the care we give them, is a touch of sanity and propriety in a disordered world where graft and political greed, terrorism, the brutal killing of innocents, and rampant crime in the streets smear our newspapers and television screens with mud and blood. The very existence of ailurophiles like you who read this book signifies that humanity has not become totally brutish and uncaring; that love and compassion still exist in the human heart—the heart that cries for the feline companion who has died.

Please do not consider it maudlin to grieve for an animal who shared so many years with you and has been, perhaps, the recipient of confidences and confessions. But be happy about the good times you had together, the times of laughter or smiles that brightened the day. This is the way to remember puss, with a smile, and with gratitude to a friend who participated in your life for a while and has left you with fond memories of a time of precious happiness and companionship.

Appendix:
Breed Organizations

The following clubs and societies constitute a special group of cat fanciers whose sole interest is in a specific breed:

Abyssinians:
The Abyssinian Cat
2 1106 River Road
Marengo, Ill. 60152

Abyssinian Cat Club of America
Wain Harding
2425 Ashby Avenue
Berkeley, Calif. 94705

Abyssinian Society of the Northwest
Henrietta Shirk, Secy
601 Sierra Vista Road
Newberg, Ore. 97132

Canadian Association for the Advancement of Abyssinians
Ms. M. Baird, Secy
4185 Fieldgate Drive #92
Mississauga, Ontario L4W 2M9
Canada

Balinese:
American Balinese Association
R.D. 2, Box 164
Columbus, Miss. 65201

Balinese Breeders and Fanciers of America
Pat Horton, Secy
16532 Ballinger Street
Sepulveda, Calif. 91343

Balinese International
7219 Larchwood
Woodridge, Ill. 60515

Eastern Balinese Association
Gayle Dennison, Secy
M.R. 1, Clearview Road
Souderton, Pa. 18964

Eastern Balinese Mews
Route #2
Hawkinsville, Ga. 31036

Bali Tales
P.O. Box 11
Livermore, Calif. 94550

Bombays:
International Bombay Society
Patt Taylor
2741 E. Sylvia
Phoenix, Ariz. 85032

Burmese:
Sacred Cat of Burma Fanciers
211 Hull Avenue
Staten Island, N.Y. 10306

United Burmese Cat Fanciers
Mrs. T. H. Griffey, Secy
14435 Chadbourne
Houston, Tex. 77079

United Burmese Cat Fanciers
2395 N.E. 185th Street
N. Miami Beach, Fla. 32604

Cameos:
Cameo Cat Club
251 Dorsey Road
Rochester, N.Y. 14616

Chartreux:
Chartreux Cat Mews
5519 Chelsea Avenue
La Jolla, Calif. 92037

Chocolate and Lilac Long-Hairs:
United Chocolate and Lilac
Longhair Society
253 Pond Street
Westwood, Mass. 02090

Himalayans:
Atlantic Himalayan Club
7908 Belmont
Ft. Pierce, Fla. 33450

Himalayan Society
Judy Twitchell, Secy
32 E. Center Street
Mohawk, N.Y. 13407

The Himalayan Society
Judy Sporer, Secy
R.D. 1, Box 424
Mohawk, N.Y. 13407

International Himalayan Society
11751 Ranchito
El Monte, Calif. 91732

Japanese Bobs:
Japanese Bob Tales
162 W. Hudson Street
Long Beach, N.Y. 11561

Korats:
Korat Cat Fanciers Association
122-7126 N. 19th Avenue
Phoenix, Ariz. 85021

Mai Pen Rai (Korat Cat Fancy)
P.O. Box A
Moriches, N.Y. 11955

Leopards:
Leopard Information Center
P.O. Box 3632
Hollywood, Calif. 90029

Maine 'Coon Cat:
The Maine Line
P.O. Box 1399
Chula Vista, Calif. 92012

Manx:
American Manx Club
13 Merrywood Road
Wappingers Fall, N.Y. 12590

Canadian Manx and Cymric Society
1402 Bethany Lane
Ottawa, Ontario K1J 8P6
Canada

The Manx Cat
P.O. Box 20072
Bloomington, Minn. 55420

Manx International
2275 W. 25th Street #22
San Pedro, Calif. 90732

Ocelots:
Long Island Ocelot Club
Shelley Starns, Secy
P.O. Box 99542
Tacoma, Wash. 98499

Persians:
Sanguine Silver Society
966 Blue Ridge Avenue N.E.
Atlanta, Ga. 30306

Sanguine Silver Society
208 Caito
Columbus, Ohio 43214

United Silver Fanciers
8 Debra Place
Syosset, N.Y. 11791

Rex:
Rex Breeders United
Sheila McMonagle, Secy
414 Normandy Drive
Lansing, Mich. 48906

Scottish Folds:
International Scottish Fold Association
664 Valerie Drive
Newton Square, Pa. 19037

Short Hair:
National Exotic Shorthair Club
P.O. Box 943
Deer Park, Wash. 99006

National Shorthair Club
1331 N. Wingra Drive
Madison, Wis. 53715

Oriental Shorthair International
2127 Ridge Street
Yorktown Heights, N.Y. 10598

Siamese:
National Siamese Cat Club
16 S. Court
Pt. Washington, N.Y. 11050

The Siamese Cat Society of
America, Inc.
Sam L. Scheer, Secy
2588-C S. Vaughn Way
Aurora, Colo. 80014

Somalis:
Somali Cat Club of America, Inc.
Evelyn Mague, Pres.
10 Western Boulevard
Gillette, N.J. 07933

Tonkinese:
Tonkinese Breed Club
156 Berkey Street
Waltham, Mass. 02154

Turkish/Angora:
International Turkish-Angora
Cat Club
P.O. Box 13737
Gainesville, Fla. 32604

Wirehair:
American Wirehair International
4438 Woodland Brook Drive
Atlanta, Ga. 30339

The following clubs and societies
are devoted to all kinds of cats:

American Cat Association (ACA)
Lois Foster, Pres.
P.O. Box 533
Georgetown, Fla. 32039

American Cat Fanciers Association
P.O. Box 203
Point Lookout, Mo. 65726

Canadian Cat Association
14 Nelson Street W., Suite 5
Brampton, Ontario, Canada

Cat Chat
Maryland Feline Society, Inc.
P.O. Box 144
Lutherville, Md. 21093

Crown Cat Fanciers Federation
Mary Jennings, Secy
P.O. Box 41
Waddy, Ky. 40075

Happy Household Pet Cat Club
439 Calle de Castellana
Redondo Beach, Calif. 90227

Happy Household Pet Club
3200 "C" Street
Sacramento, Calif. 95816

The International Cat Association (TICA)
Georgia A. Morgan, Secy
220 E. Arroyo Drive
Harlingen, Tex. 70808

Index

Italicized numerals indicate the page location of an illustration.

Cattery *(cont.)*
   name registration and taxes, 146–147
   run materials, 145–146
   stud section, 145
   work area, 146
"Cat That Walked by Himself, The" (Kipling), 28
Cave lion *(Felis spelaea)*, 6
Celebrated Cats (Brooks), 28
Cellini, Benvenuto, 31
Cellulitis, 197
Cenozoic era, 3, 4, 5
Central nervous system, disorders of, 266–269
Cerebellar hypoplasia, 272–273
Cervantes, Miguel de, 28
Cézanne, Paul, 33
Chagall, Marc, 32, 33
Championship class, 153
Champfleury (Jules Husson), 28, 32
Chandler, Raymond, 29
Chartreux, 62
Chaucer, Geoffrey, 28
Cheetah *(Acinonyx jubatus)*, 35, 39–40
Child with a Cat (Gainsborough), 32
China, 22, 30, 37
Chinese long-hair, 74
Cholelithiasis, 240–241
Chromosomes, 108–110, 111
Chronic anemia, 256–257
Chronic interstitial nephritis (CIN), 244–245
Chronic pancreatitis, 242
Church Book of Bottesford (England), 23
Chylothorax, 227
Circulation, *see* Respiration and circulation
Circulatory system, diseases of, 250–258
Cirrhosis of the liver, 240
Civets, 4
Classes, 153–154
Clouded leopard *(Neofelis nebulosa)*, 35, 38–39
Coat length, 117–118

Cobb, Richard, 68–70
Cobb, Mrs. Virginia, 69
Coccidiosis, 213
Colette, 26, 28
Colitis, 238–239
Coloboma, 281
Color breeding, 115–117
Color and pattern recognition, 49–52
Color-point long-hair, *see* Himalayan
Columbus, Christopher, 11
Commercial cat food, 87
Communication, 15–18
Community cages and runs, 144–145
Competition, 157; *see also* Shows and showing
Conditioned response, 98
Congenital glaucoma, 280
Congenital malformations, 175–176
Congenital nystagmus, 281
Congenital renal diseases, 246
Control, teaching, 98
'Coon, *see* Maine 'coon cat
Cornish rex, *see* Rex cat
Cougar, *see* Puma
Courbet, Gustave, 32
Cross eyes, 281
Crossing-over (of chromosome pairs), 111
Crown Cat Fanciers, 156
Crusaders, 10
Cryptococcosis, 199
Cryptorchidism, 139, 176
Cuneo, Michele de, 11
Cyprian cat, 74
Cystic endometritis, 137–138
Cystitis, 247

Dacryocystitis, 284
Daniel in the Lion's Den (Rubens), 31
Darwin, Charles, 13, 27, 81, 105, 106
Da Vinci, Leonardo, 31
Deafness, 81
Death, 298–299
Defense, means of, 14
Delacroix, Eugène, 32
Demodectic mange, 273
Demonology, 11
Dental disease, 234–235